POSTCARD HISTORY SERIES

Salinas

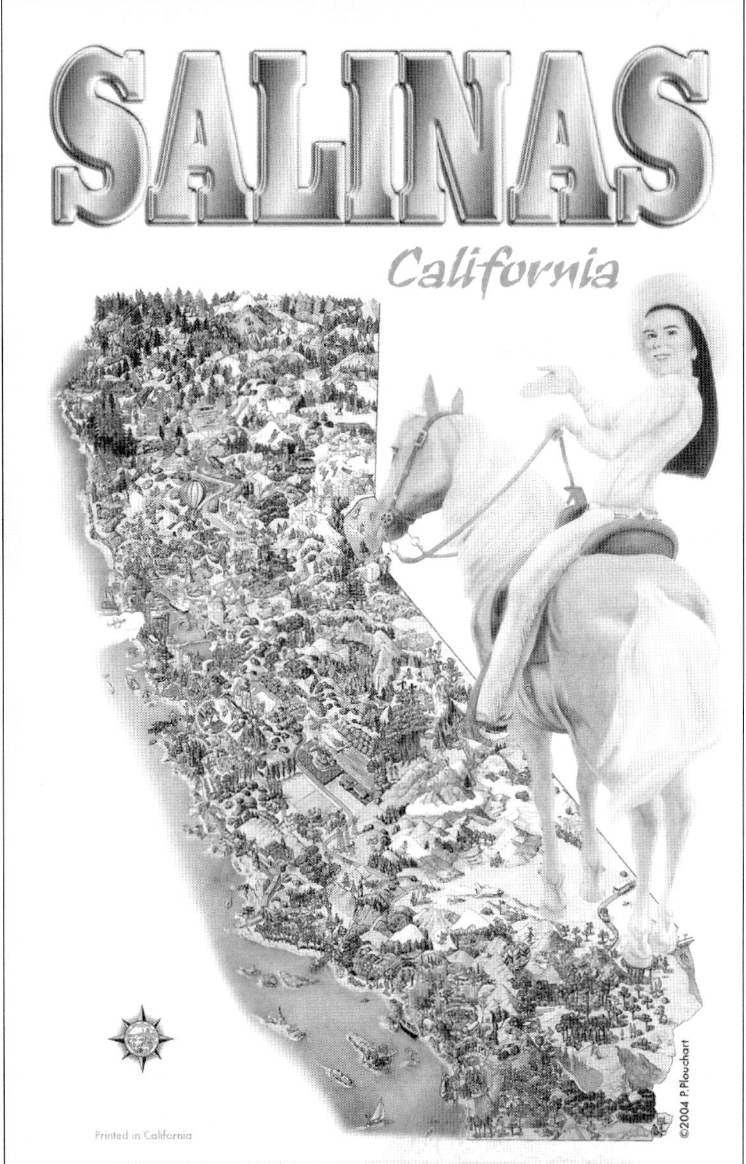

This promotional postcard shows a cowgirl on horseback welcoming visitors to California. While it looks more vintage by design, this card's copyright is actually 2004. (Courtesy of Philippe Plouchart.)

On the Cover: Pictured is Main Street, looking north. The famous "Salinas" sign with the big hat hung over Main Street for many years. (Courtesy of the Monterey County Historical Society.)

On the Back Cover: Several cowgirls show off their Levis jeans in the summer of 1939. (Courtesy of the Monterey County Historical Society.)

POSTCARD HISTORY SERIES

Salinas

Monterey County Historical Society

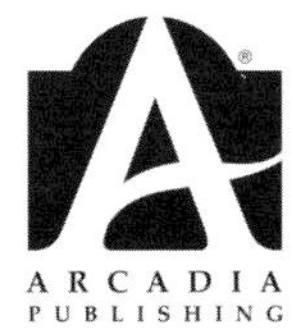

ISBN 978-1-4671-3002-8

Published by Arcadia Publishing
Charleston, South Carolina

Printed in the United States of America

Library of Congress Control Number: 2013944404

For all general information contact Arcadia Publishing at:
Telephone 843-853-2070
Fax 843-853-0044
E-mail sales@arcadiapublishing.com
For customer service and orders:
Toll-Free 1-888-313-2665

Visit us on the Internet at www.arcadiapublishing.com

Contents

ACKNOWLEDGMENTS

This work is being produced on behalf of the Monterey County Historical Society. The authors wish to thank all of the hardworking members of the society and the community who have contributed so much to gather and maintain the early photographs, memorabilia, and stories from Salinas's early beginnings. We wish we had room to name them all, but the list would be far too long. Special thanks go to Barbara Brown and James Perry. All images, unless otherwise noted, are courtesy of the Monterey County Historical Society.

INTRODUCTION

The area that later became Salinas was first used by local Indians for thousands of years, then by the Spanish for pasturing the vast herds associated with the Presidio of Monterey. Important land grants during the Mexican era included Rancho Nacional, site of Hilltown; Rancho Llano de Buena Vista, where Spreckels and the famous sugar factory were built; Rancho El Alisal, site of Hartnell's first college and the country home of Gov. Juan Alvarado; Rancho El Sausal, site of the Sherwood/Castro Adobe and major portions of Salinas today; and Rancho Rincón del Sanjón, located west of Salinas and the site of the Boronda Adobe.

The more recent history of Salinas begins at the Big Bend in the Alisal Slough, when an entrepreneur named Deacon Elias Howe acquired 80 acres of land and built an establishment at the junction of two stage routes. Situated halfway between Monterey and San Juan Bautista, it soon became known as the Half Way House. Business boomed as it became a popular stage stop, beating out the competition at Natividad, which eventually closed. Howe was able to attract customers by serving the best brandy in the area and setting up bets on which stage would arrive first. The winners would receive free brandy.

Charley Parkhurst was frequently the winning stage driver. Whole cases of whiskey were bet on Charley's prowess. Only after Parkhurst's death in 1879 was it discovered that "Charley" was really Charlotte Parkhurst.

After owning his successful Half Way House for only 18 months, Deacon Howe sold it and the 80 acres surrounding it to Alberto Trescony. Born in Italy, Trescony had a fascinating career prior to his arrival in Monterey in 1842, and his life history has become something of a legend in Monterey County. One of his skills was as a tinsmith; he was able to sell his wares to prospectors for high prices. Within a short time, he saved enough to start purchasing properties, and acquired hotels in both Monterey and San Juan Bautista. Near the Half Way House, at the edge of the slough, he built a small hotel, general merchandise store, a blacksmith shop, and a stable. This expansion marks the true beginnings of Salinas—the small wooden hotel stood on the site of the future Abbott House, later the Cominos Hotel. For years, this hotel dominated the 100 block of Salinas and formed the heart of the community, until it was demolished in 1989 for a parking lot.

As Salinas grew, it became the economic center of the valley, fueled by agriculture, and eventually encompassed several outlying communities such as Natividad, Santa Rita, and the site of Salinas's first post office, Hilltown.

Trescony hired Austin Smith and Charles McFadden to manage the hotel in the early 1860s, and Smith accepted the job as postmaster when the Salinas Post Office was moved from Hilltown in 1864. Later, Smith and McFadden operated the general merchandise store.

The initial expansion of Salinas coincided with the drastic reduction in the Spanish-style cattle industry, partially due to the growing availability of American beef in the late 1850s. Then, on December 24, 1861, heavy rains began that lasted for nearly a month, and many cattle drowned. John Steinbeck included a graphic description of cattle washing down the Salinas River in the opening chapter of his classic novel *East of Eden*. The winter was severe everywhere, and snows were frequent; even Monterey experienced six inches of snow. Then, in 1863 and 1864, the valley was struck by a drought. Within two years, the cattle population dropped from between 70,000 and 100,000 to only 13,000.

In spite of the disasters to the Spanish range cattle, a few foresighted individuals saw where the future would lead. In about 1865, William Bardin Sr. noted that, very soon, dairy cattle would be brought into the Salinas Valley and that there would be a great many farmers. True to his vision, in that same year, Carlisle S. Abbott, a well-known dairyman from Marin County, drove 500 dairy cattle to the Salinas Valley. He rented 9,000 acres in the area of Rancho Llano de Buena Vista, southeast of Salinas, including the area that would become the town of Spreckels. By 1875, Abbott was not only milking 1,500 cows and producing 200,000 pounds of butter annually, but he also owned the land. Abbott was not alone; as early as 1869, there were a total of 30 dairymen with 5,500 milk cows. The wharf at Moss Landing allowed products for the first time to be shipped long distances, and the acreage planted in grains increased drastically. The sheep population around Salinas declined, but up the Salinas Valley, where land was cheaper, huge herds continued to prosper. Monterey County was the leading wool producer in the state in both the 1870 and 1880 censuses.

By 1869, Bardin was able to write to a friend that:

> Now you see extensive fields of grain in place of immense herds of stock. Nearly every acre of arable land of the mouth of the Salinas River and full width of the valley to the stage road leading from Hilltown . . . to Natividad is under cultivation and most to . . . Soledad . . . and occasionally a farm . . . for twenty miles [beyond] . . . in one or two years . . . all the land on Salinas [Plain] will be farmed.

Jacob Leese sold the rest of Rancho El Sausal to Eugene Sherwood in either 1859 or 1860. Sherwood converted the rancho to farming and raised wheat. He leased all but 2,000 acres of the original rancho and became an active leader in the development of the now prosperous agricultural region of the Salinas Valley.

The same year, in a move precisely opposite that of Sherwood, Alberto Trescony sold his Salinas property, the Half Way House, and about 160 acres to developers A.B. Jackson and Alanson Riker. He wanted to concentrate on ranching in southern Monterey County.

Sherwood entered into a partnership with the new owners of the Half Way House, and in 1868, they laid out Salinas City on adjoining portions of El Sausal and Rancho Nacional, granting a road right-of-way and land for a depot. This persuaded the Southern Pacific Railroad Company to locate its tracks and depot in Salinas rather than in Santa Rita.

No sooner was the town laid out than settlers began to arrive. The first new business was Michael Hughes's harness shop. The I.J. Harvey family, arriving in 1868, counted only 12 to 14 buildings, some not yet completed. The structures were the American Hotel, a livery stable, two blacksmith shops (one with a residence), a butcher shop, two saloons, two general stores (one unfinished), and three other buildings. By the end of the year, there were 125 buildings, with half again as many under construction. Ford & Sanborn's lumber mills were hard pressed to meet the demand. But the expansion was uneven. A visitor in August 1869 reported 17 saloons, with another being built, but as of yet, no church.

One

Early Salinas's Growth and Development

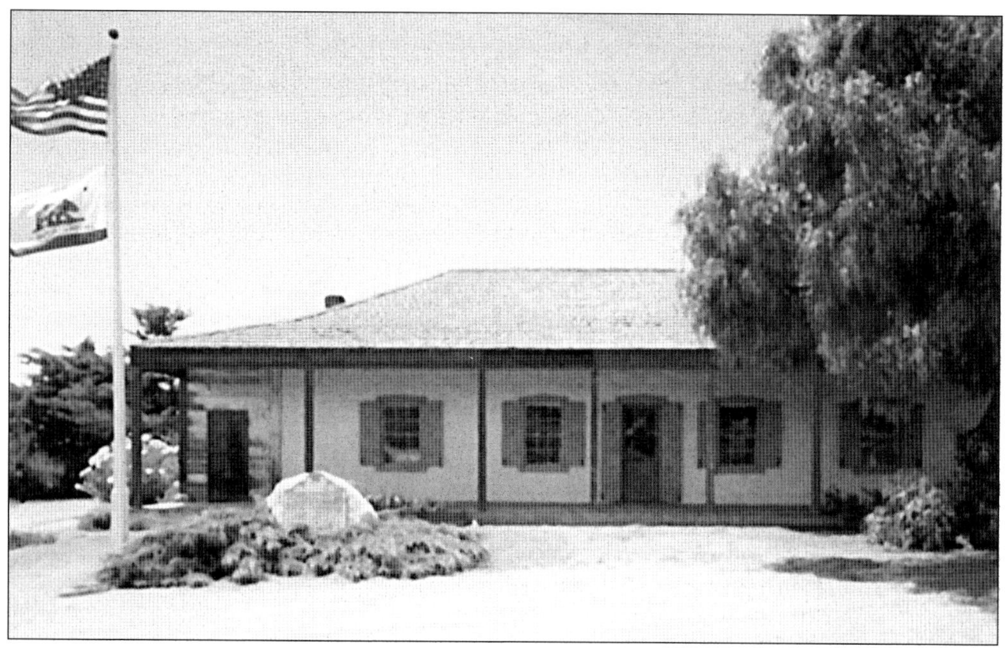

The earliest building in the Salinas area is the José Eusebio Boronda Adobe, constructed around 1846. This adobe is listed in the National Register of Historic Places and is a California Historical Landmark. It is currently owned by the Monterey County Historical Society and was completely restored between 1972 and 1974.

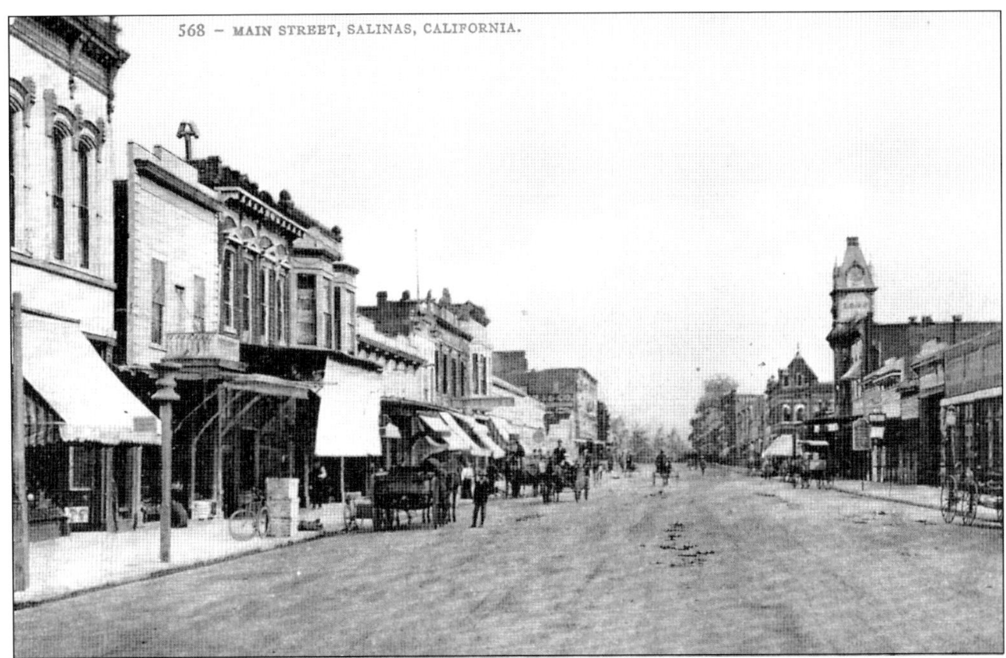

Here is an early photograph of Salinas. Note the dirt streets. Neither telephone lines nor electric lines had yet been installed when this photograph was taken.

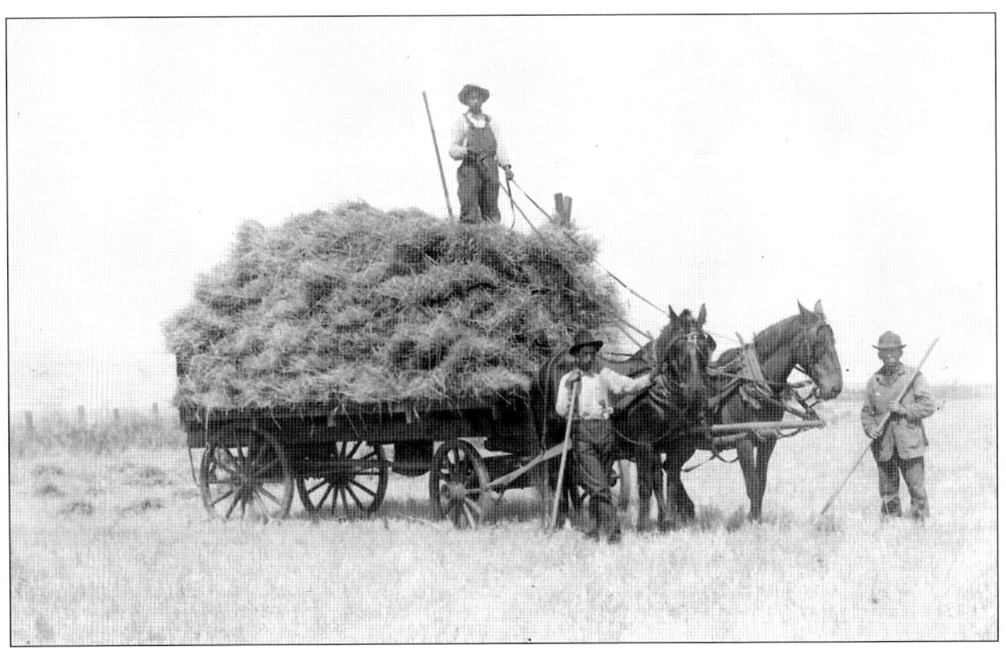

Prior to the introduction of irrigation, dry farming was practiced in the Salinas area. Hay and grain went primarily to feed horses and to the many dairies in the valley. Beans, potatoes, and other crops fed the local communities.

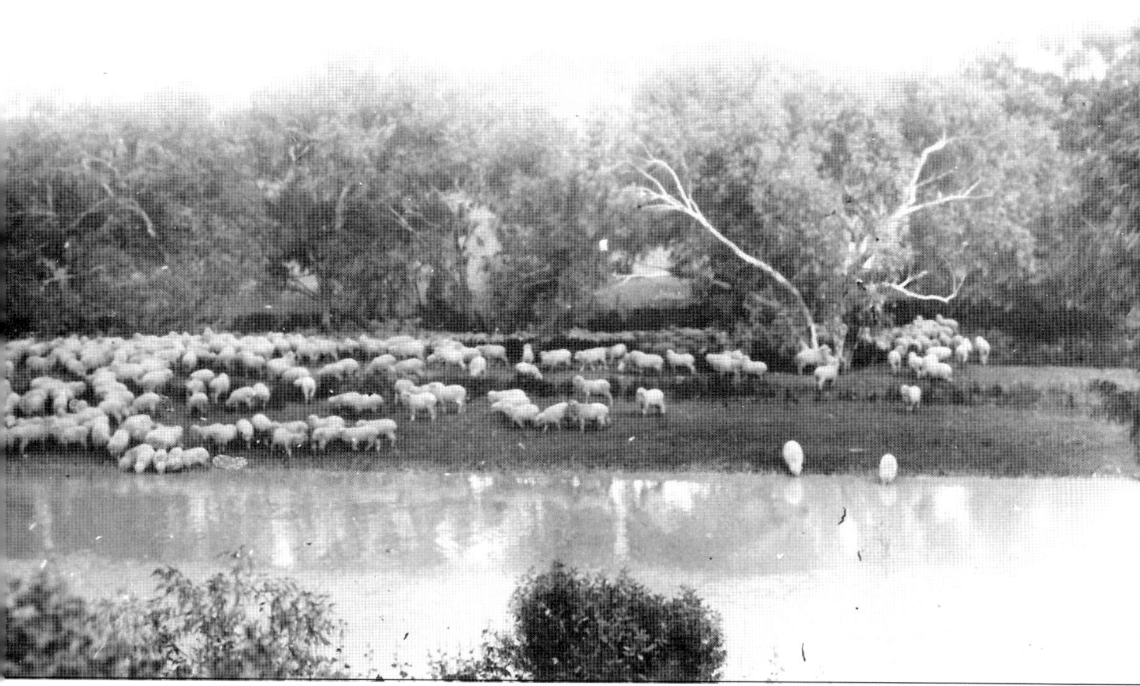

Although the Salinas area is closely associated with agriculture, early industries included cattle and sheep raising as well. Monterey County was the leading wool producer in California in both the 1870 and 1880 censuses. The sheep population around Salinas declined due to the success of agriculture, but up the Salinas Valley, where land was cheaper, huge herds continued to prosper. This vintage real-photo postcard shows one such herd grazing by the river.

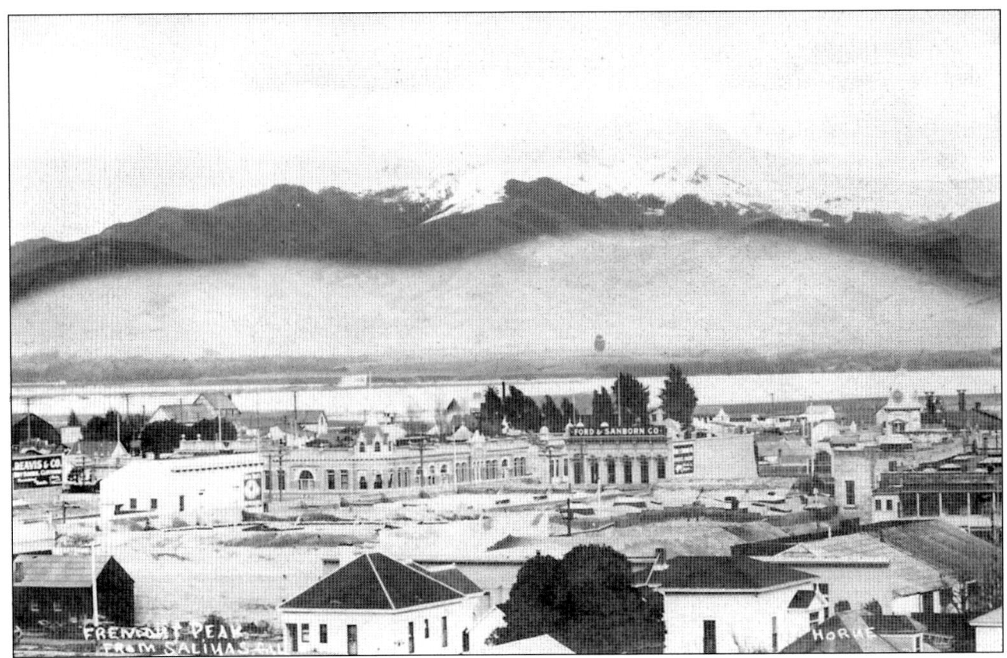

Pictured here is an early winter view of downtown Salinas. Snow is visible on the Gabilan Mountains in the background.

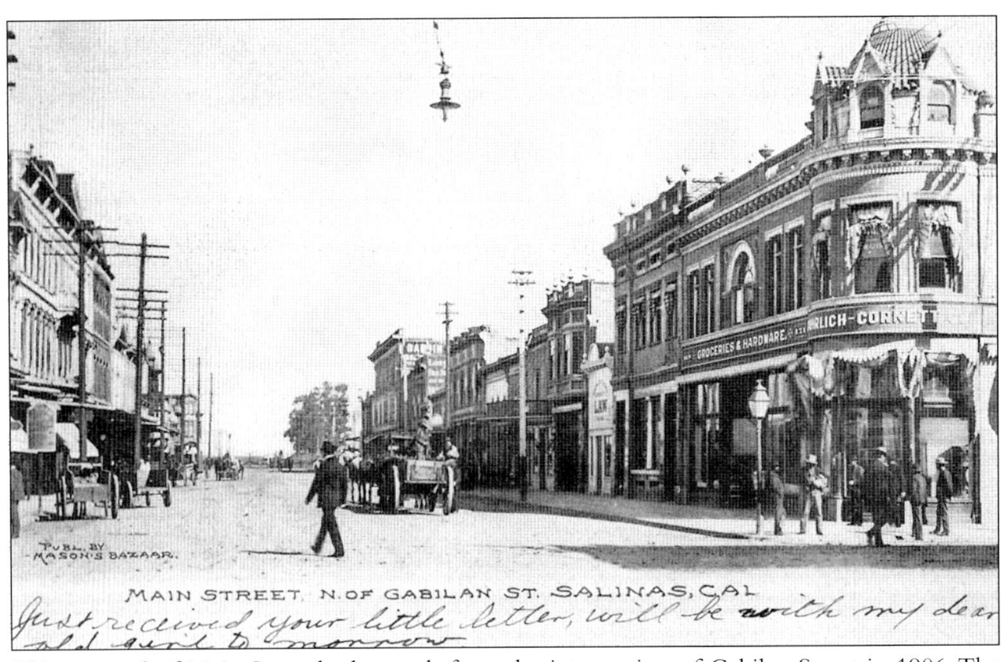

This postcard of Main Street looks north from the intersection of Gabilan Street in 1906. The McDougal Building (1898) is in the foreground, and the Bardin House is on the right. On the left are the Salinas City Bank (1873), Abbott House (1874), the Fashion Livery Stable, and Opera House. This postcard was mailed to a Mrs. Baker in Pacific Grove. Note the sender's message: "Just received your little letter, will be with my dear old girl tomorrow."

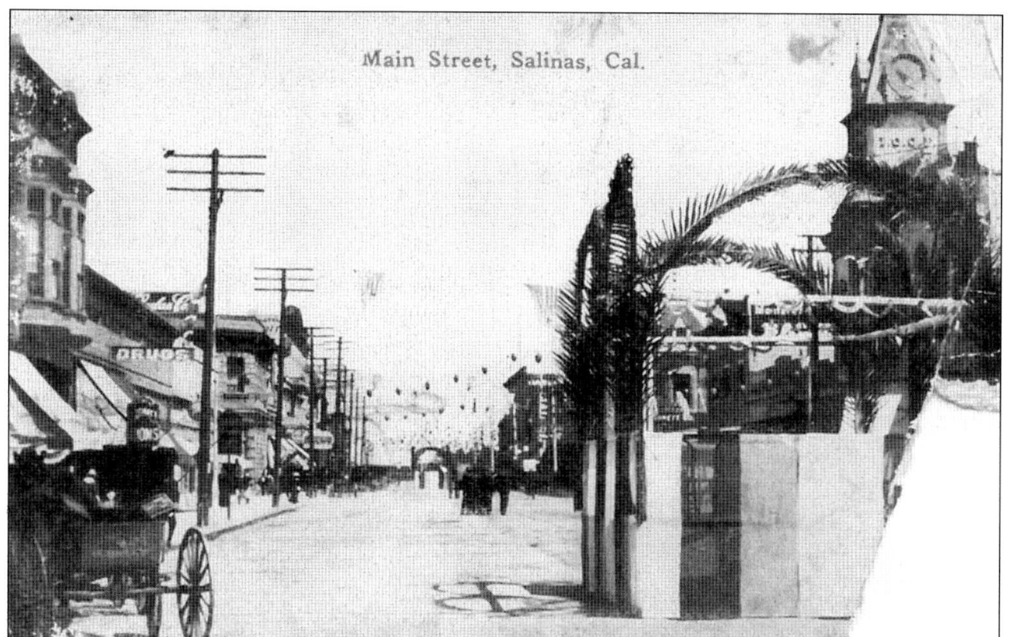

Here is another early view showing downtown Salinas. Note the Chinese lanterns decorating Main Street. To the right is the tower of the local Independent Order of Odd Fellows (IOOF) building. This serves as an easily identifiable landmark in many of the Main Street photographs that follow.

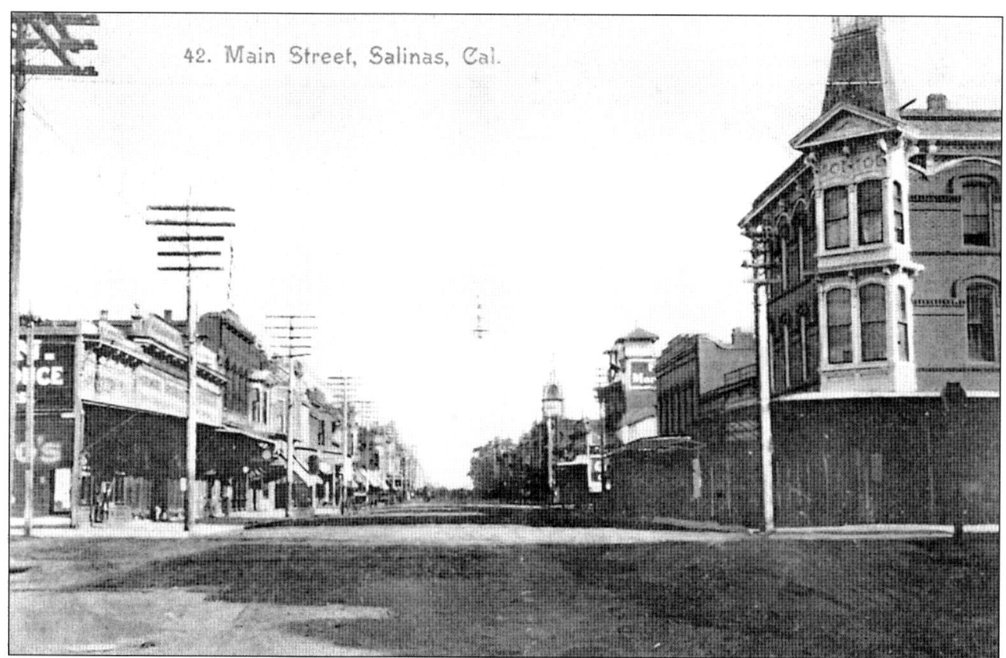

Main Street of Salinas is pictured here as it looked in 1908. On the right is the Hotel Jeffrey, which served as a stage stop for many years. The hotel opened on New Year's Day in 1888.

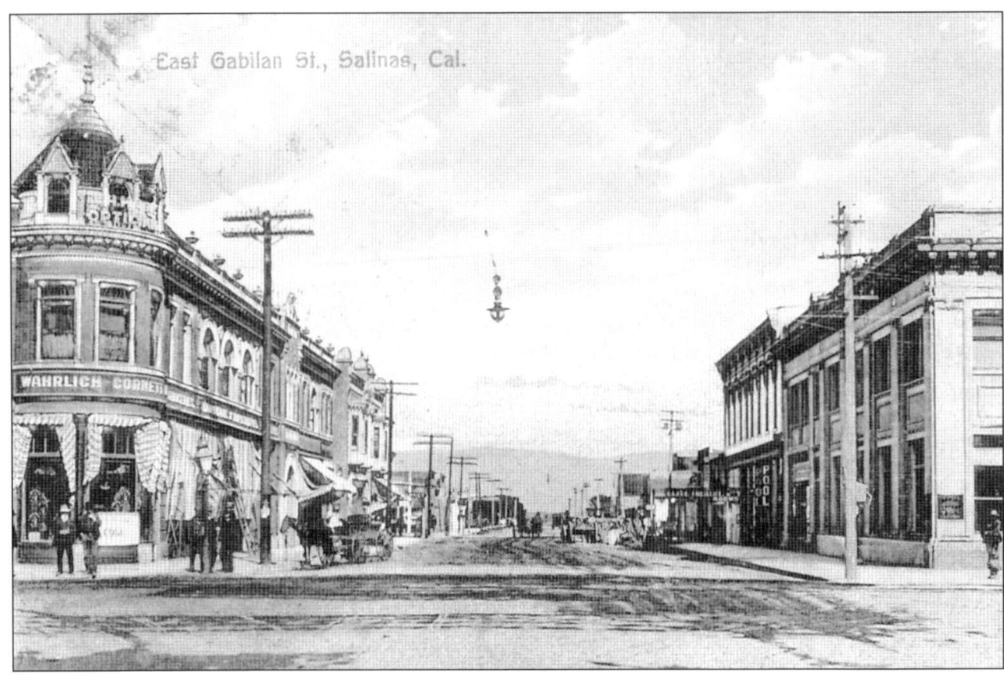

The view on this postcard looks east from Main Street on Gabilan Street in 1910. Gabilan Street had not yet been paved at that time. Of interest is the lone streetlight hanging in the center of the intersection. It appears that during those times, a streetlight was hung in the center of each intersection on Main Street.

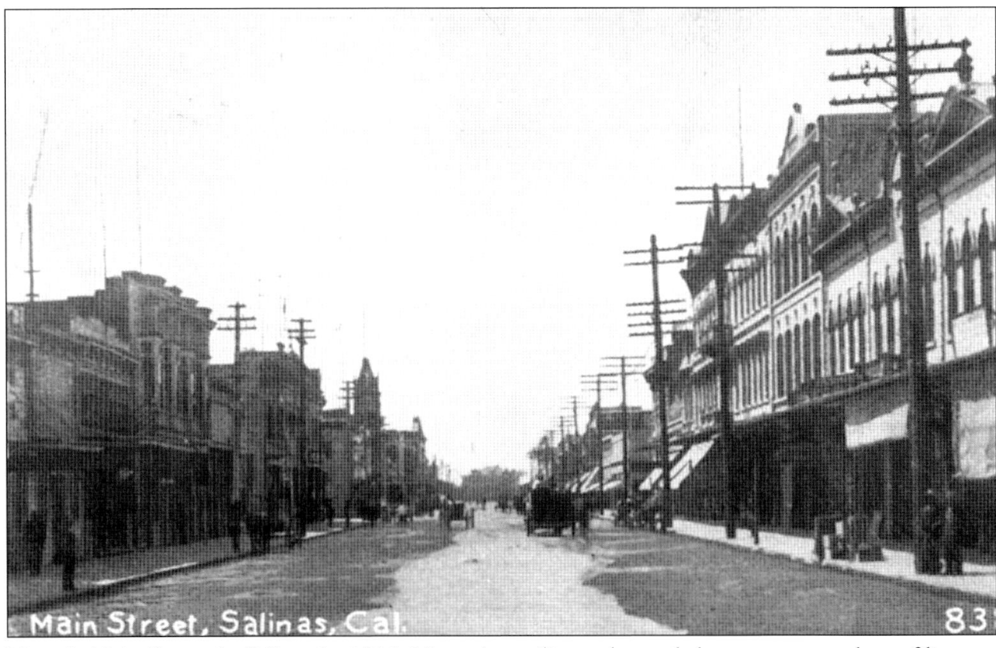

Here is Main Street in Salinas in 1914. Note the utility poles and the greater number of lines as compared to the previous image (above), taken just four years earlier. Sidewalks are in place, but the streets are still unpaved.

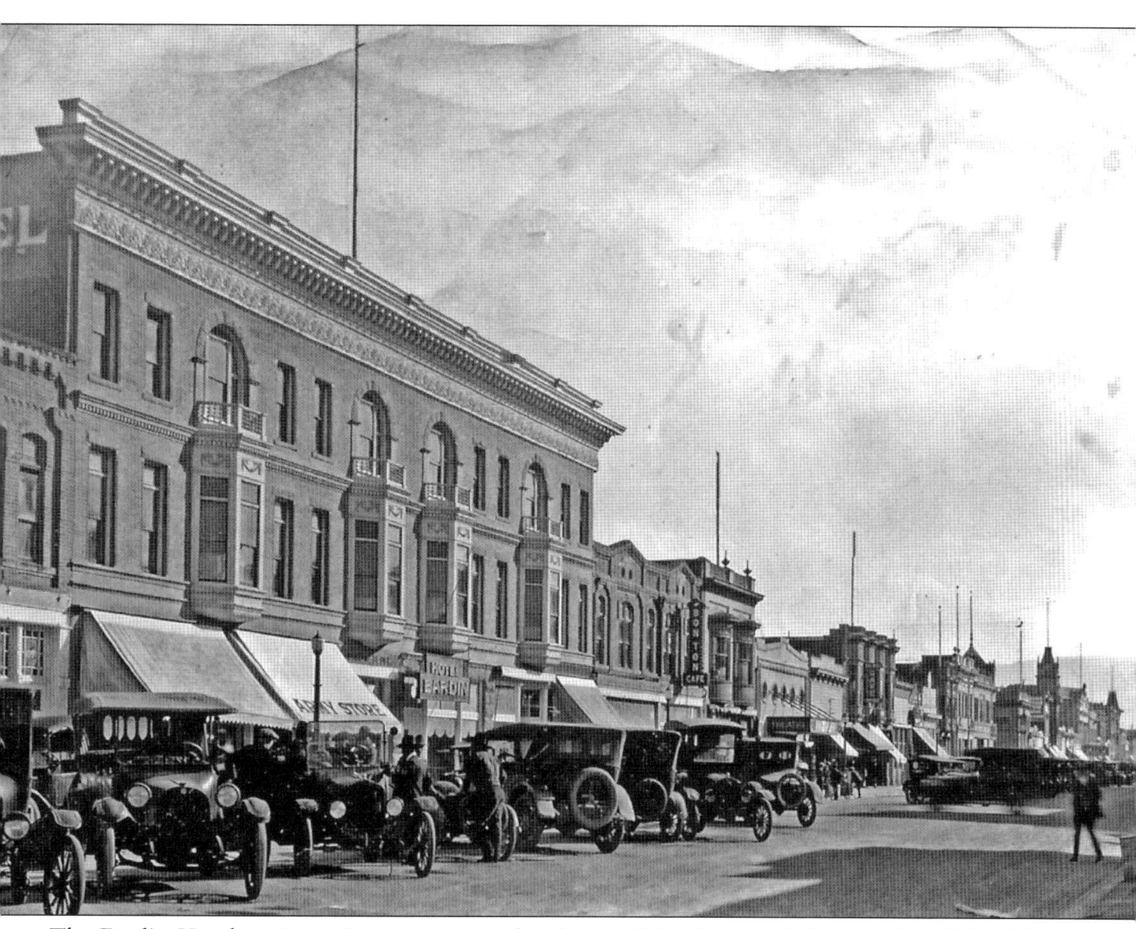

The Bardin Hotel on Main Street was considered one of the finest in Salinas in the 1920s. This later became the Franciscan Hotel, which was destroyed by fire in 1945.

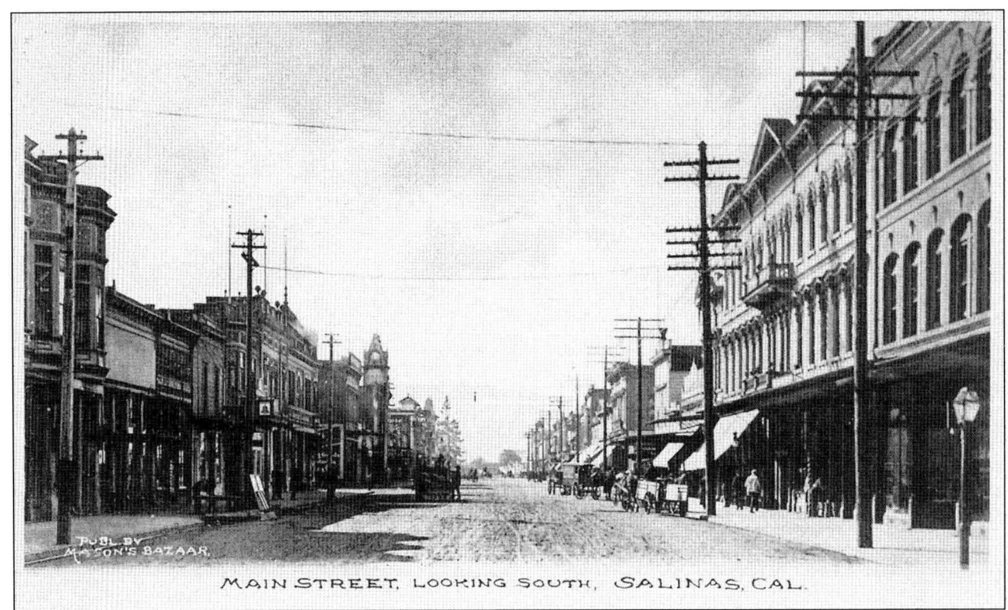

Looking south along Main Street, the Abbott House, built in 1873, is on the right. It was one of the finest hotels on the central coast.

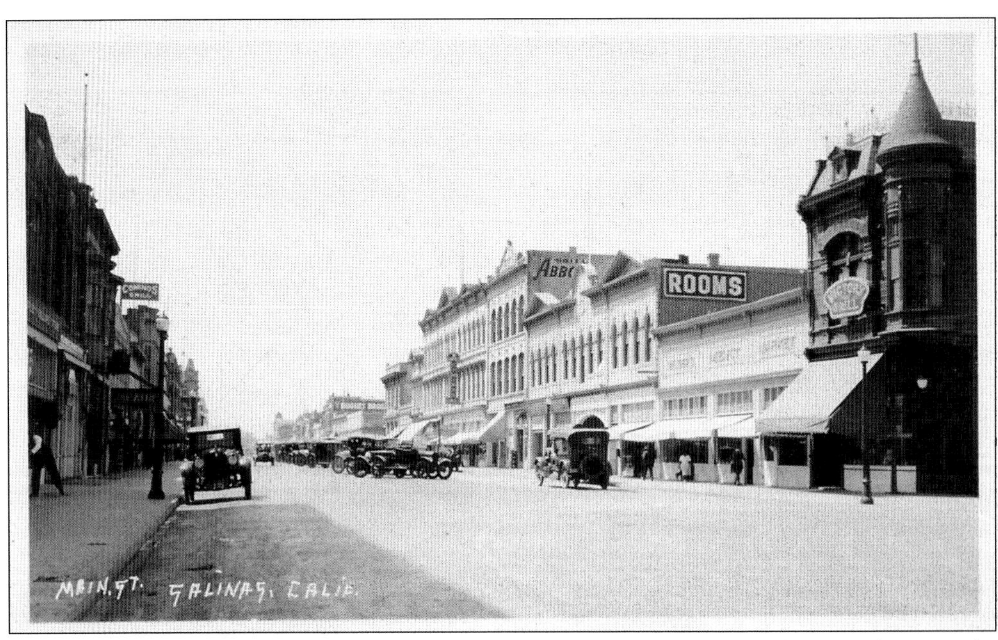

Another view shows Main Street from the early 1920s. The Abbott House has now become the Cominos Hotel, although the sign on the side of the building has not yet been changed.

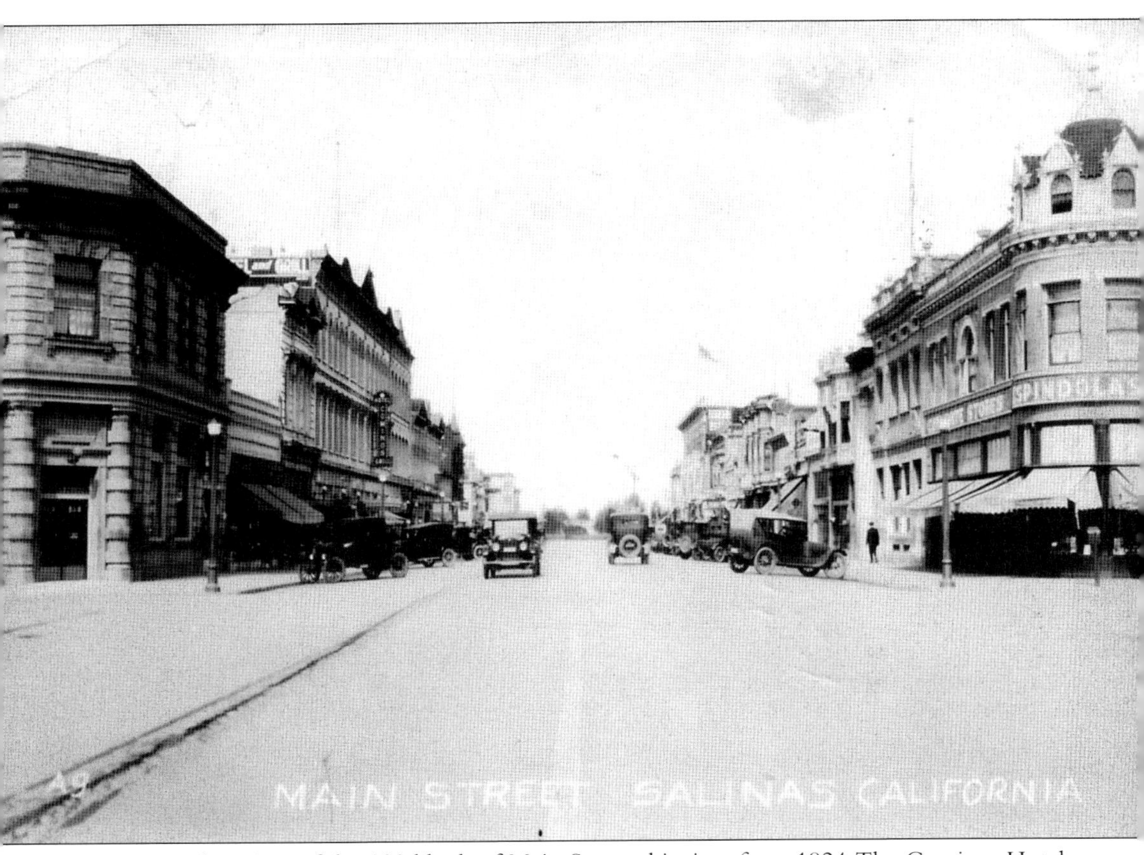

Here is another view of the 100 block of Main Street, this time from 1924. The Cominos Hotel is the large building in the center of the block. Note there are no utility poles and that hanging streetlights have been replaced with standing streetlamps.

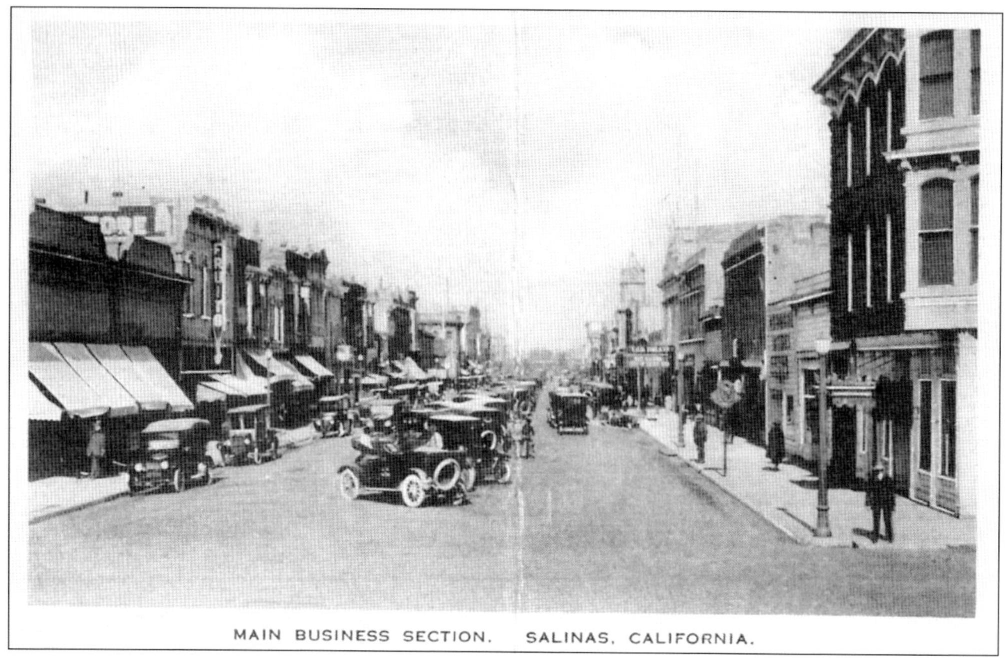

MAIN BUSINESS SECTION. SALINAS, CALIFORNIA.

The 200 block of Main Street is pictured here in 1923. This postcard shows that the town is bustling with activity and many automobiles are even parked in the center of the street.

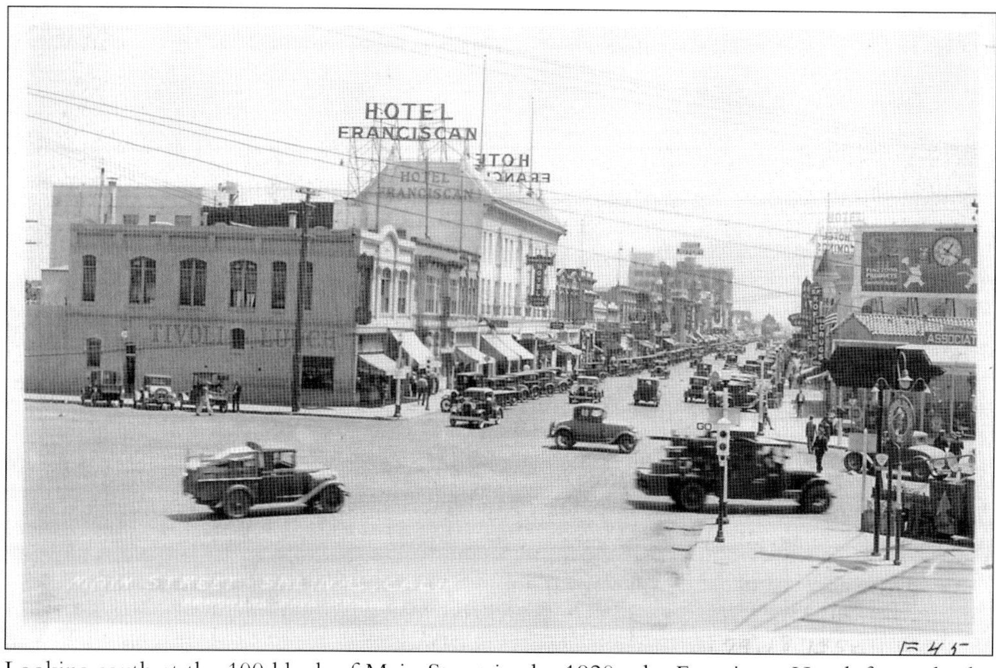

Looking south at the 100 block of Main Street in the 1920s, the Franciscan Hotel, formerly the Bardin Hotel, dominates the east side of the block. Meanwhile, the Cominos Hotel dominates the west side.

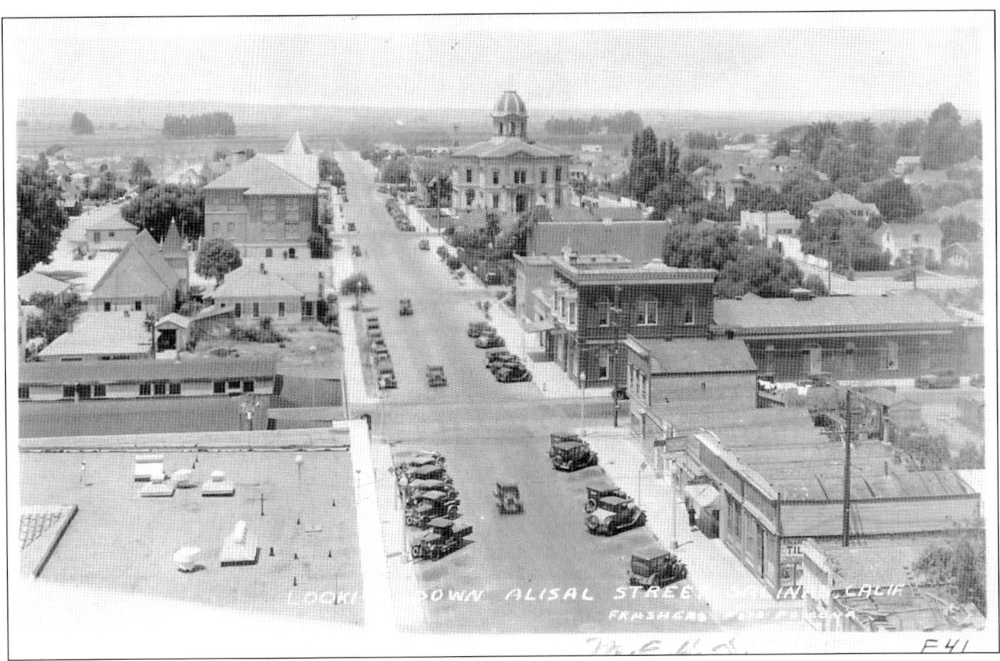

Here is a view looking west along Alisal Street in the 1920s. Buildings include the armory, on the right just past the first intersection, and the courthouse on the next block. The tall two-story building on the left is the Salinas High School.

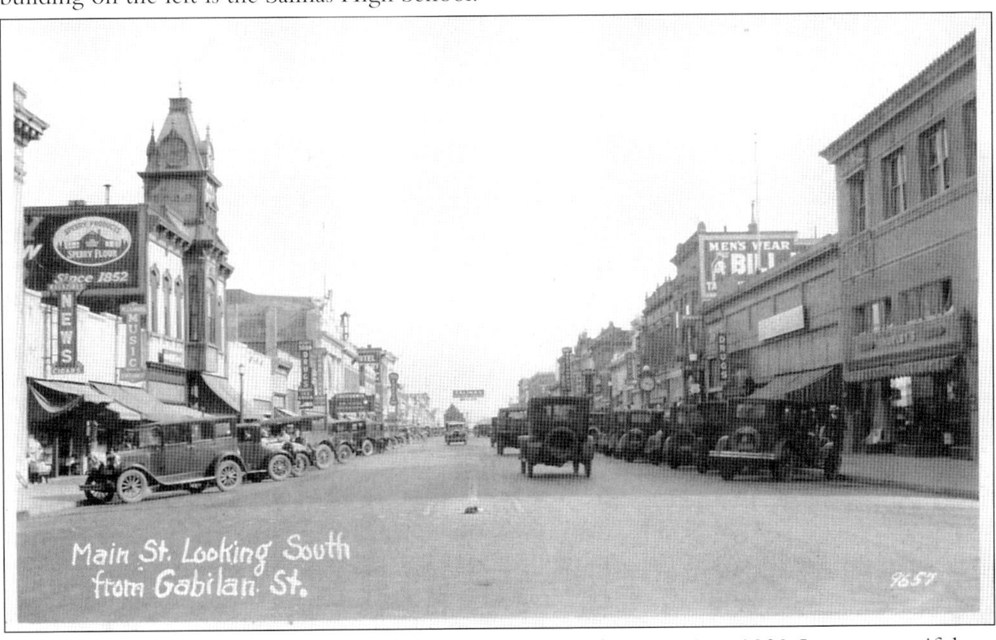

Pictured here is a view of the 200 block of Main Street in about 1929 or 1930. It appears as if there are hardly any parking spaces available. On the left, the first sign reads, "Magazines, News, Cigars," and the second says, "Alexander Music and Stationery." Farther down the block, the sign reads, "Soda, Drugs and Ice Cream." The marquee of the California Theater is visible but unreadable. On the right side, the signs say "Drugs," "Diamonds, Jeweler," "Candy," and "Restaurant." At the very end of the street is the famous Salinas Rodeo and Chamber of Commerce sign.

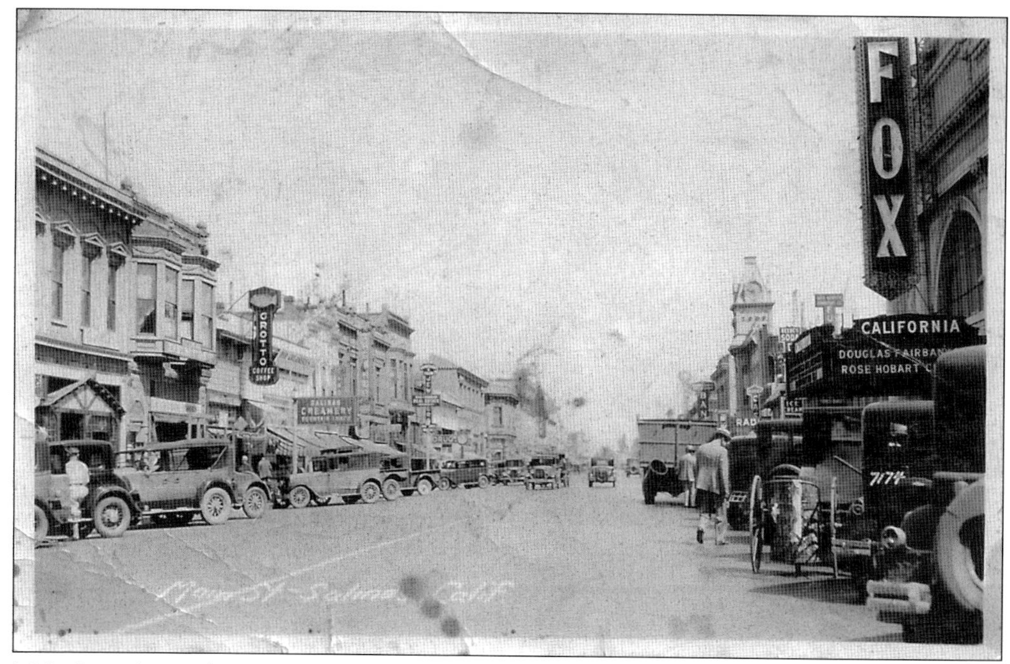

Main Street is seen here in 1931. The date is established by the movie playing at the Fox California Theater: *Chances* starring Douglas Fairbanks Jr. and Rose Hobart.

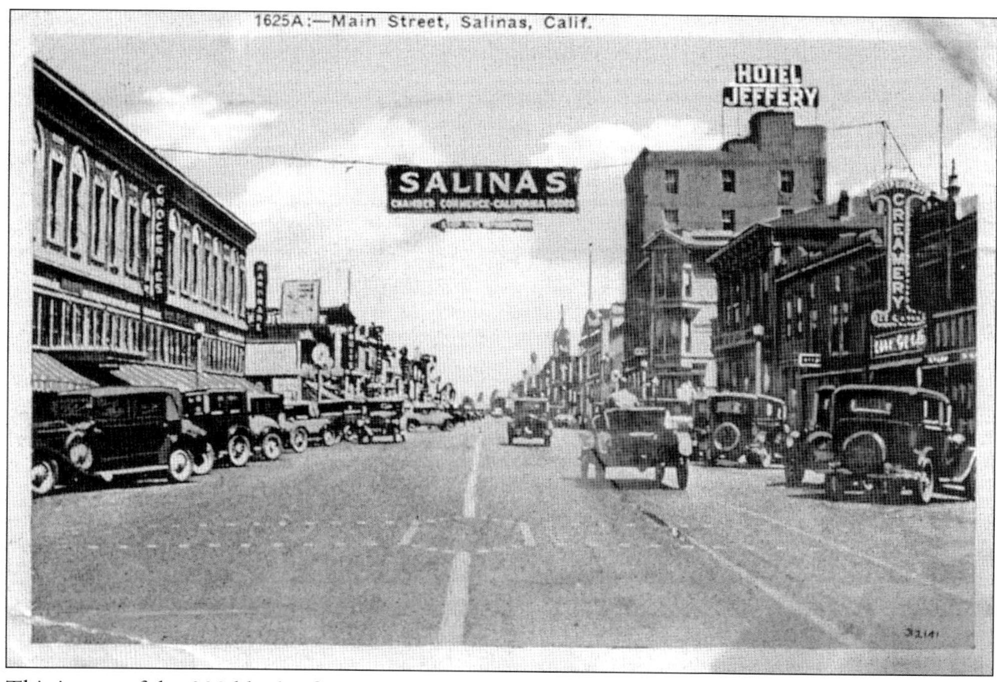

This image of the 300 block of Main Street, dating to 1925, shows the famous sign that decorated the center of town for many years. In 1915, under the leadership of Salinas mayor Chris N. Thorup, the Big Week Sign Committee was granted permission to erect the large sign over Main Street to advertise both the rodeo and the chamber of commerce.

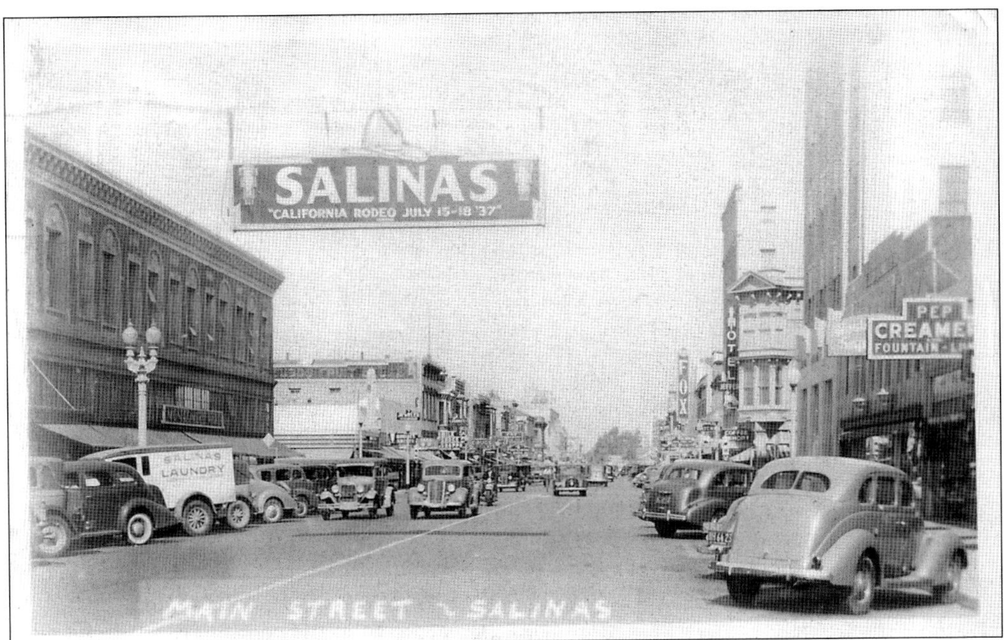

This 1937 view is similar to the previous postcard on the opposite page. The big hat was attached to the sign in later years, and the chamber of commerce signage was removed and replaced with that of the California Rodeo; the dates were changed every year to advertise the event.

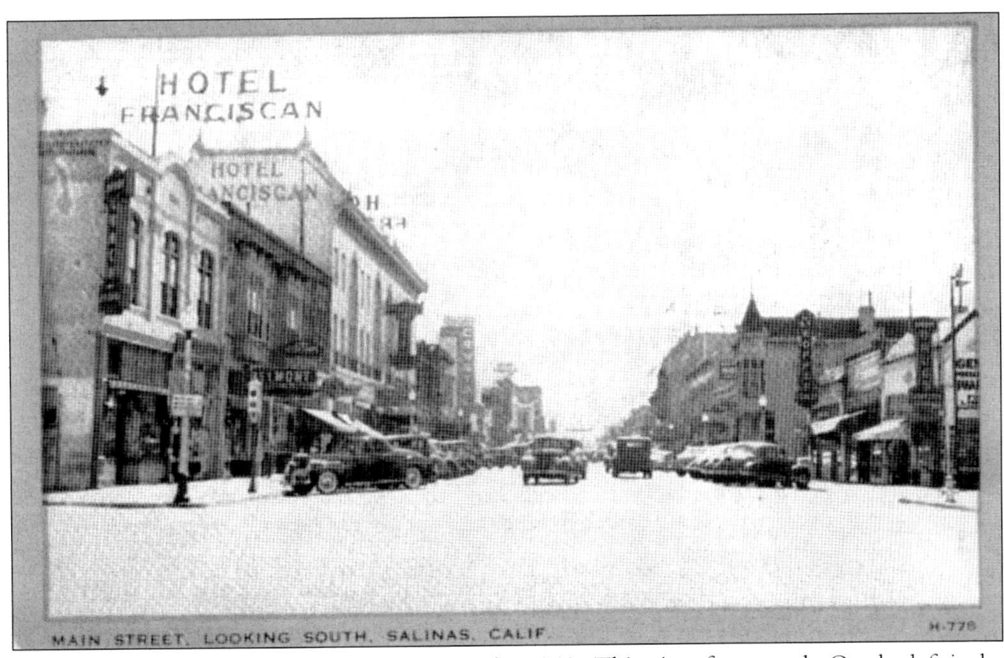

The 100 block of Main Street is seen here in the 1940s. This view faces south. On the left is the Hotel Franciscan, and farther down the street is the Crystal Theater marquee, located at 153 Main Street. The theater was demolished in late 2003, and in 2005, the Mayan Theater with 16 screens opened on its site. The facade of the Mayan is a replica of the Crystal Theater.

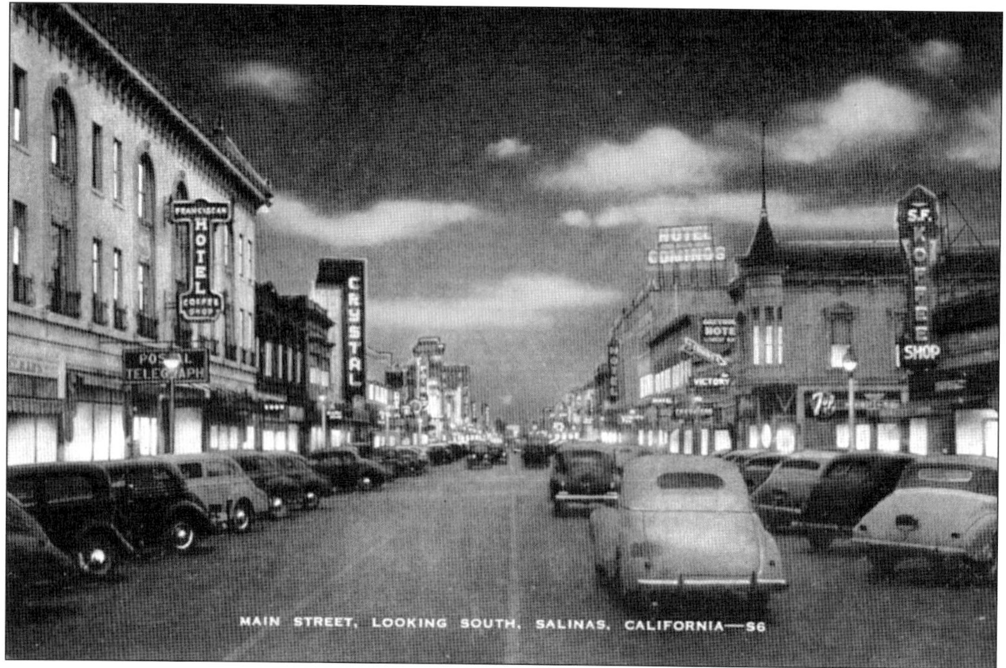

This unusual nighttime view shows Main Street in the 1940s. On the right are the S.F. Koffee Shop, Victory Bar & Grill, and the Cominos Hotel. On the left are the Franciscan Hotel and Crystal Theater.

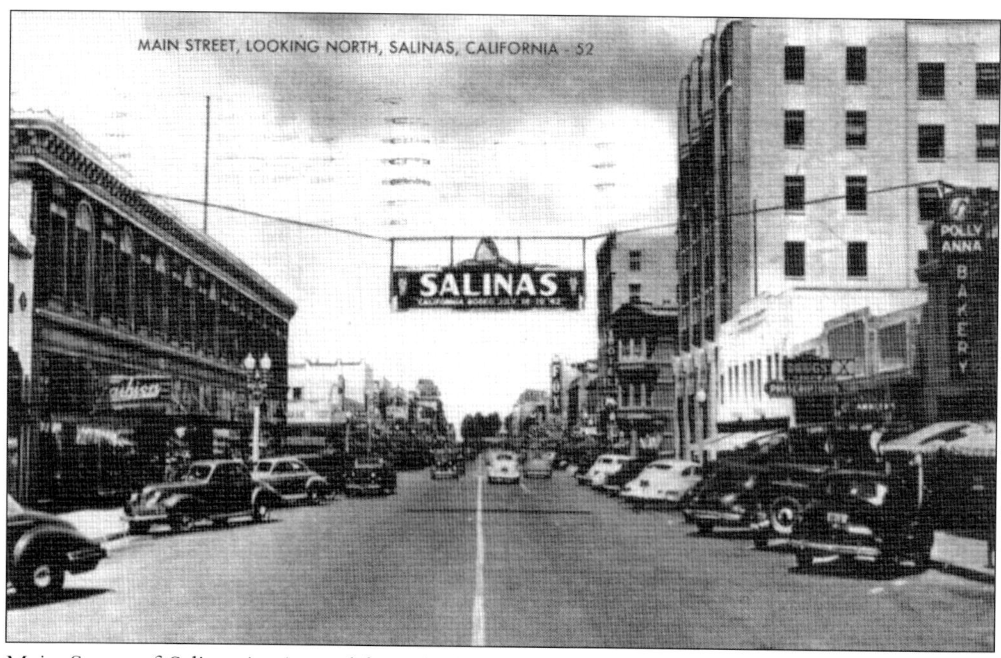

Main Street of Salinas is pictured here in 1942. This is another view of the famous sign that decorated the center of town for many years.

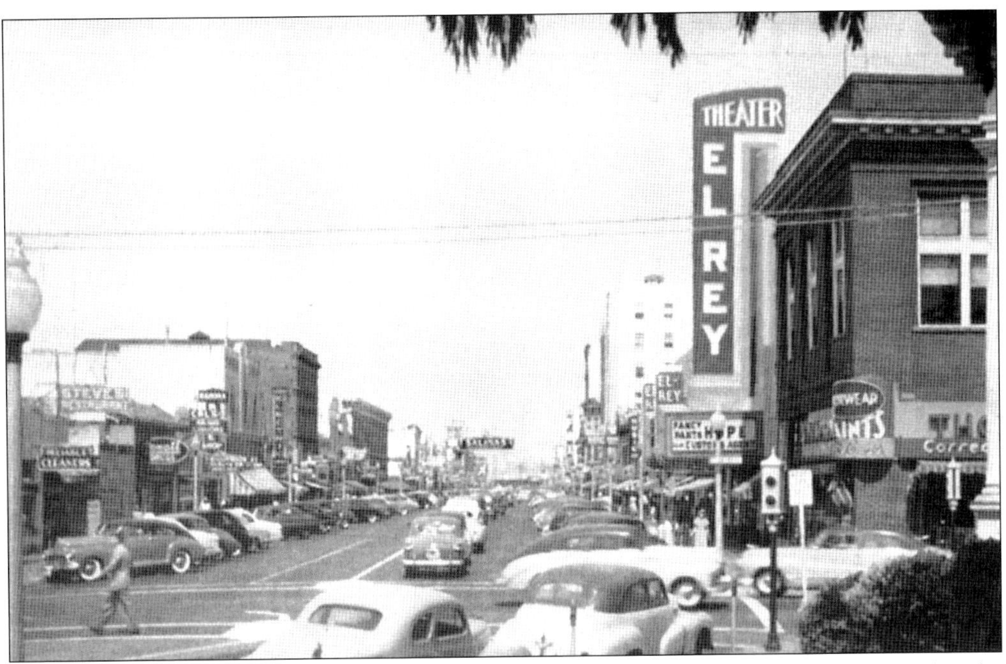

The 300 block of Main Street is seen here in 1950. Bob Hope and Lucille Ball are featured at the El Rey Theater, starring in *Fancy Pants*.

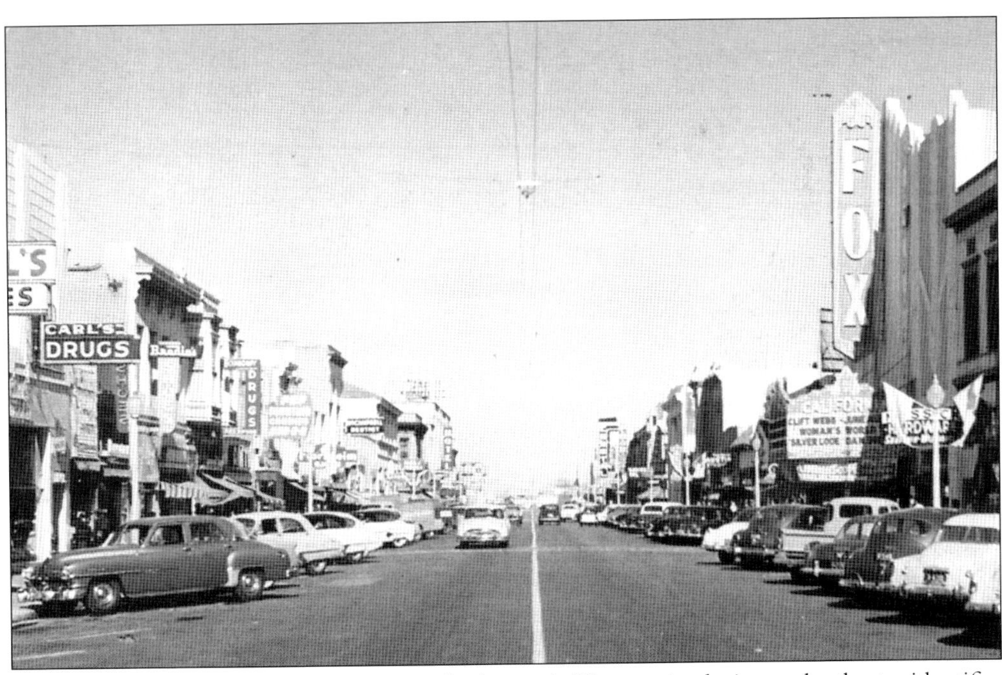

This view of the 200 block of Main Street looks north. The movie playing at the theater identifies this postcard as being from 1954.

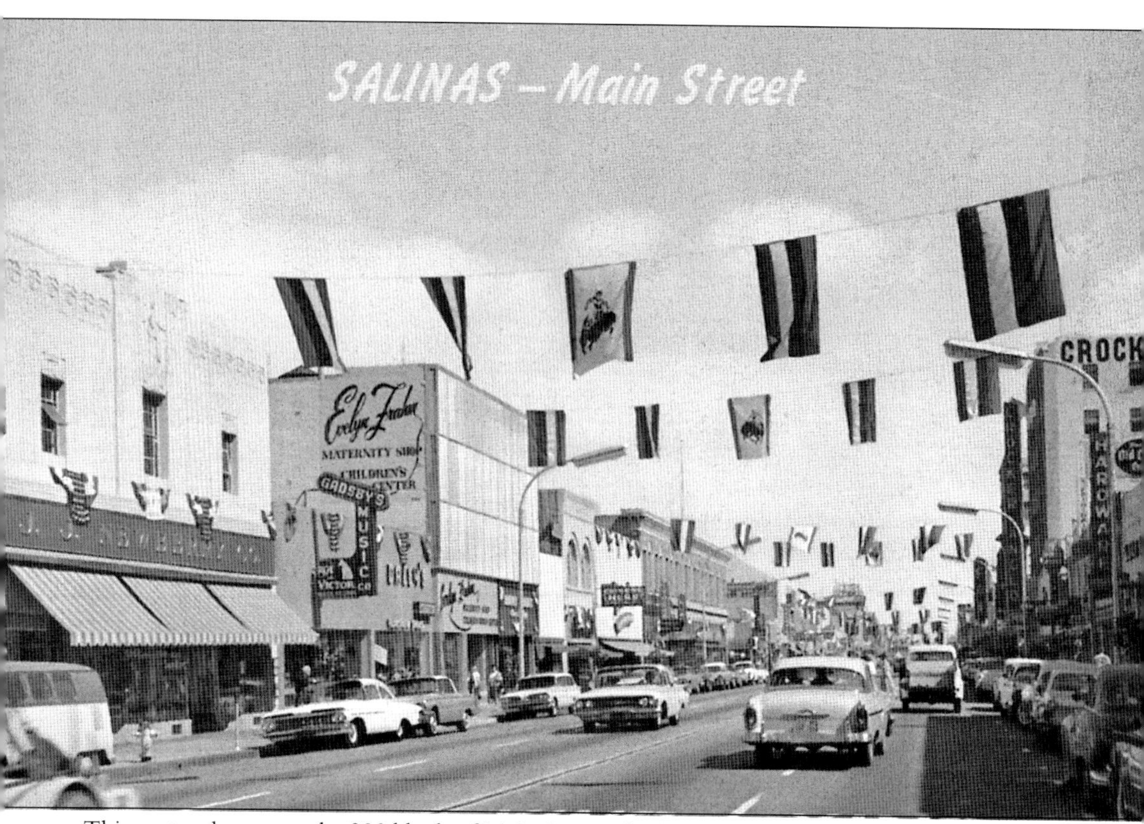

This postcard captures the 300 block of Main Street of Salinas in the 1960s. Pictured on the left are J.J. Newberry Co., Gadsby Music, The Lady Shop, Chinese Herbs, and Woolworth's.

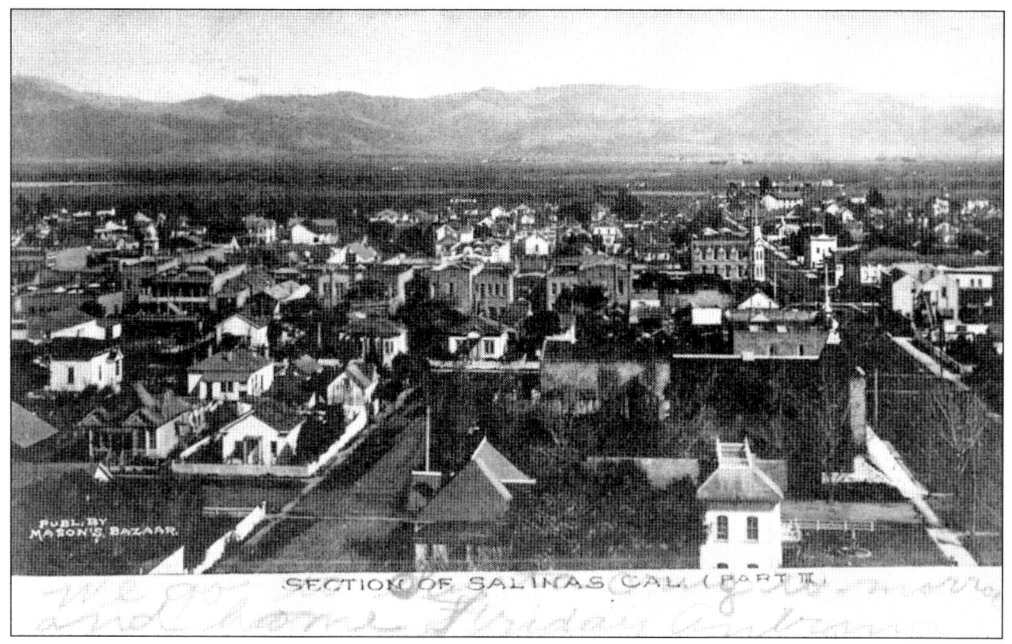

Here is a rooftop view of Salinas in 1906.

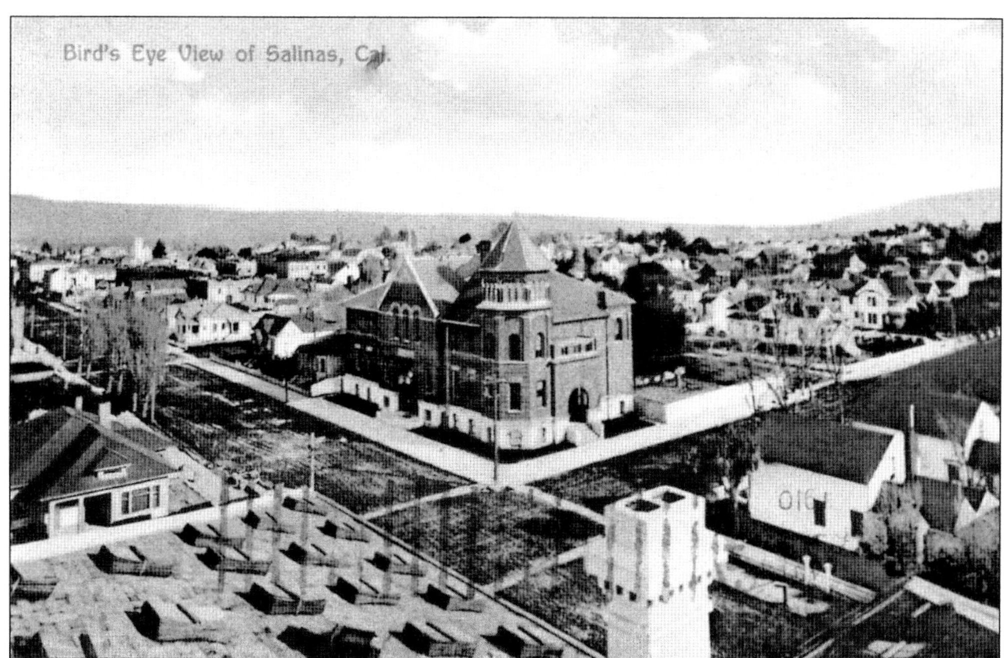

Here is another rooftop view, this one from 1910. The building in the center is the original high school, known as "the brickyard."

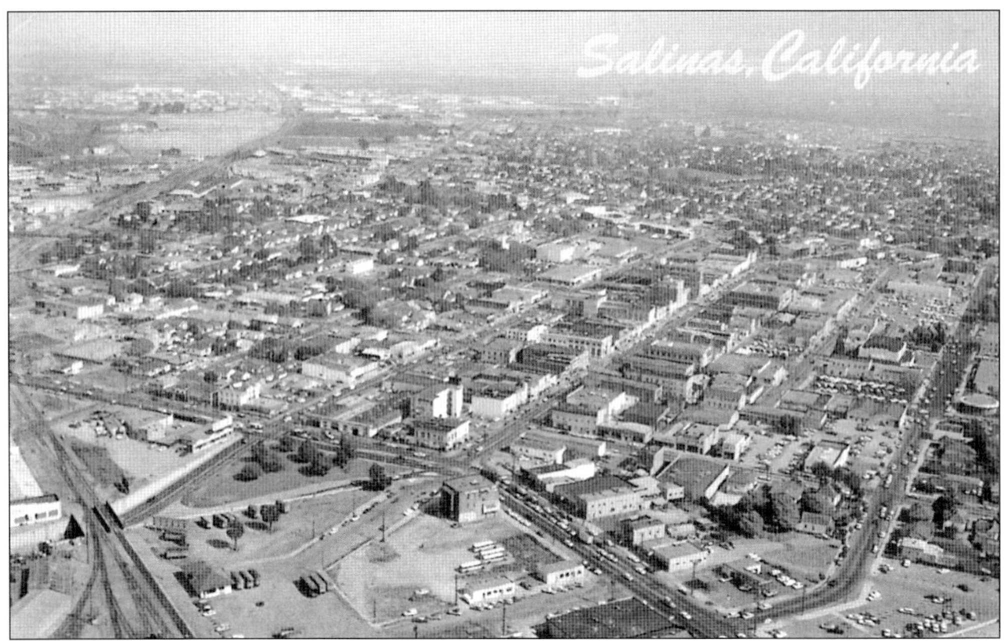

This c. 1960 aerial view of Salinas shows how much the city had grown in the second half of the 20th century. In the left-hand corner at the bottom is the Salinas Rail Road Station, located at 11 Station Place, one block north of Market Street.

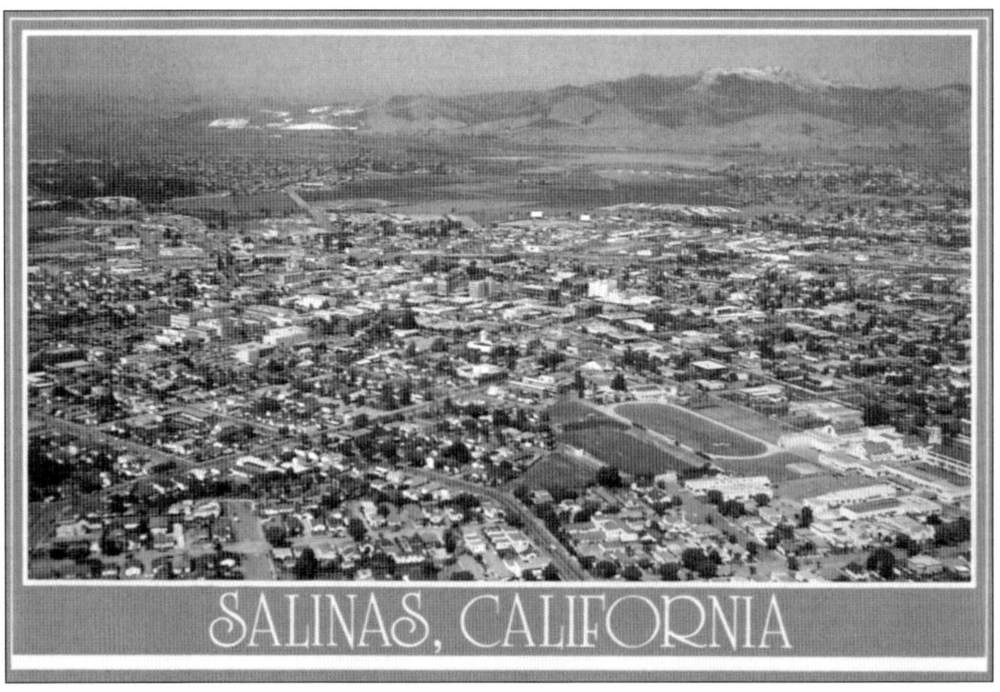

The aerial view on this postcard dates to 1987. As evidenced by this image, the town has started to sprawl.

Two

Historic Homes

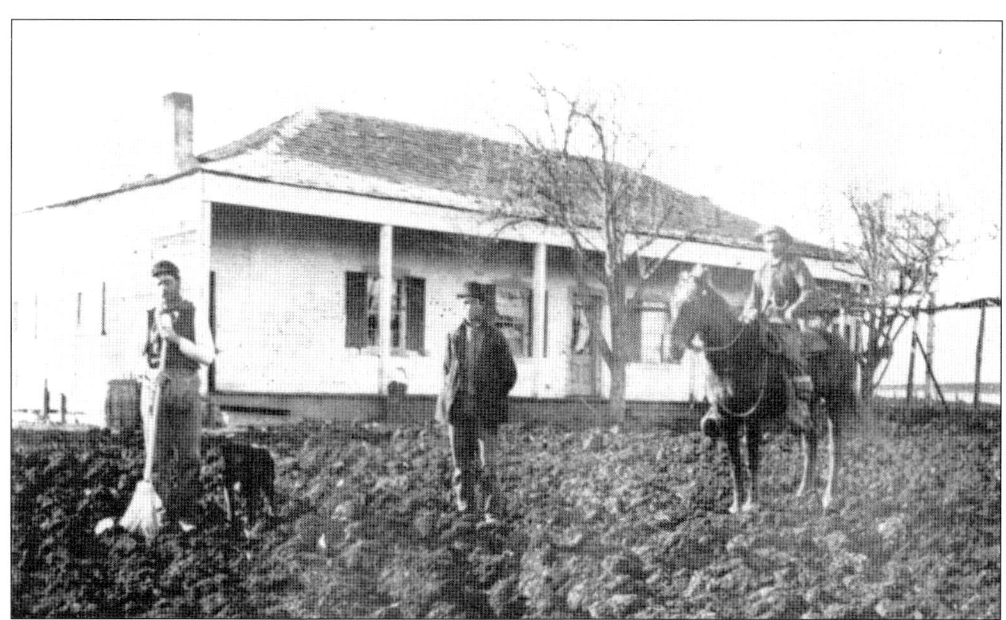

This early view shows the José Eusebio Boronda Adobe. Built about 1846, this is the oldest building in the Salinas area to retain its original design and setting. Pictured are some of the family members of William Anderson and Ines Boronda de Anderson, daughter of José Eusebio Boronda. This building is listed in the National Register of Historic Places and is a California Historic Landmark (No. 870).

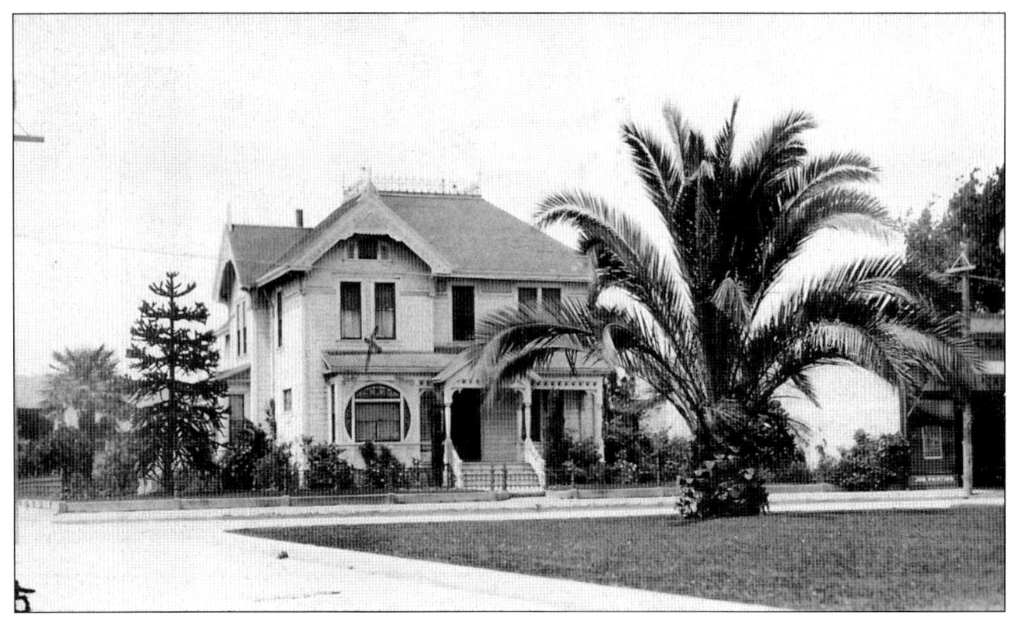

This home was owned by early Salinas resident Jesse Carr. It was built on Church and Howard Streets north of the county courthouse. This house with five fireplaces was considered the finest private residence in the city. The structure was demolished when the new courthouse was built in 1930. The Monterey County Historical Society has several of the fireplace mantels in its collection.

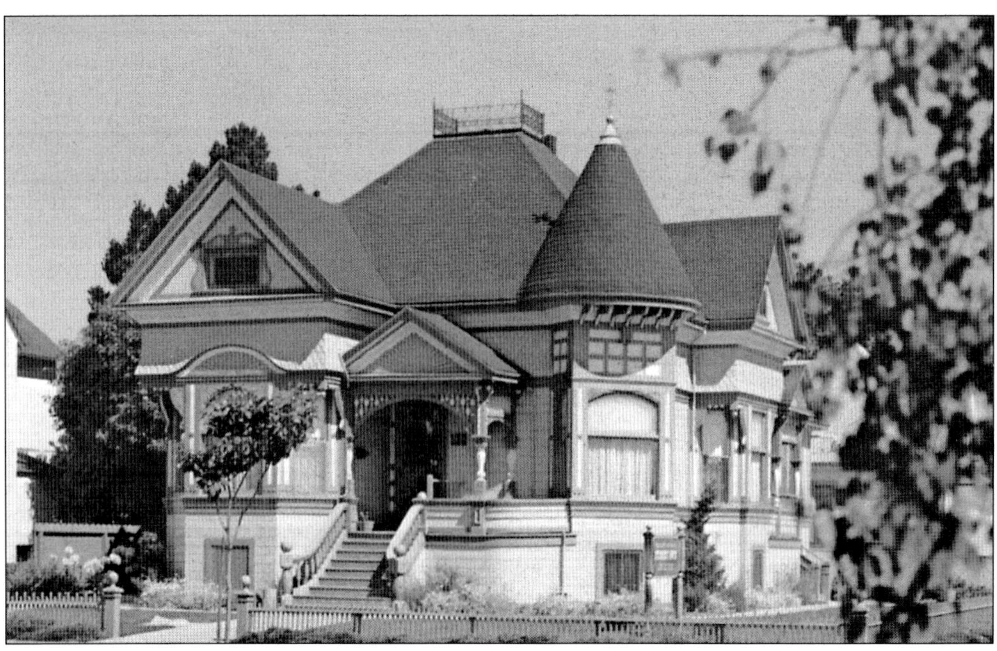

The boyhood home of author John Steinbeck was three blocks west of Main Street on Central Avenue. The home was originally built in 1897 for J.J. Connor. The building has been restored and is operated by the Valley Guild as a luncheon restaurant.

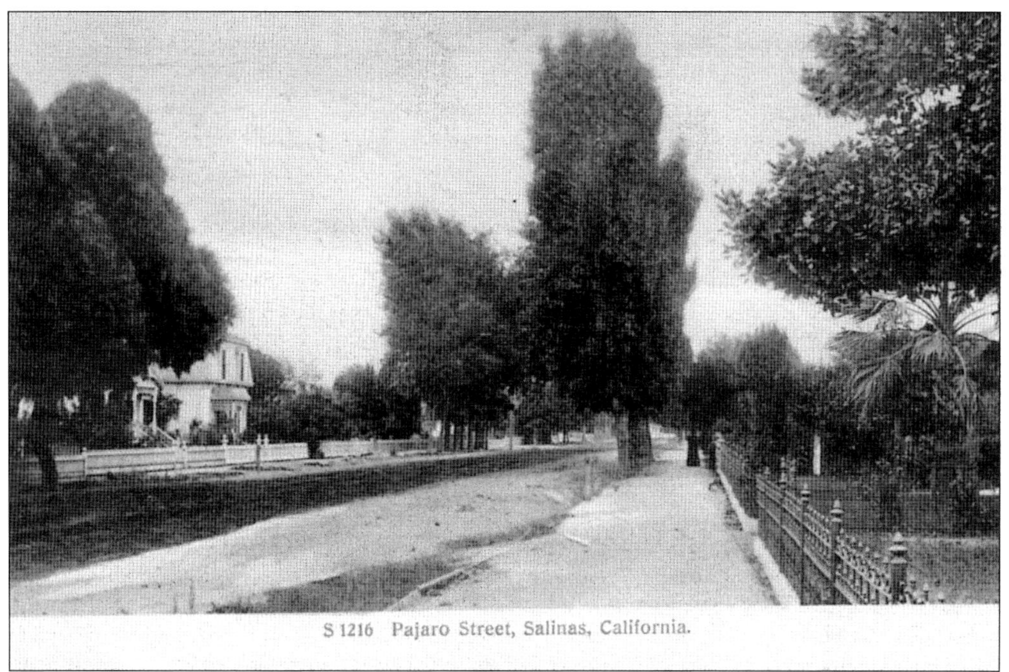

This residential street was not far from Main Street. The 1909 view has a serene, quiet feeling with the beautiful trees and quaint fences lining the simple walkway.

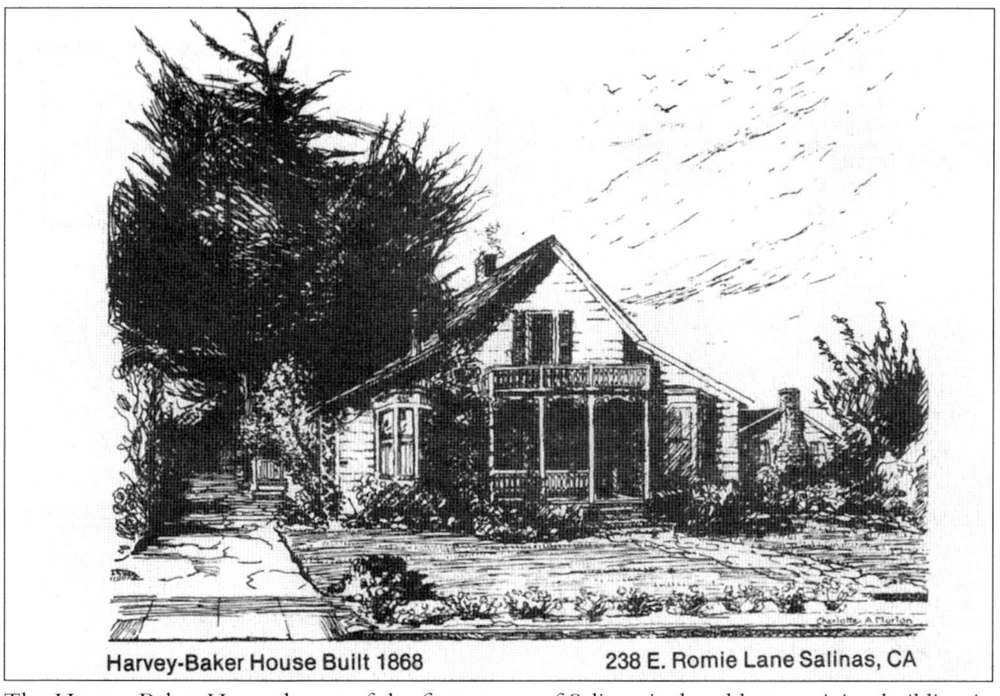

The Harvey-Baker House, home of the first mayor of Salinas, is the oldest surviving building in town. It has been moved several times and is now located at the Salinas Transportation Center in downtown Salinas. It is now a historic house museum.

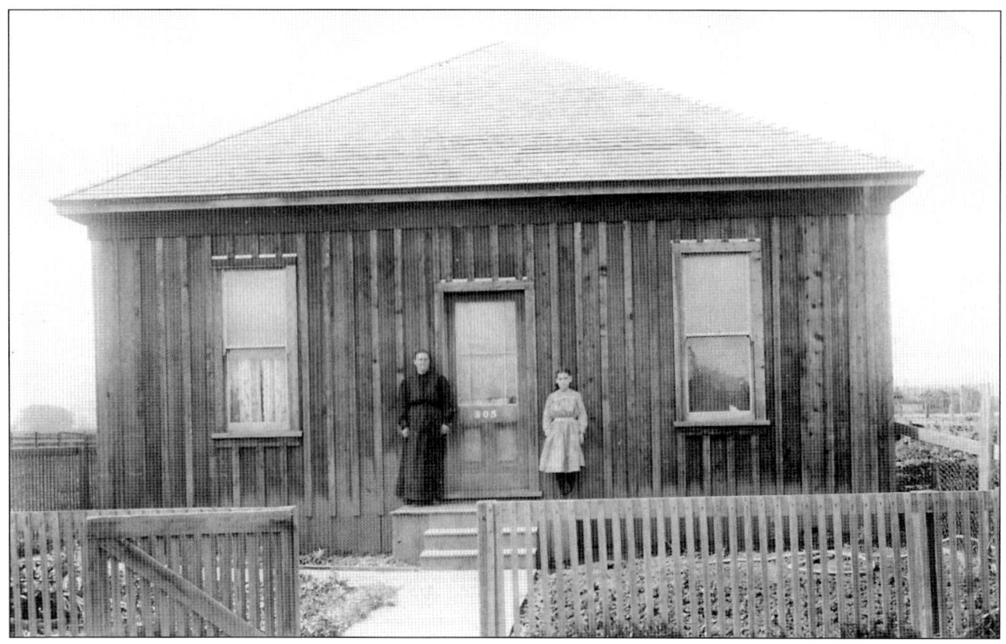

The Worthington Home, a one-story board-and-batten bungalow cottage at 305 Geil Street, is pictured here about 1911. Present are Mrs. Abbie West and her niece, Clara Worthington.

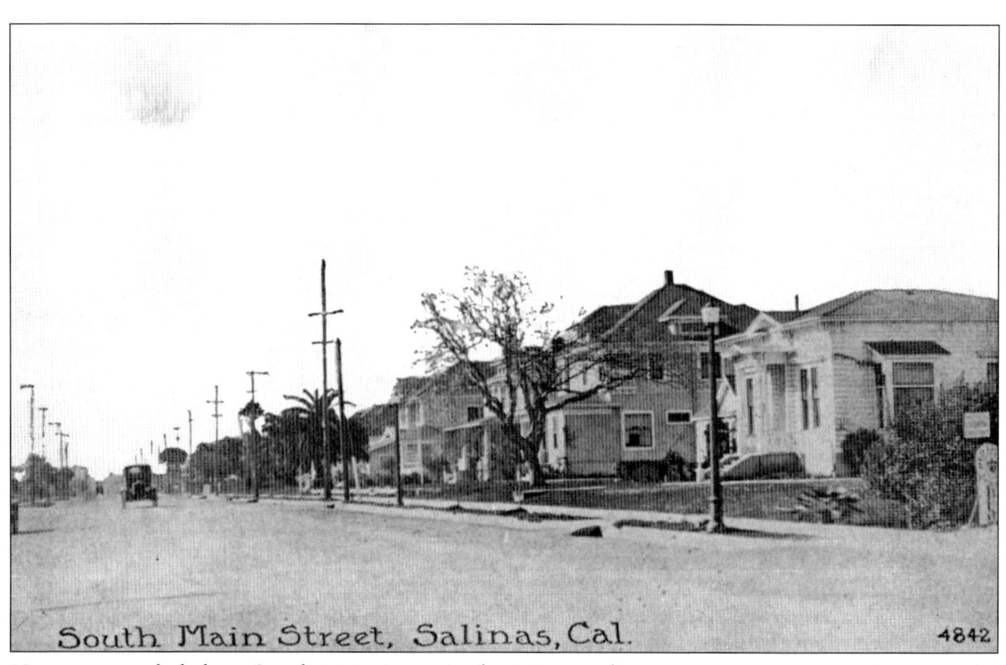

Homes expanded along South Main Street in the 1920s as the town grew. In 1924, Salinas was the wealthiest city in America per capita.

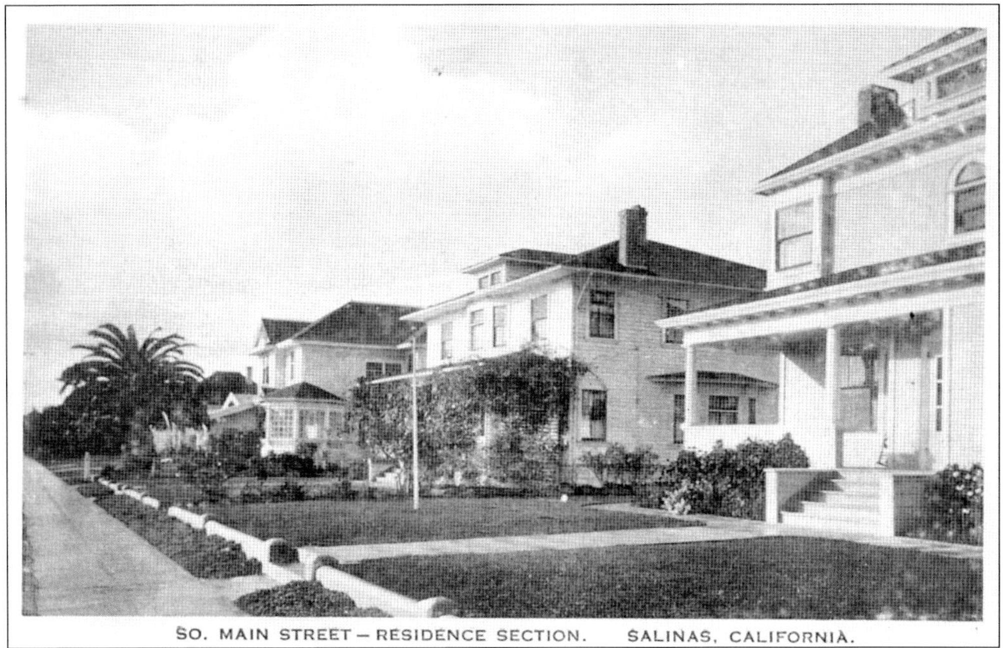

Pictured here is another view of South Main Street; this image was captured in 1927.

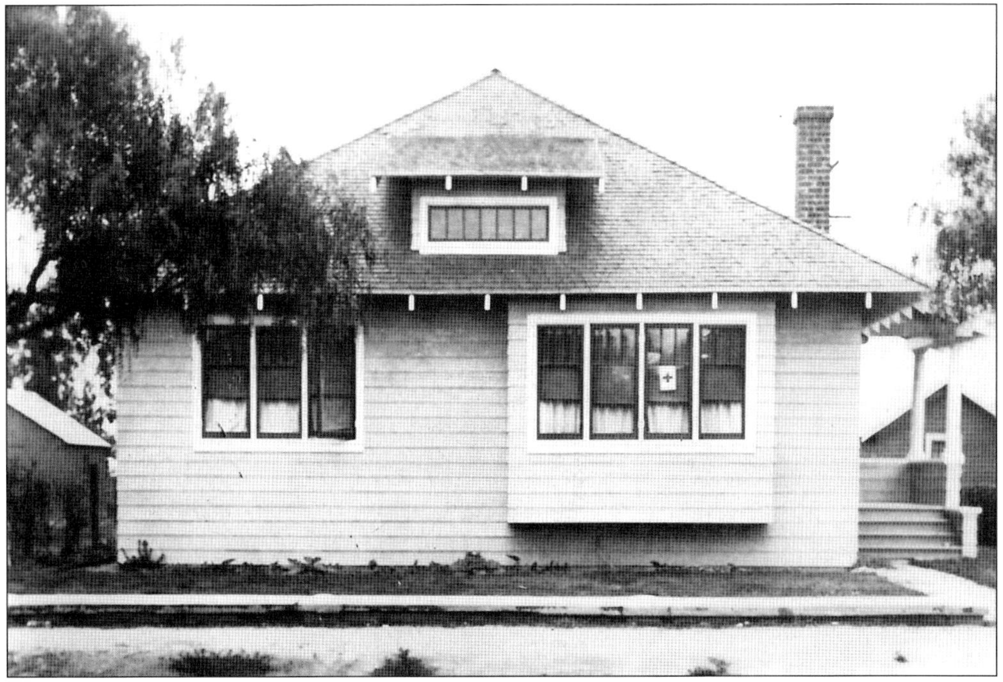
The red cross in the window of this house denotes that there was a case of scarlet fever there.

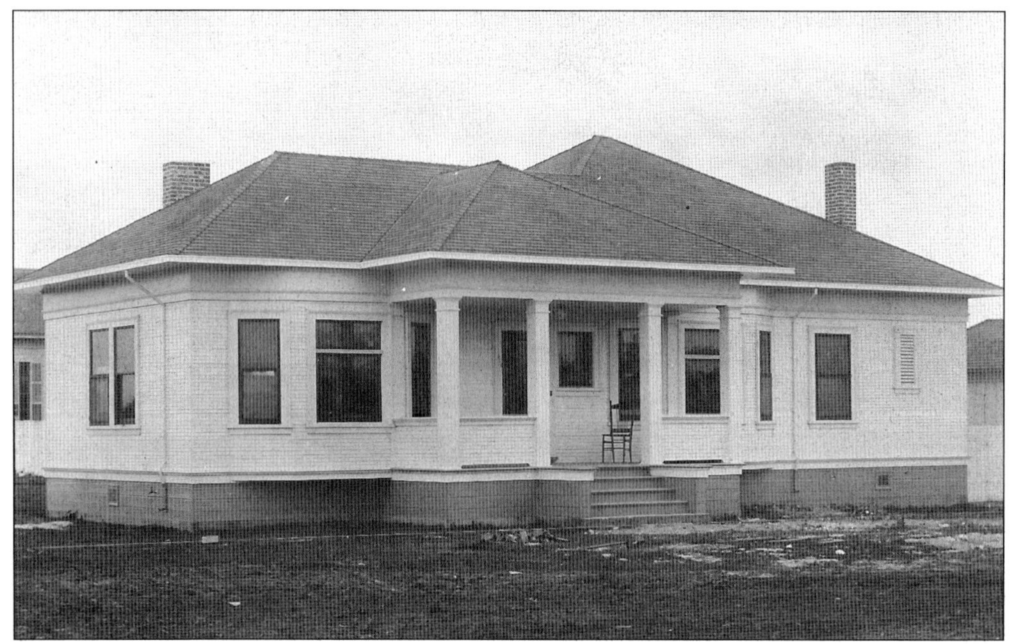

This picture was taken of the house at the northwest corner of Cayuga and Clay Streets shortly after it was finished.

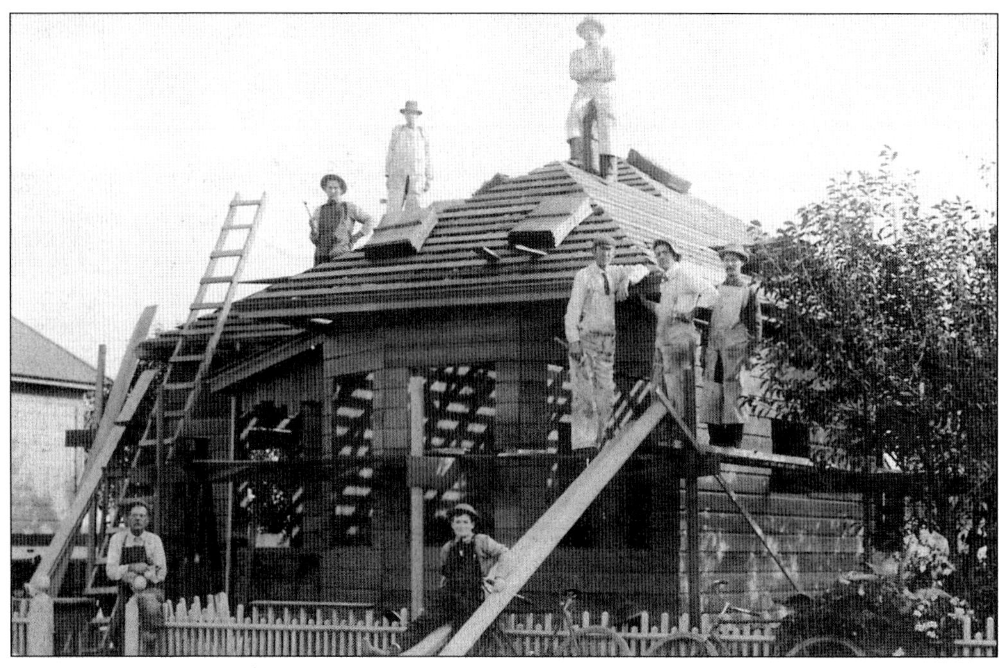

This postcard captures the common construction methods in November 1908. Most, or perhaps all, of the men are wearing ties.

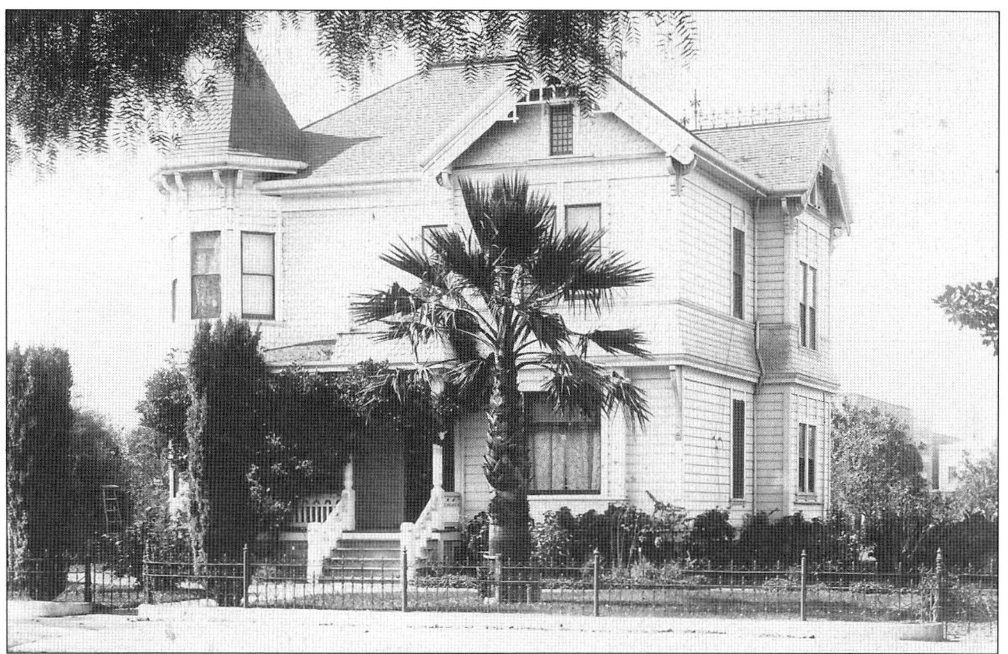

The Iverson home at 226 Pajaro Street was constructed around 1890 for E.P. Iverson, who was a partner with his brother James Iverson of one of the first blacksmith shops in Salinas. In later years, he was in partnership with two others and purchased 1,500 acres of land on Carr Lake for farming.

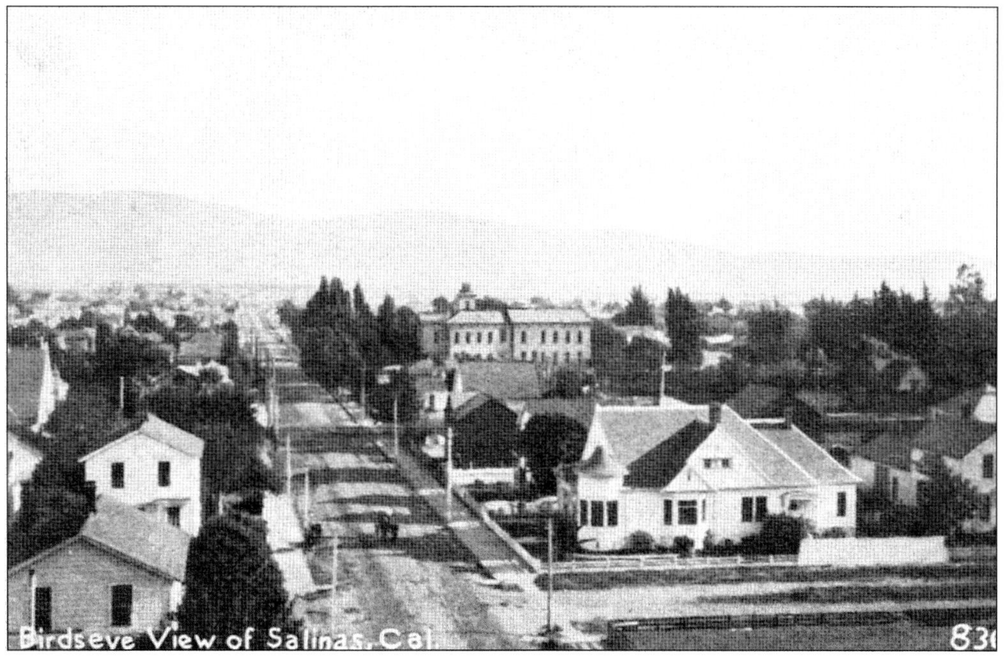

By 1912, the town was spreading out in all directions.

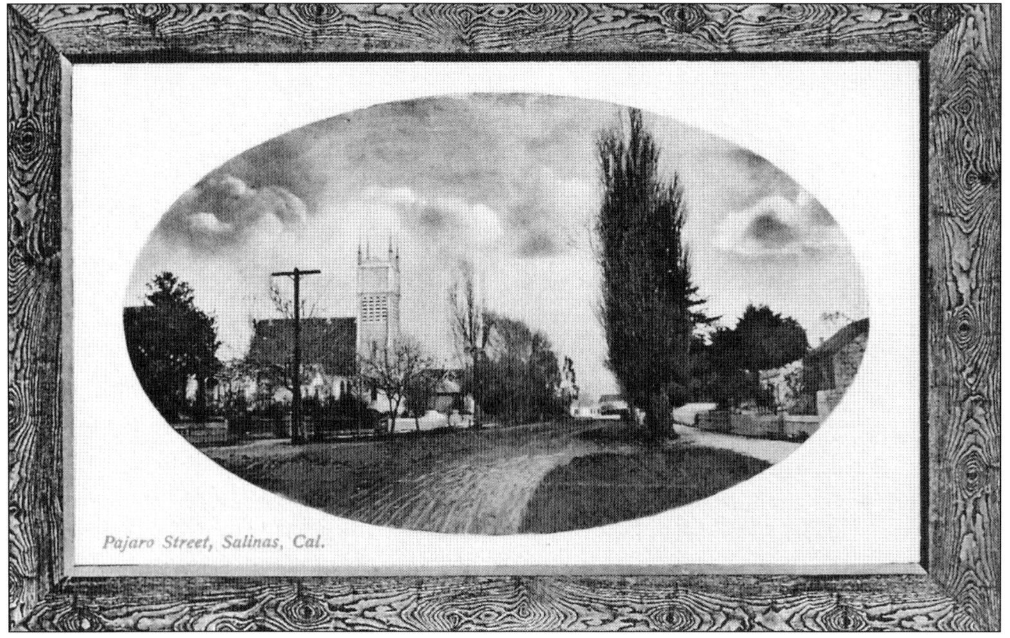

By the early 1900s, many Victorian homes had been built on Pajaro Street, just two blocks east of Main Street.

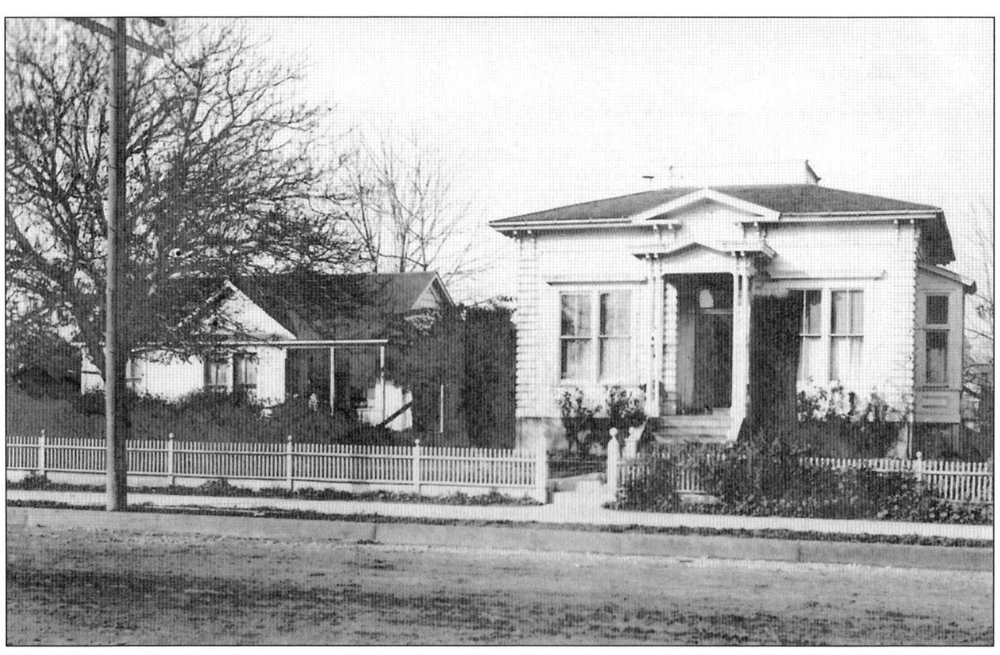

The Thomas Duncan home was located on Lincoln Avenue, which paralleled Main Street two blocks to the west.

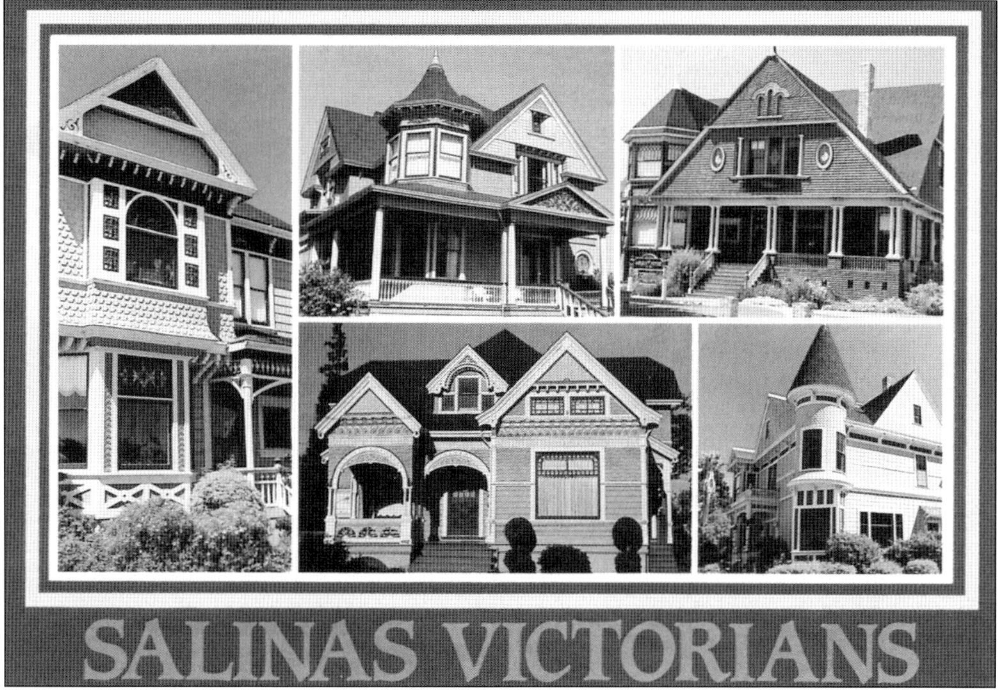

This postcard shows off some of the town's Victorian homes. At left is Austin House, built c. 1896; upper center is Black House, c. 1896; upper right is the Sargent House, c. 1896; lower center is Piini House, 1898; and lower right is the Corey House at Las Palmas Ranch, 1891. The Austin House was owned by the mother of one of the authors, and she was very careful to make sure that it would be preserved when she sold it.

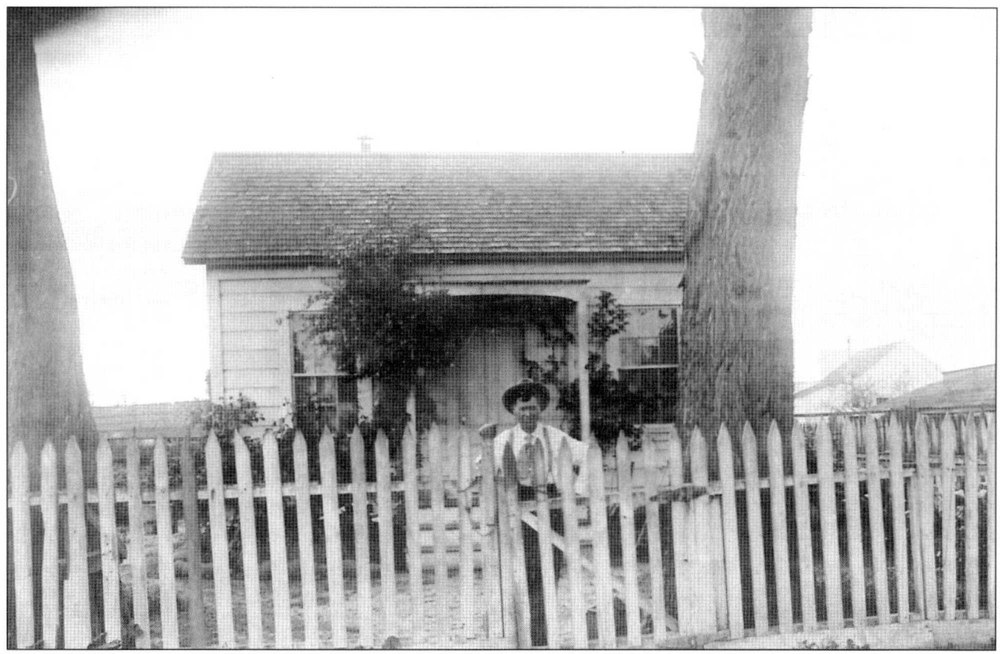
Here is an unidentified early dwelling. Not all homes were built in the Victorian style.

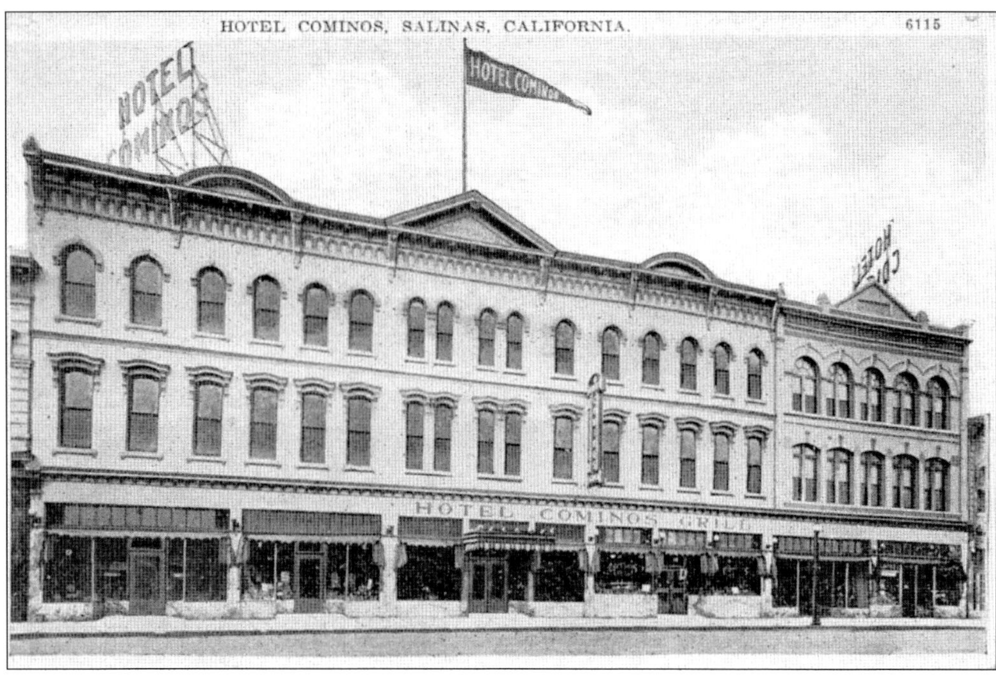

Throughout the years, the primary landmark on Main Street was the Cominos Hotel, originally established as the Abbott House in 1873. It was demolished by the city following the 1989 Loma Prieta earthquake. Below is a more recent view of the Cominos Hotel, most likely taken in the 1950s.

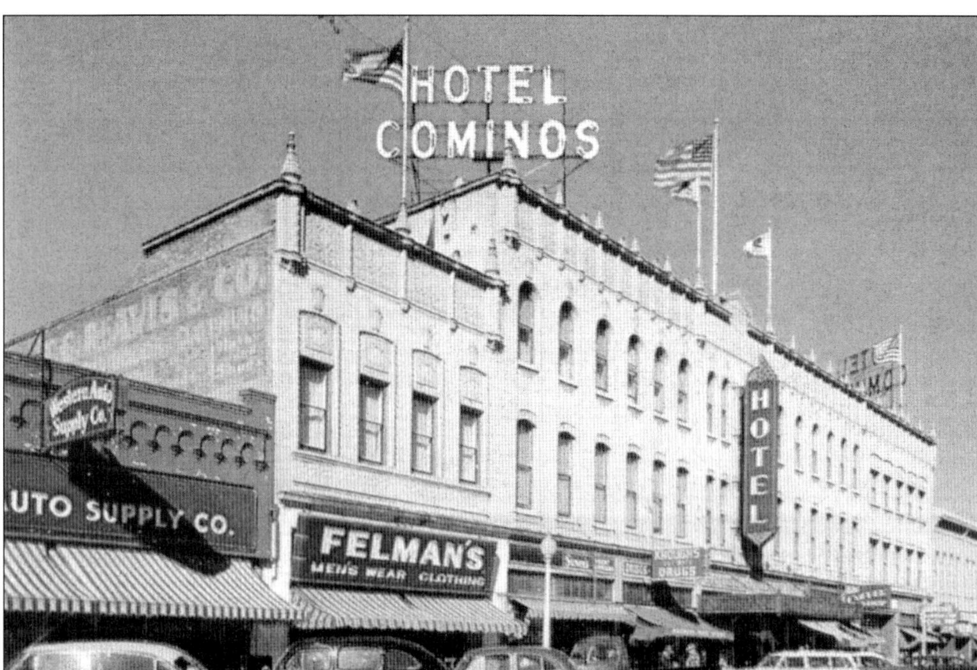

Three

Business, Commerce, and Major Public Buildings

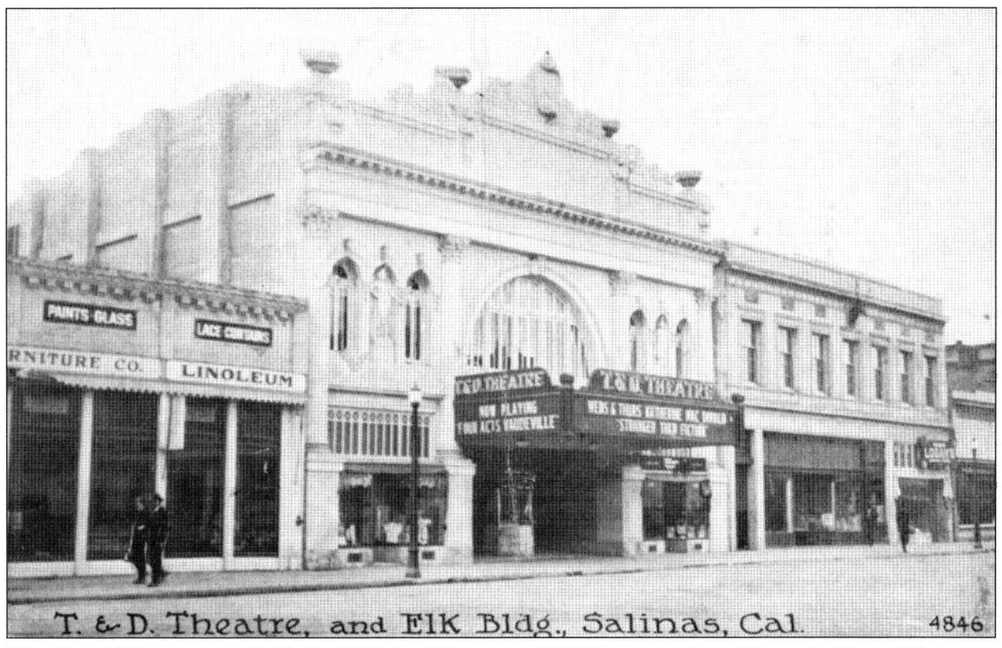

The T&D Theater was built in 1921 by Turner and Dakin to replace Brown's Opera House as Salinas's main theater. The theater had the most up-to-date operating room on the coast and a state-of-the-art organ in the orchestra pit. It was built for live theater and vaudeville and secondarily for silent films, which were new at that time. The marquee identifies the Wednesday and Thursday movie as *Stranger than Fiction*, an action-drama from 1921 starring Katherine MacDonald.

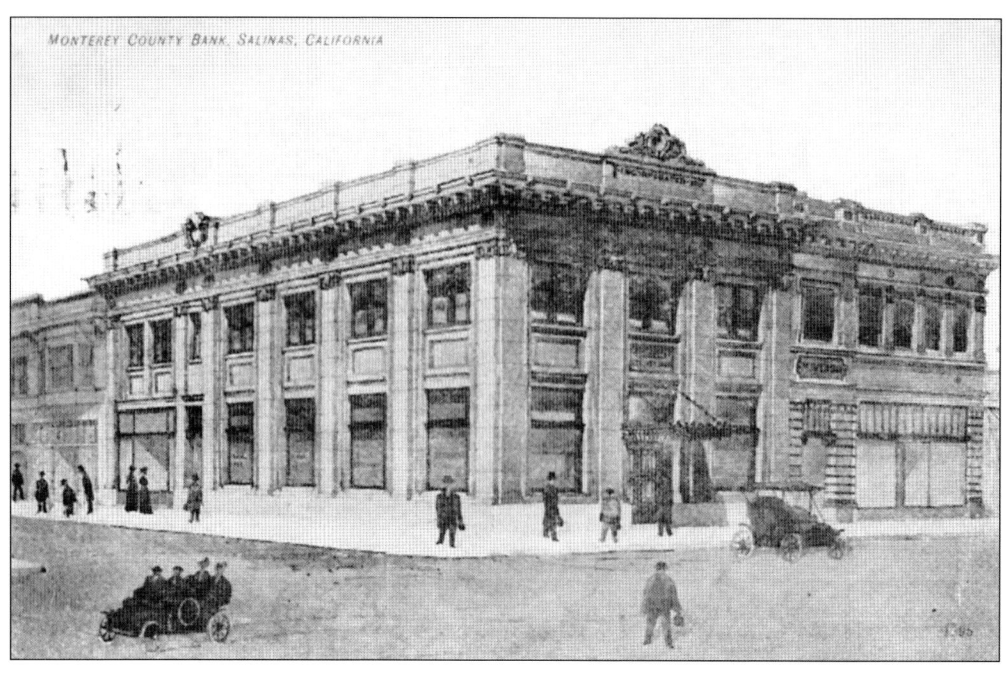

Monterey County Bank, seen above in 1906, was designed by William Weeks and is a two-story, concrete, classical building. It was remodeled in 1927. Pictured below is the reverse of the above postcard. This was clearly sent to potential customers.

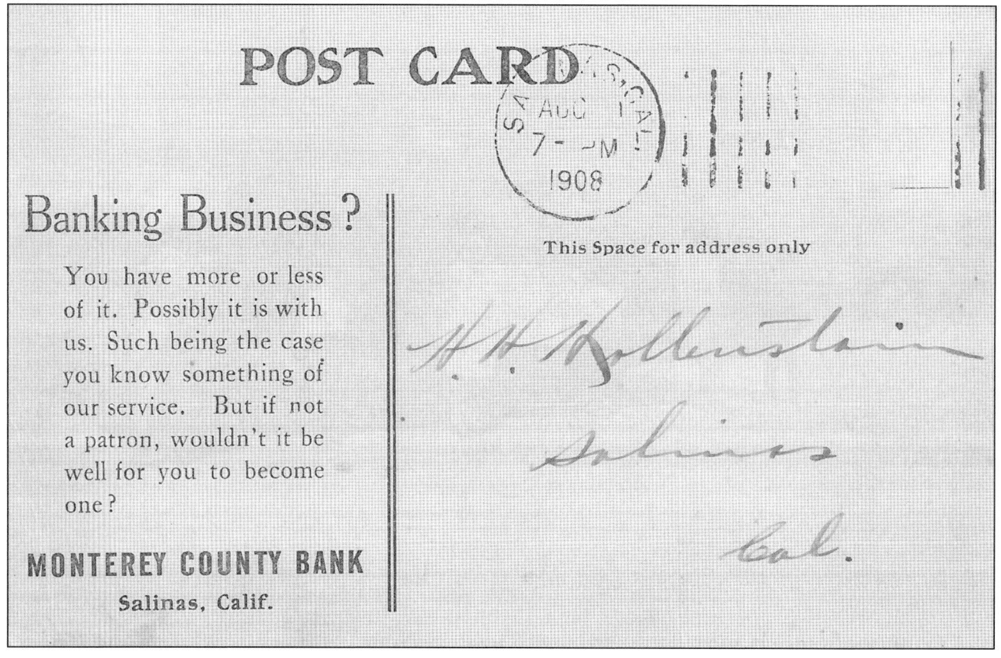

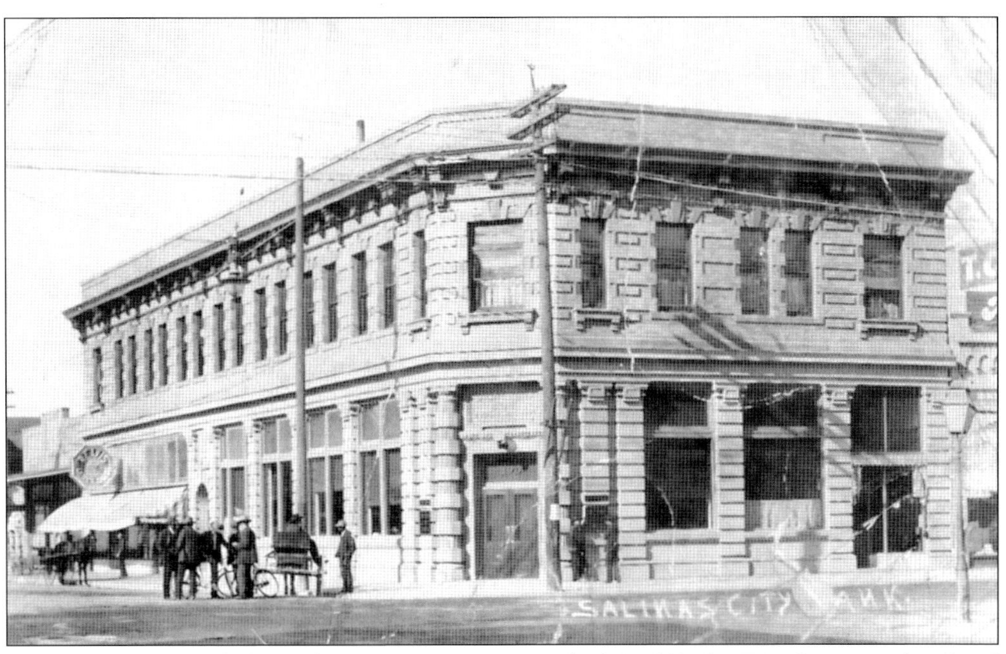

The Salinas City Bank, located at 172 Main Street, was built in 1907 by W.E. Greene and replaced a wooden-frame drugstore that was originally erected there.

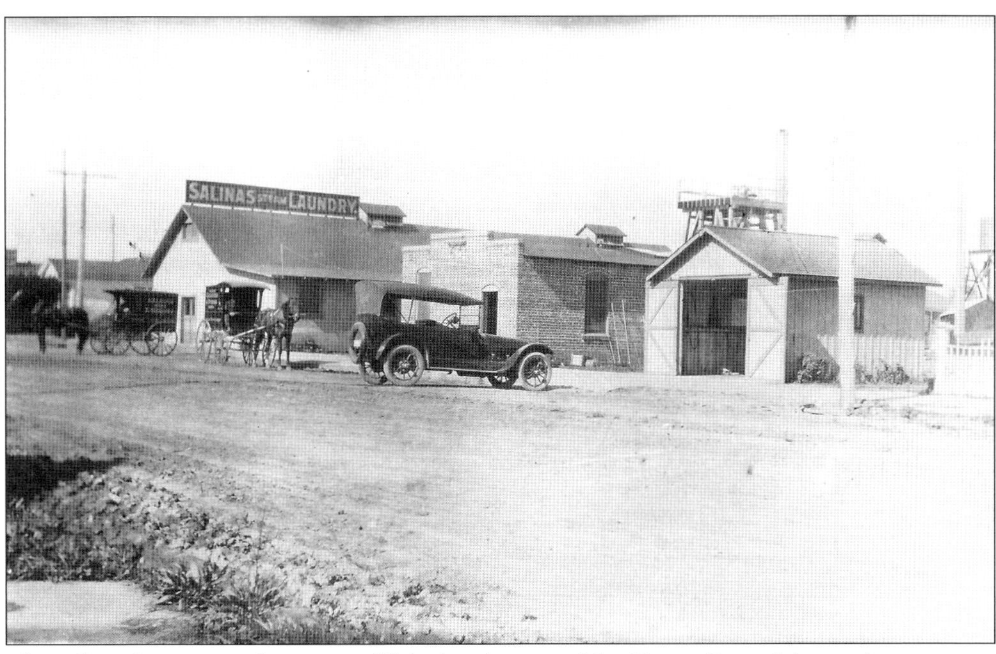

The Salinas Steam Laundry was established and operated by Henry Gross. A horse-drawn wagon picked up laundry from around town and as far away as the Spreckels Sugar Factory.

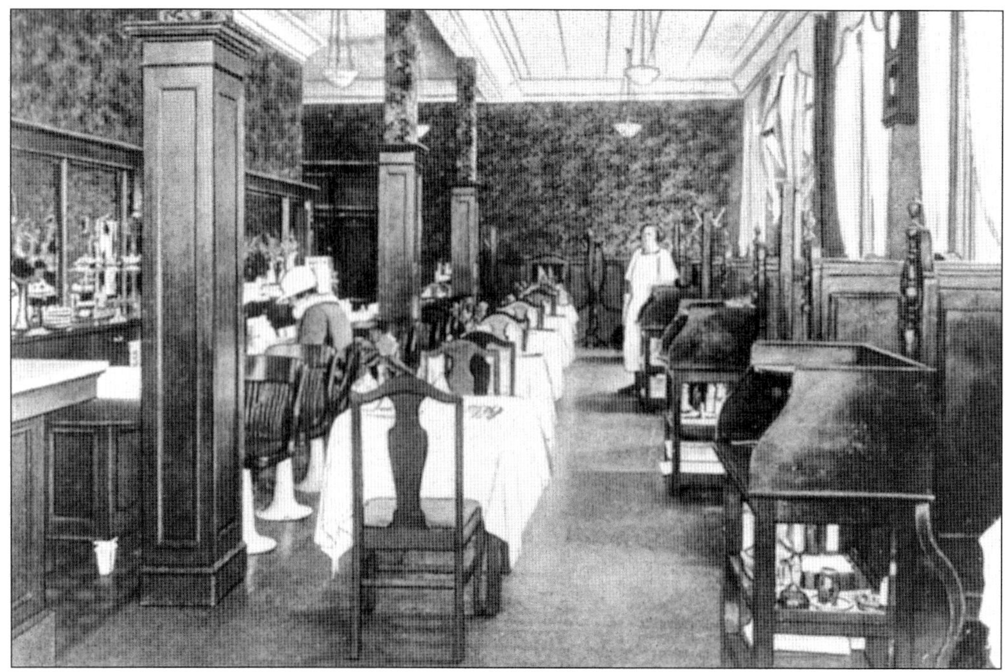

The Jeffery House was the center of hospitality in Salinas since 1883. The coffee shop boasted of fresh eggs and milk from James Jeffrey's own ranch, as well as its own recipes from his wife. Real Spanish enchiladas, barbecue sauce, and strawberry shortcake were some of the famous ones. In 1966, the last meal was served at the hotel, as it closed its doors that year.

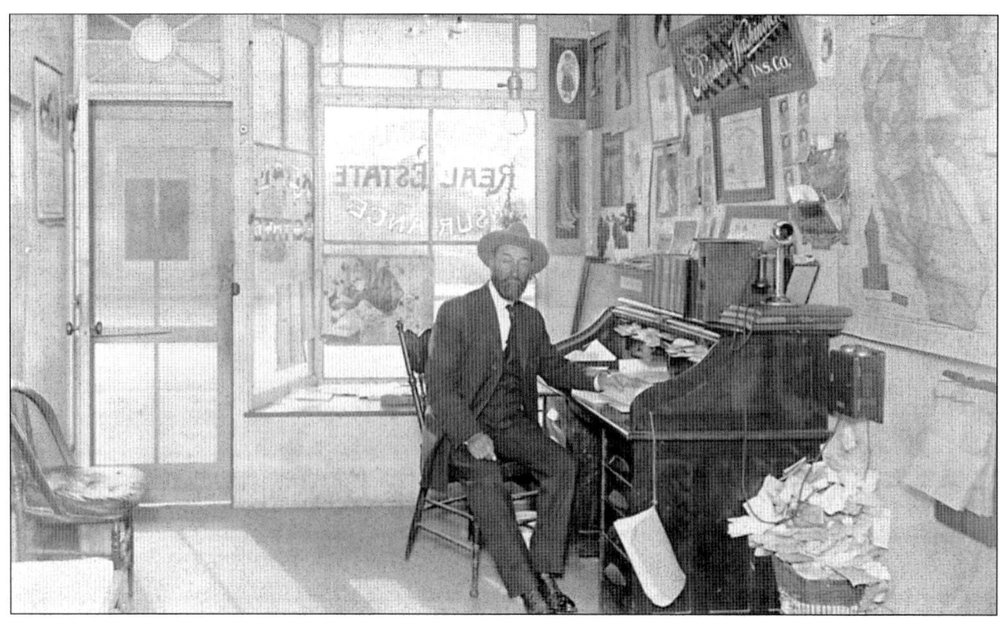

A total of $11,563,146.10 worth of construction was done in Salinas from 1922 to 1937. Real estate was booming, and the B.A. Soberanes Real Estate and Insurance Office was busy.

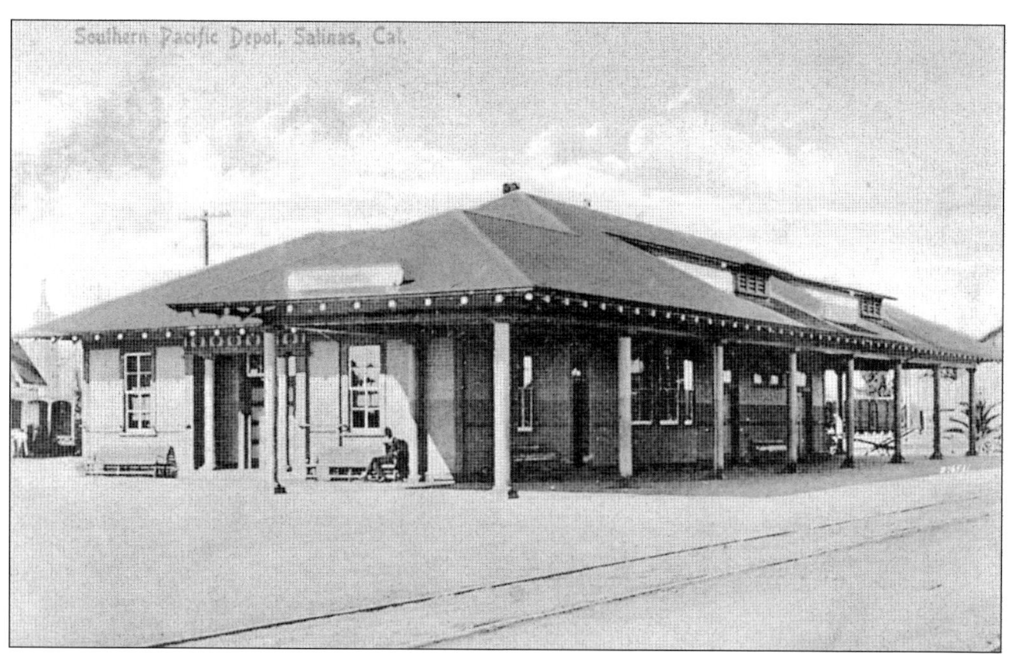

The Southern Pacific Depot in Salinas is pictured in 1909. Eugene Sherwood offered the Southern Pacific Railroad free acreage for the right-of-way and a depot, which opened its doors for business in 1872.

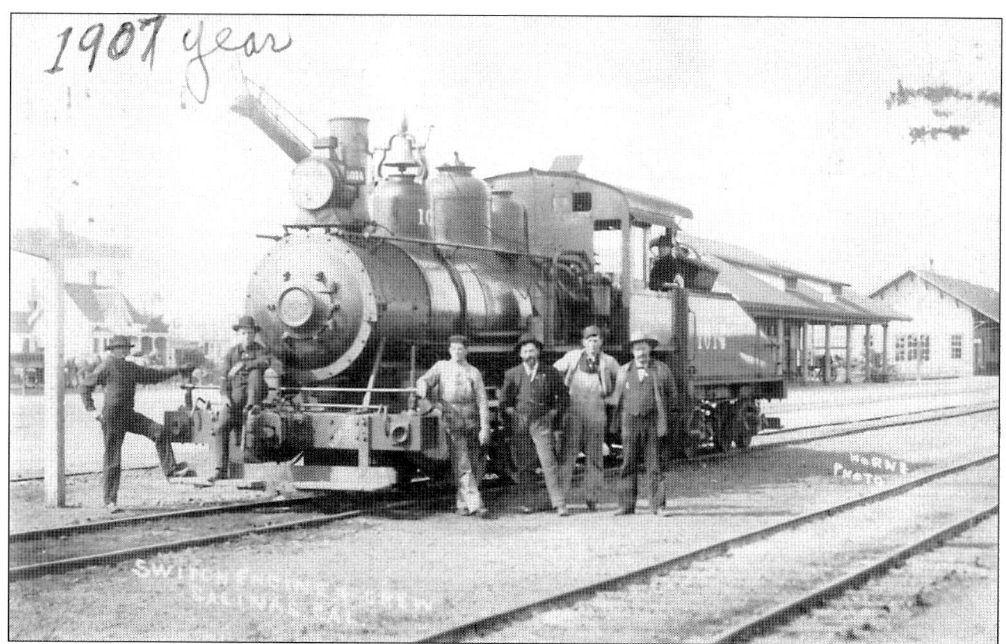

The engineer and six-man depot switching crew pose for a real-photo postcard shot in 1907. The depot building can be seen in the background.

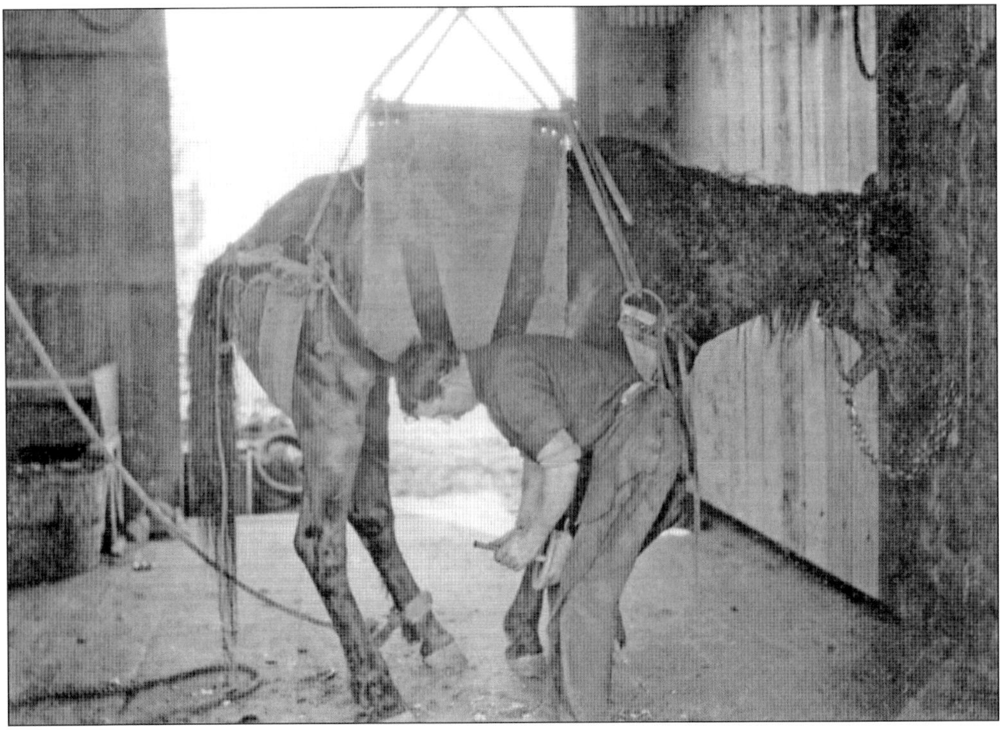

Pictured here is the interior of the Lacey Blacksmith Shop about 1890. The Laceys were among the first to come to Salinas when it was in its infant stages. When automobiles came to the forefront, they opened the Lacey Garage on Market and Monterey Streets. This method of shoeing horses does not seem to have caught on.

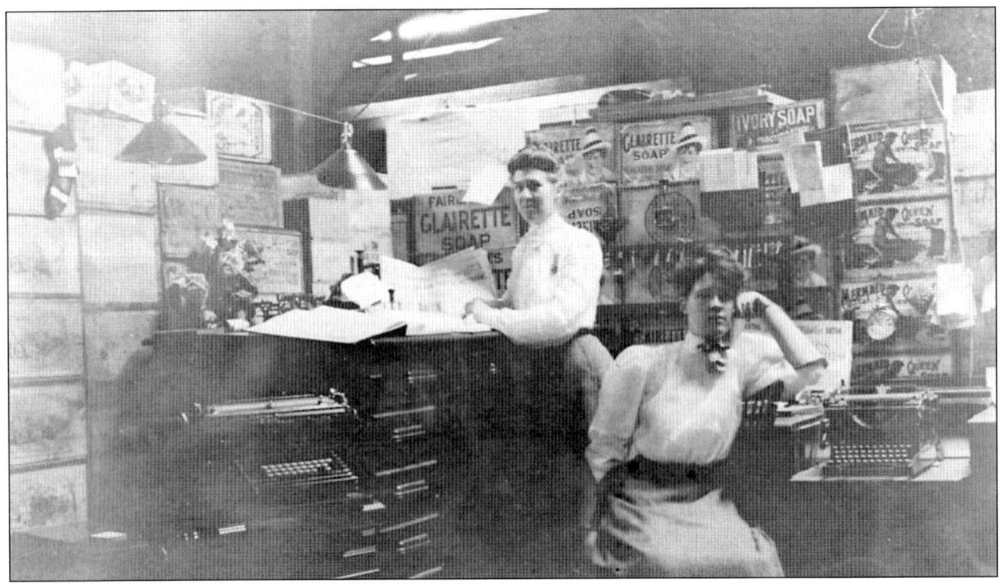

Seen here is the interior of the Ford and Sanborn Co. department store's business office, located at the corner of Main and Gabilan Streets. Note the old typewriters.

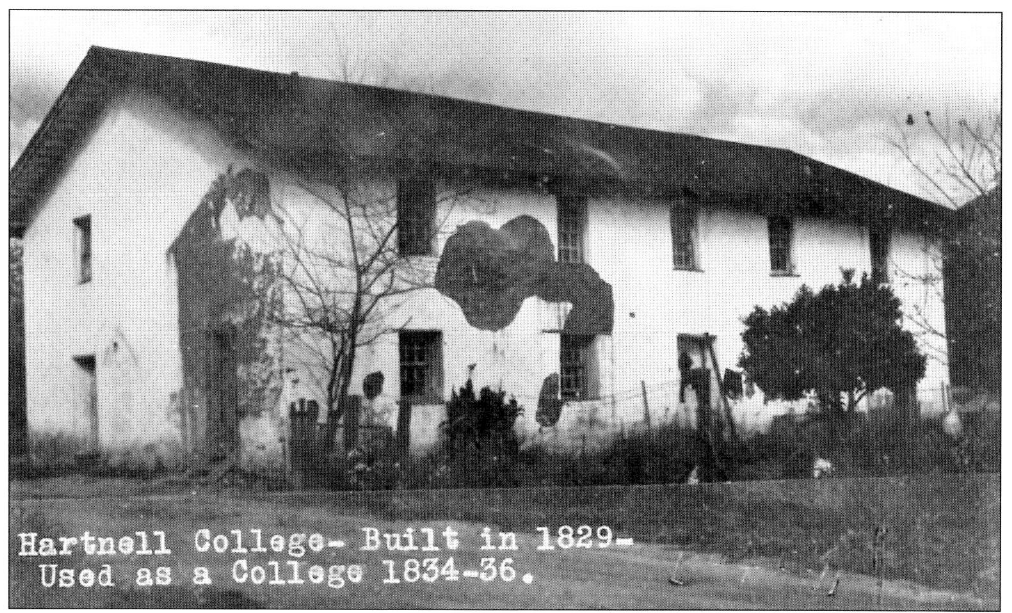

The Hartnell College adobe, used by William Hartnell to establish the first college in California, is seen in this postcard. It was founded on January 1, 1834. In 1833, when Hartnell had announced that he would open a "*seminario or casa de educación*," the announcement declared that tuition would be available in English, German, and Latin grammars, arithmetic, bookkeeping, mathematics, and philosophy. The algebra was equivalent to that required for graduation from Hartnell College today.

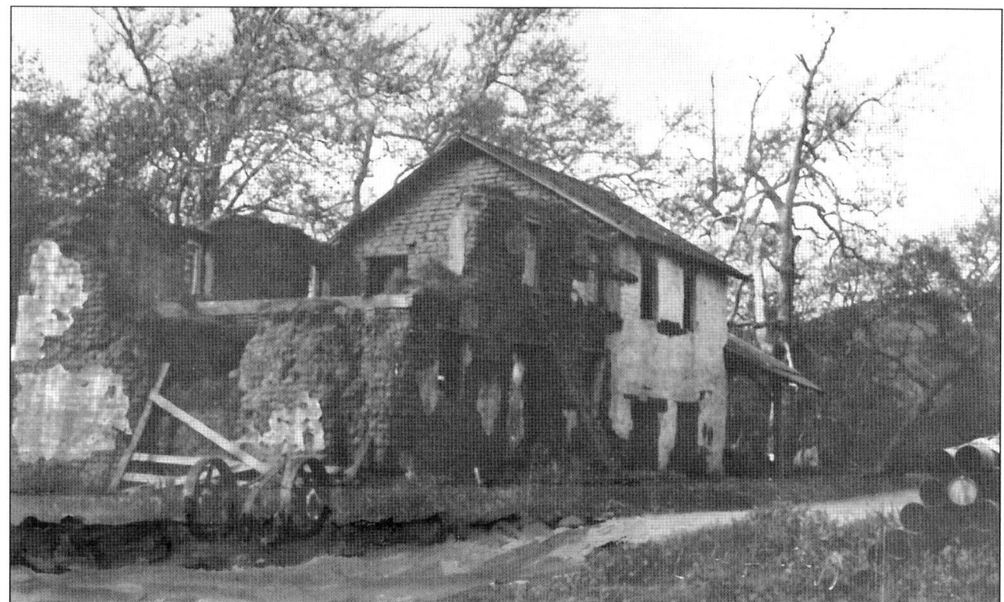

The old adobe building fell into disrepair and was eventually demolished, leaving only memories of a time long past.

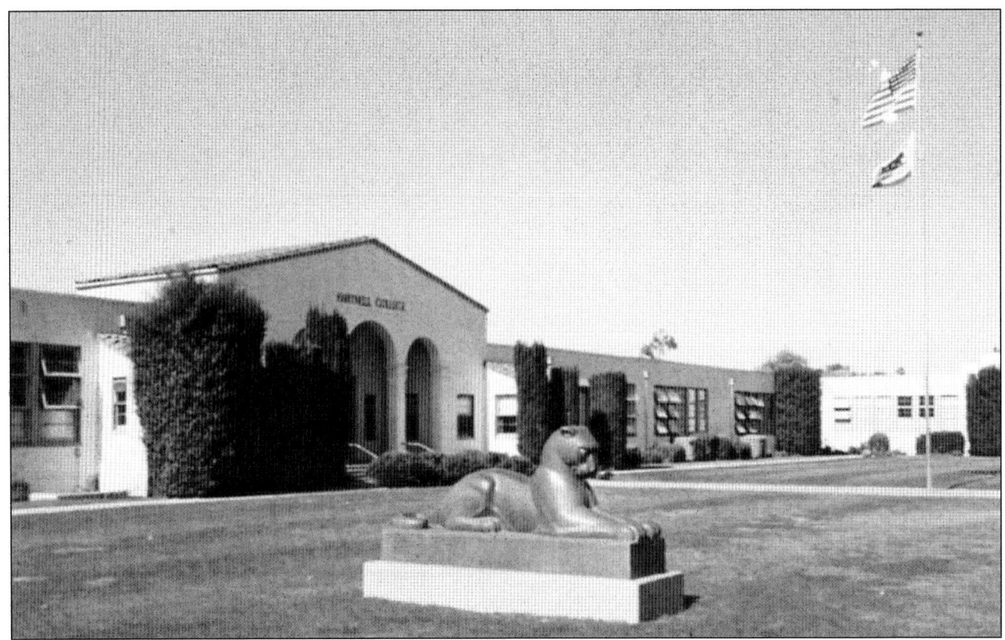

In 1935, a bond issue was passed making it possible to purchase 15.3 acres of land on what was then the western edge of Salinas on Homestead Avenue and build a new Salinas Junior College. The land was purchased, and the Spanish-style buildings were built that same year. In 1948, the students petitioned the school board to change the name to William Edward Petty Hartnell in honor of the man who started the first college in California, and the school became Hartnell Junior College. The large black granite panther, sculpted by Raymond Puccinelli under the Federal Arts Program, was placed on the campus by the class of 1940. It was nicknamed "Oscar," and as the school's mascot, it still occupies a prominent place on the campus today.

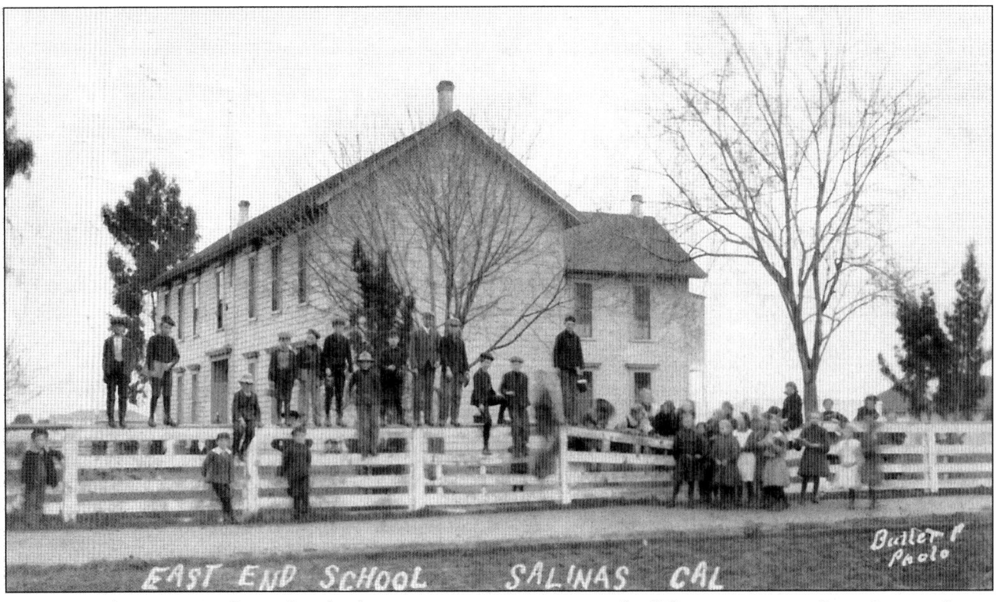

In 1870, Salinas got its first school when a two story, two room building was erected on the southeast corner of Front and East Alisal Streets. It was later enlarged to become the East End School.

This schoolhouse in Spreckels was three stories high and designed by W.H. Weeks. It was erected in 1899 and demolished in 1936. When the building was demolished, the bell was taken to the University of California, Davis, where it is still used to signal scores at football games. The bell was named the Tavernetti Bell, and is dedicated to the memory of Thomas Fredrick Tavernetti.

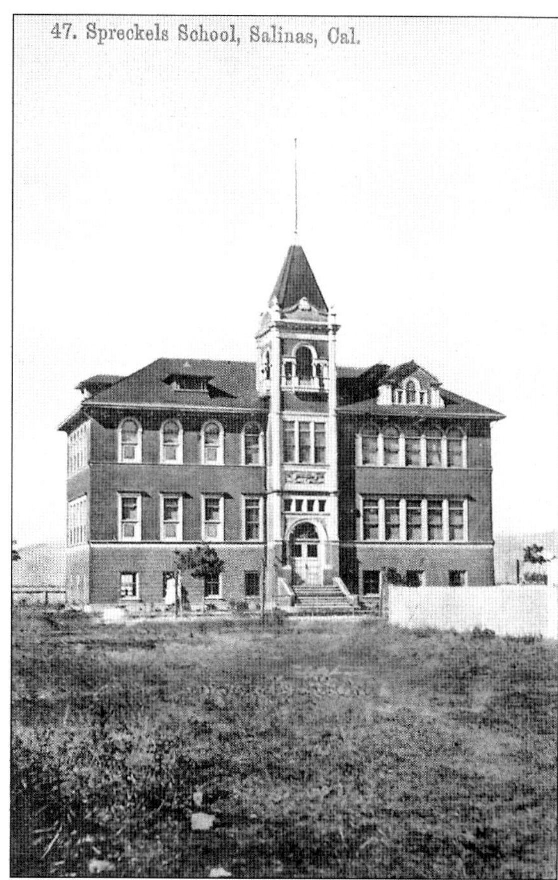

The original Salinas High School was located on West Alisal Street. It was nicknamed "the brickyard." The lot where it stood is now the parking lot opposite the post office on West Alisal Street. This postcard is from 1909.

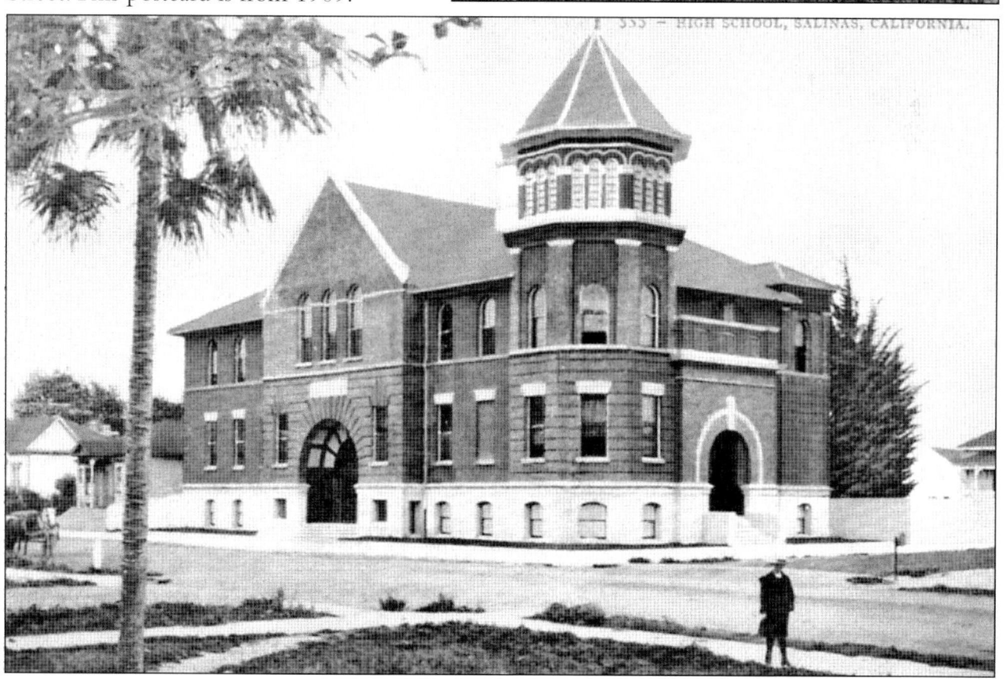

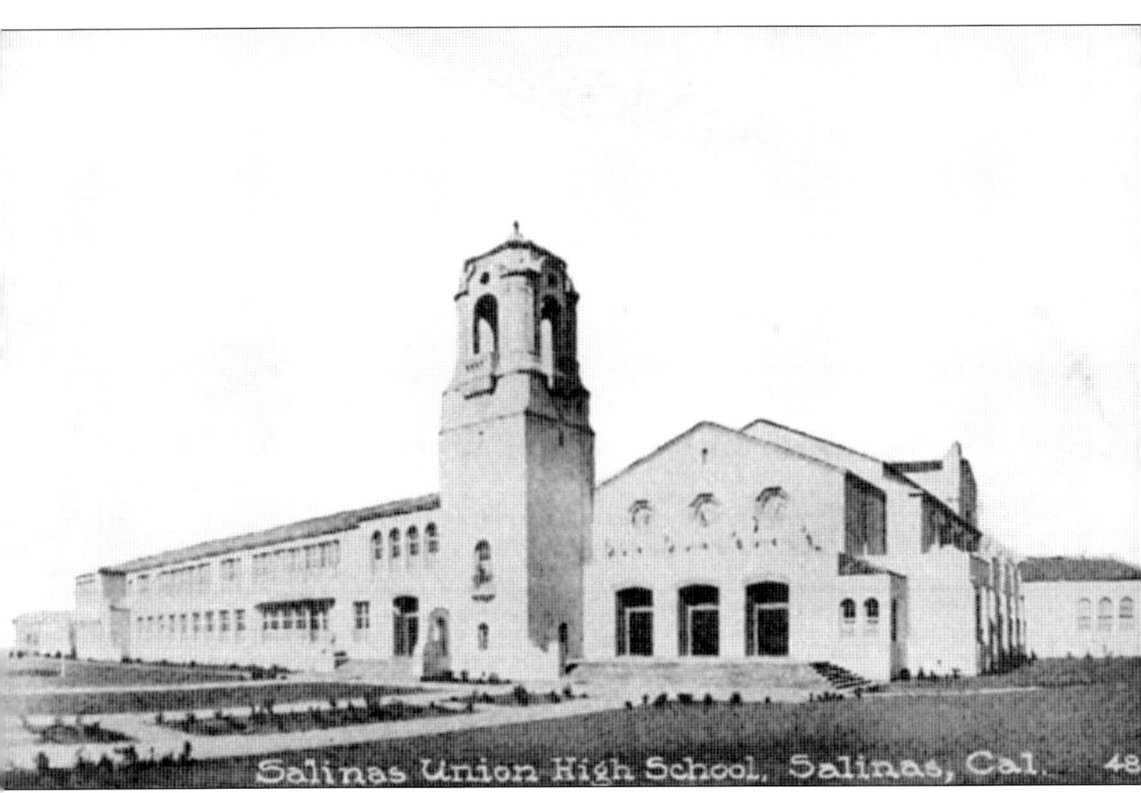

The new Salinas High School on South Main Street began operation in 1920 and is still in use today. A few years ago, the school district was faced with the question of restoring and refurbishing the original school or building a new facility. They wisely chose to preserve the historic building.

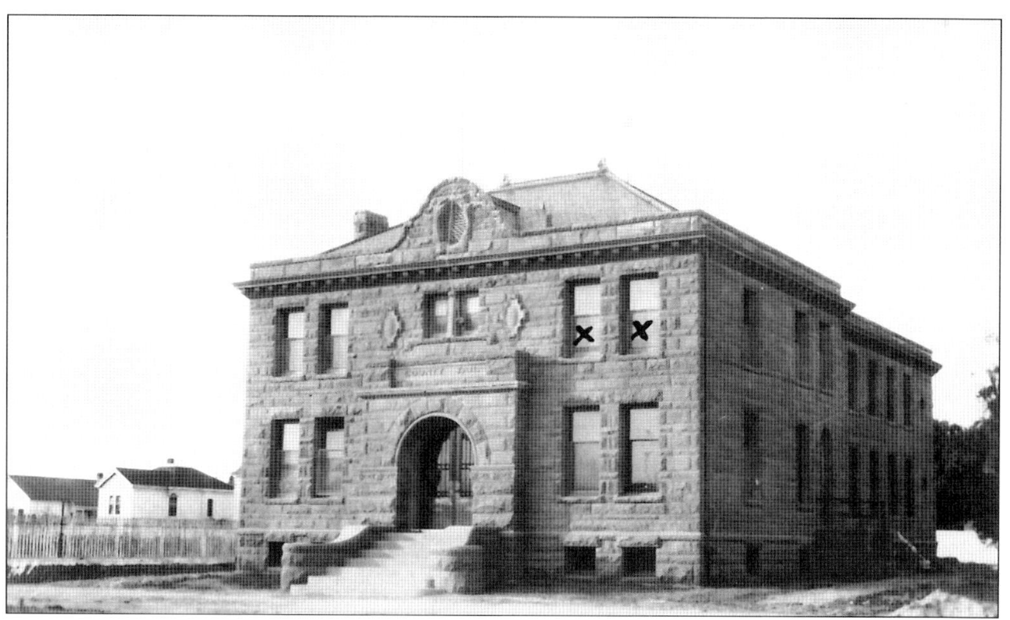
The old Monterey County Jail, built in Salinas in 1904, is featured on this postcard.

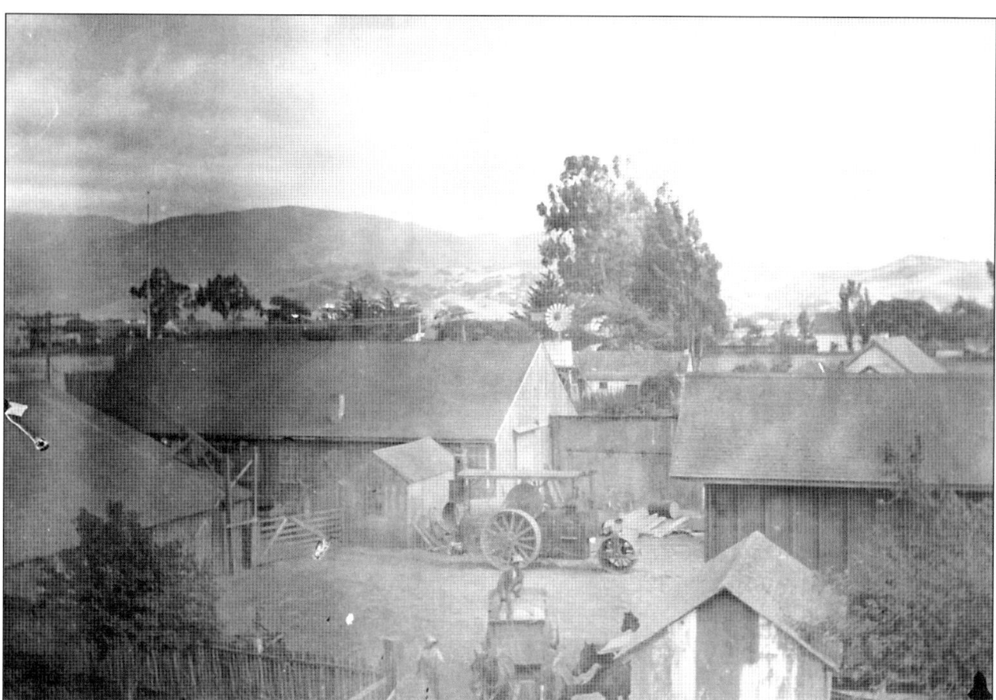
Pictured here is the Fenton blacksmith shop at Confederate Corners, situated just south of Salinas. This small area received its name when a group of southerners, including two former Confederate army captains, settled there in the late 1860s.

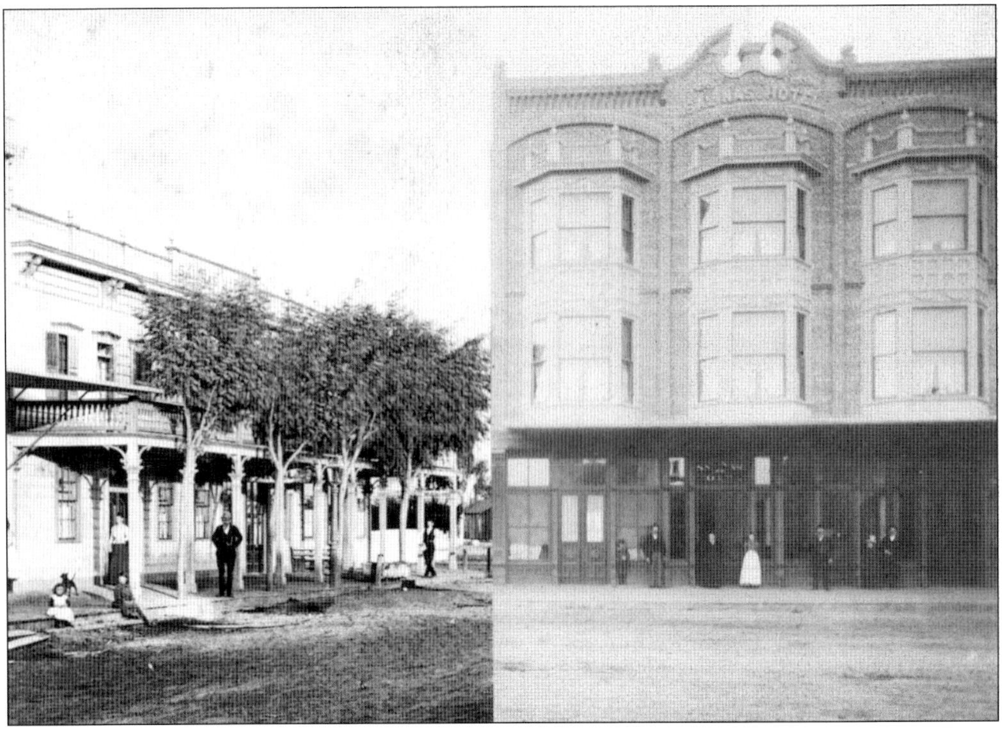

This postcard shows two views of the Salinas Hotel, located on the northwest corner of Market and Main Streets. The original wooden building (left) was built in 1870; note the wooden sidewalks and unpaved street. The masonry annex, constructed in 1895, survived the 1906 earthquake but was demolished following the 1989 Loma Prieta earthquake.

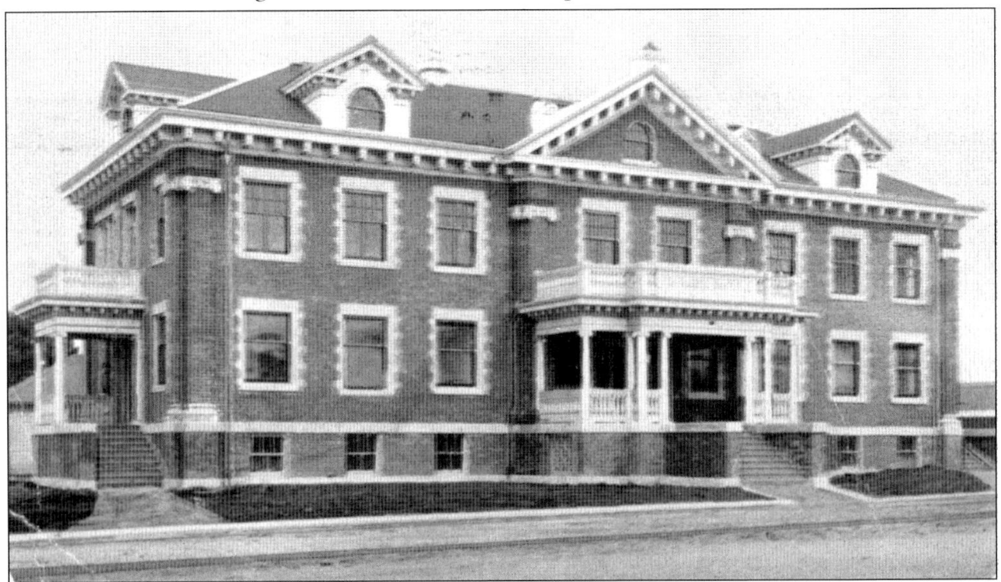

The James Bardin Hospital was just south of the 300 block of Main Street, where the street makes a bend. It was the first fully equipped and up-to-date hospital in Salinas. The hospital could accommodate 22 patients and served as a training school for nurses, providing many women with a vocation when other opportunities were limited.

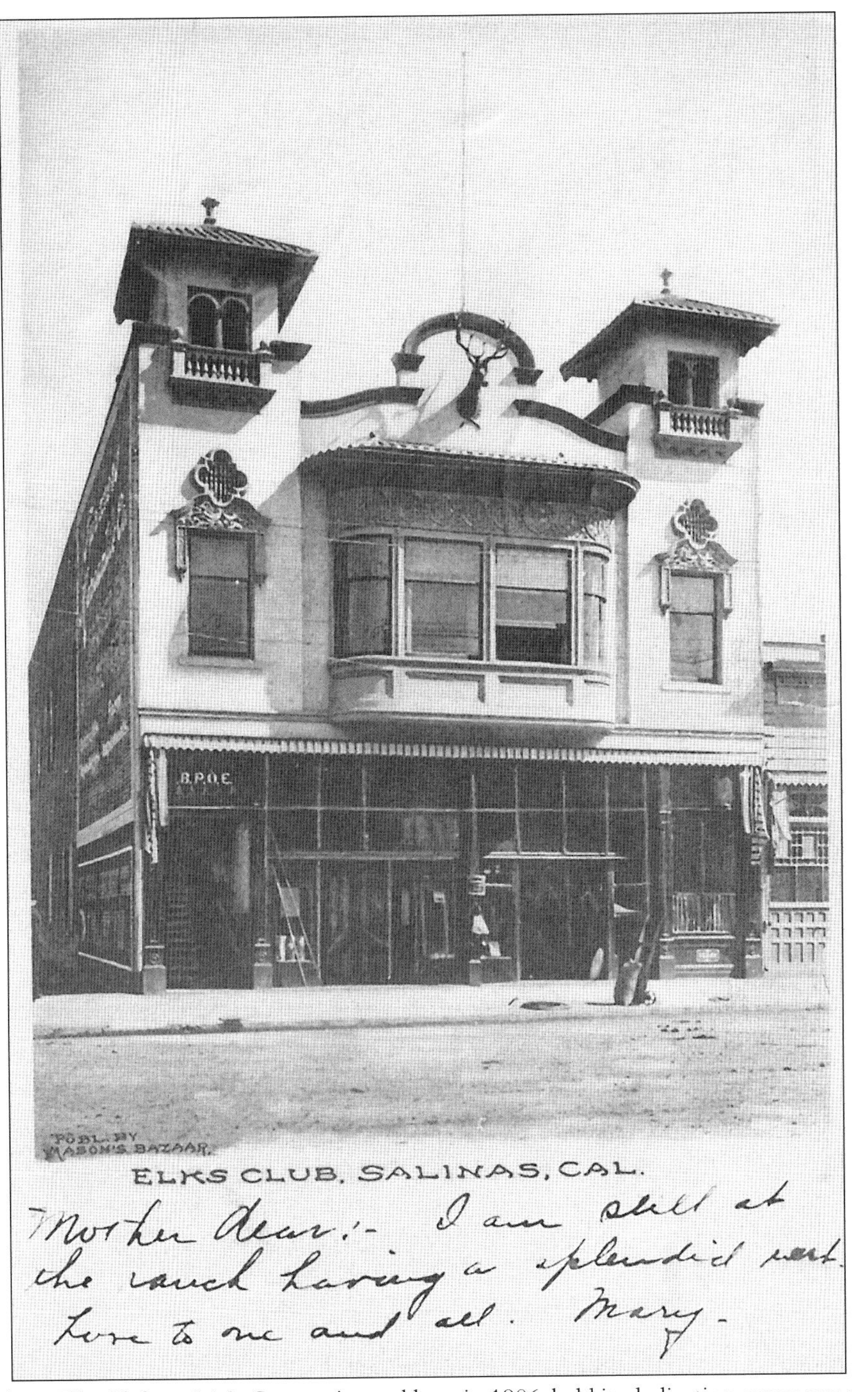

The Salinas Elks Club on Main Street, pictured here in 1906, held its dedication ceremony on May 10, 1905. Salinas Elks Club No. 614 was established on August 25, 1900, with 35 members. They held their meetings in the Abbott House, and by 1905, when their building was dedicated, had over 260 members. On February 17, 1965, they bid farewell to the old building that had served them so well and moved to their new location at 614 Airport Boulevard with a total of 1,462 members. The new Elks Lodge is still in use today.

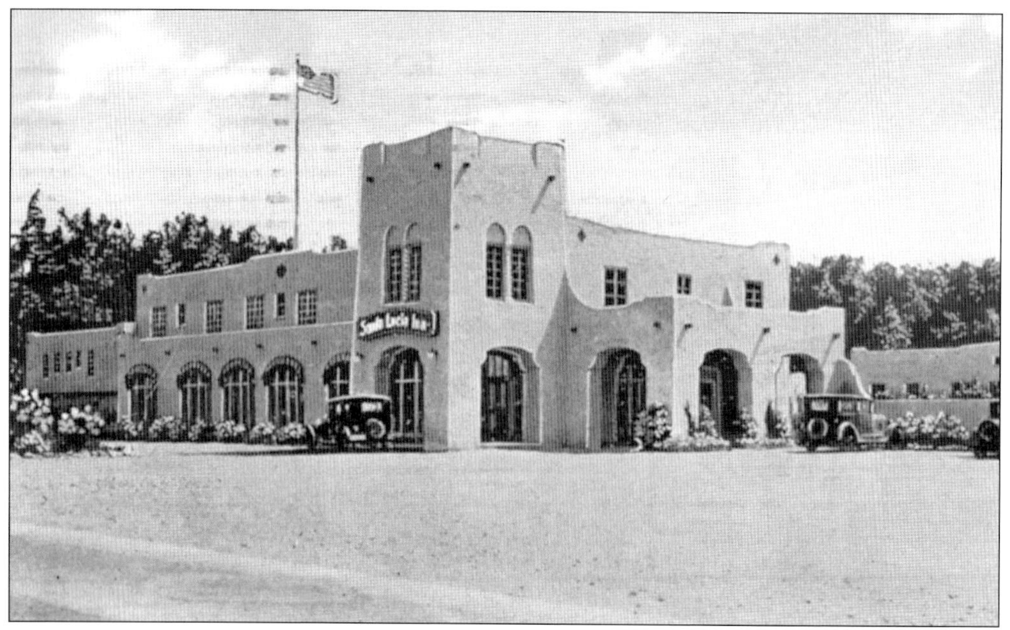

The Santa Lucia Inn, pictured here in 1930, was located at 808 North Main Street. The inn opened its doors on June 24, 1927. It cost $100,000 to build, and was ahead of its time in that everything ran on electricity. It was the stopover between Los Angeles and San Francisco, hosting such celebrities as Marilyn Monroe and Joe DiMaggio. The movie *East of Eden* was filmed in Salinas and many members of the cast stayed at the inn, including Burl Ives, Julie Harris, and Raymond Massey. In 1957, it was moved across the street to become the Frontier Inn. It is no longer standing.

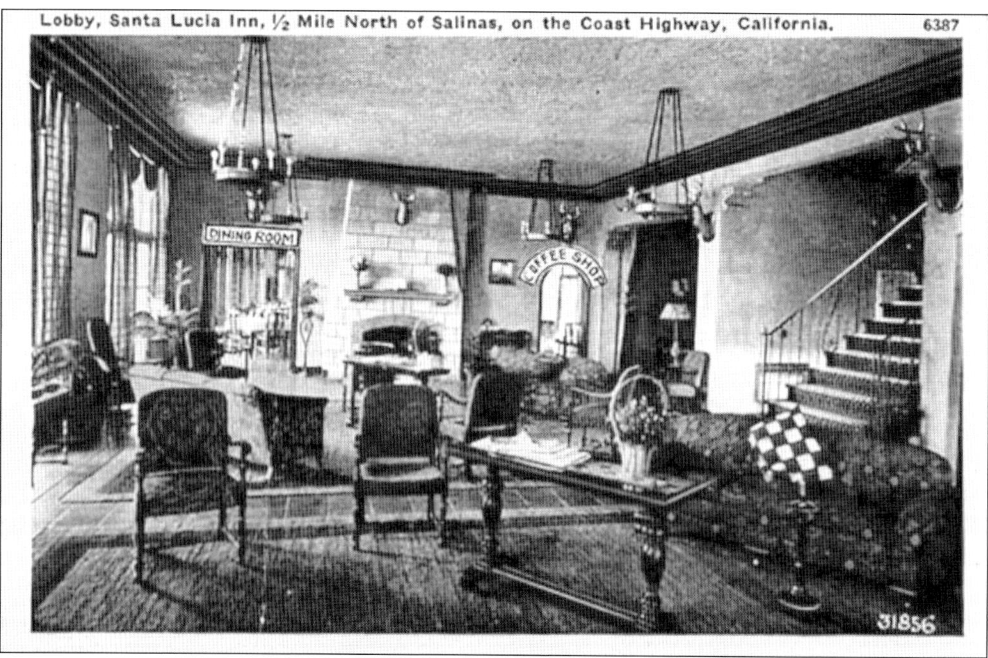

This interior photograph of the Santa Lucia Inn's lounge shows massive wrought iron chandeliers hanging from the ceiling, as well as plush couches and chairs enhanced with a large brick fireplace.

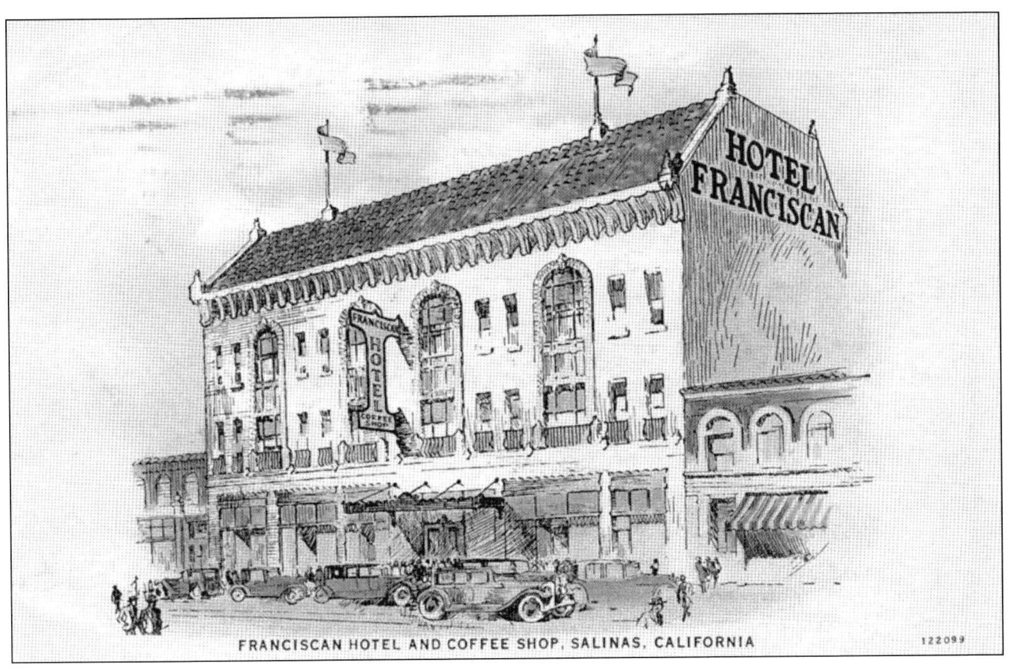

In its day, the Franciscan Hotel was one of the premier establishments in Salinas. It was originally the Bardin Hotel. A fire destroyed the hotel in 1945, and the National Steinbeck Center was built on its site. Pictured below is the reverse of the postcard above. The Franciscan featured 120 "modern" rooms, a dining room, and coffee shop, and billed itself as the "headquarters for Lettuce and Produce Men."

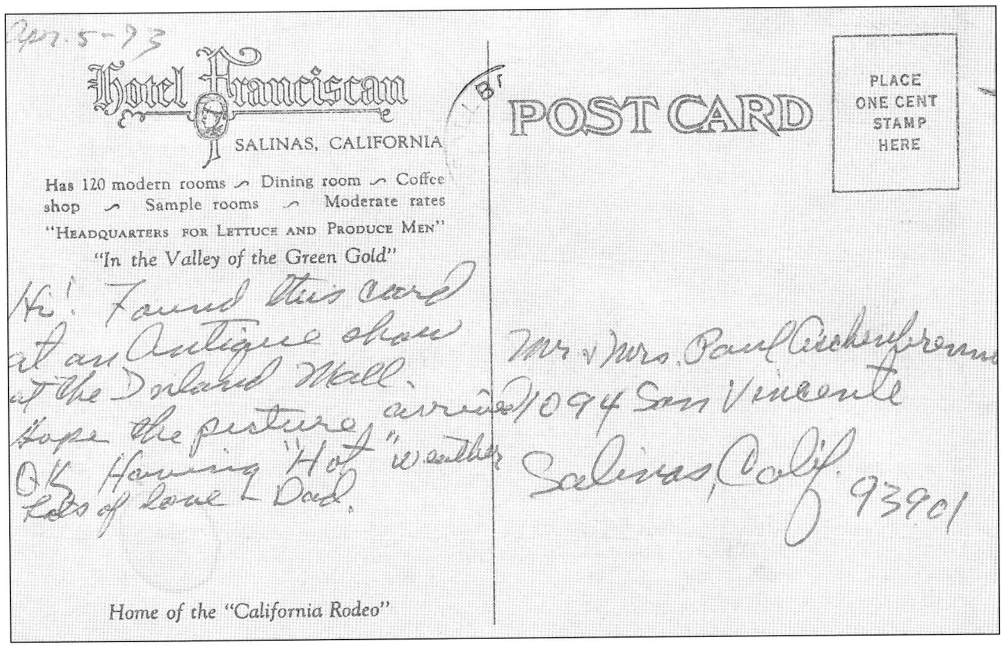

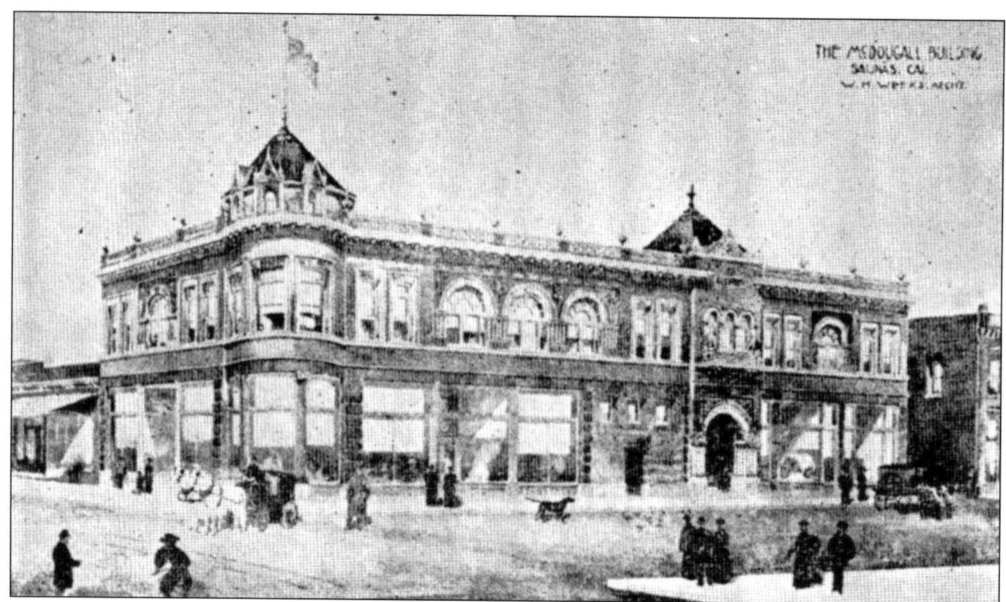

The McDougall building at the northeast corner of Main and Gabilan Streets in Salinas was built by James McDougall, a leading merchant and community leader who served at one time as city postmaster and county tax collector. The building was contracted in 1898 by William H. Weeks and was the most elaborate commercial building in town. The up-to-date steel reinforcement used to carry seismic loads withstood the 1906 earthquake and served as a model to architects and contractors in the rebuilding of Salinas after the great disaster.

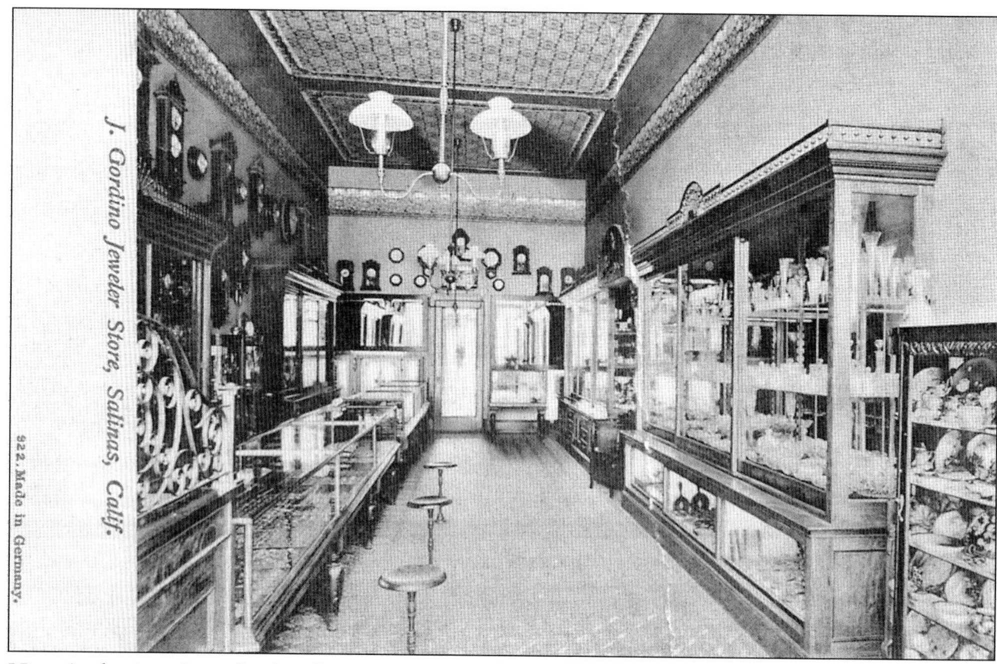

Here is the interior of a jewelry store operated by J. Gordino. Notice the array of clocks, fine crystal, and china. This building dates to approximately 1910.

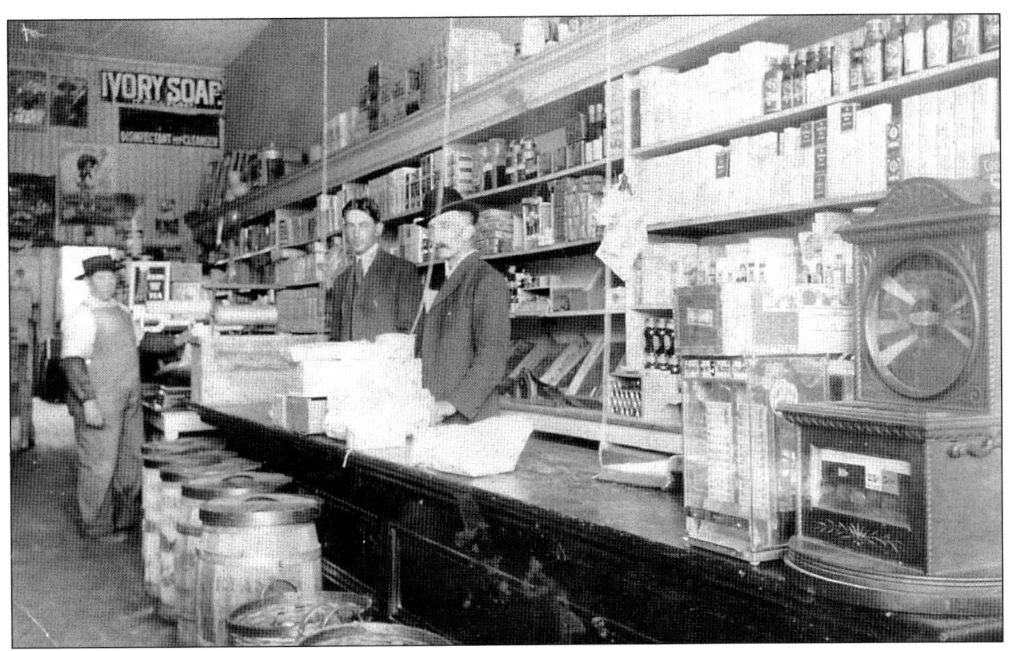

This postcard shows a business interior in 1919. The gentlemen in the photograph are identified on the reverse, reproduced below. Their names are quite difficult to read, though it looks like they may be W.G. Anderson, Lonnie (B.?), and Arthur Thatcher.

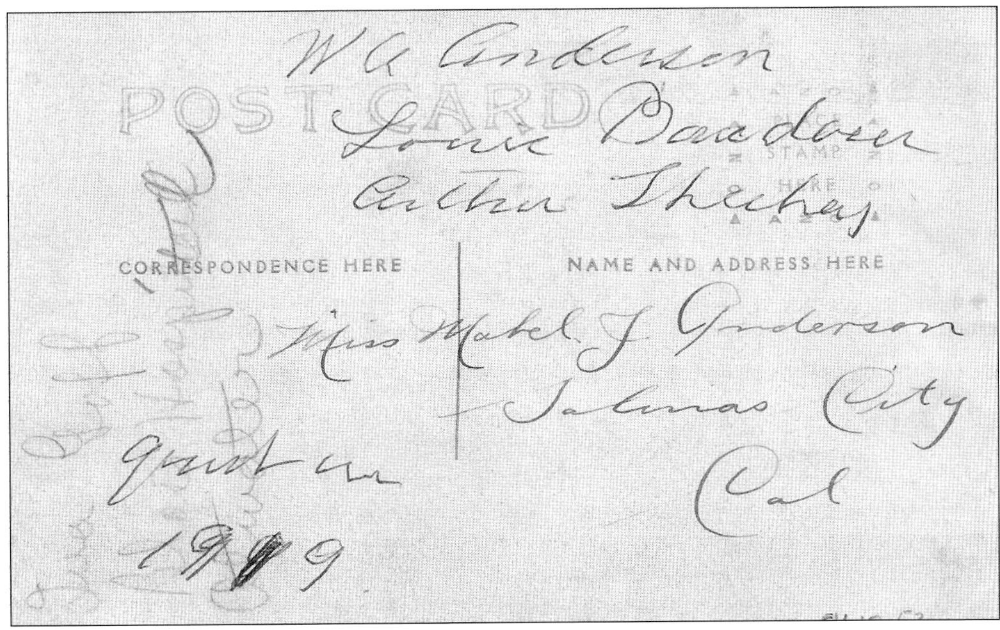
W G Anderson

POST CARD

STAMP HERE

CORRESPONDENCE HERE

NAME AND ADDRESS HERE

Miss Mabel J. Anderson
Salinas City
Cal

1919

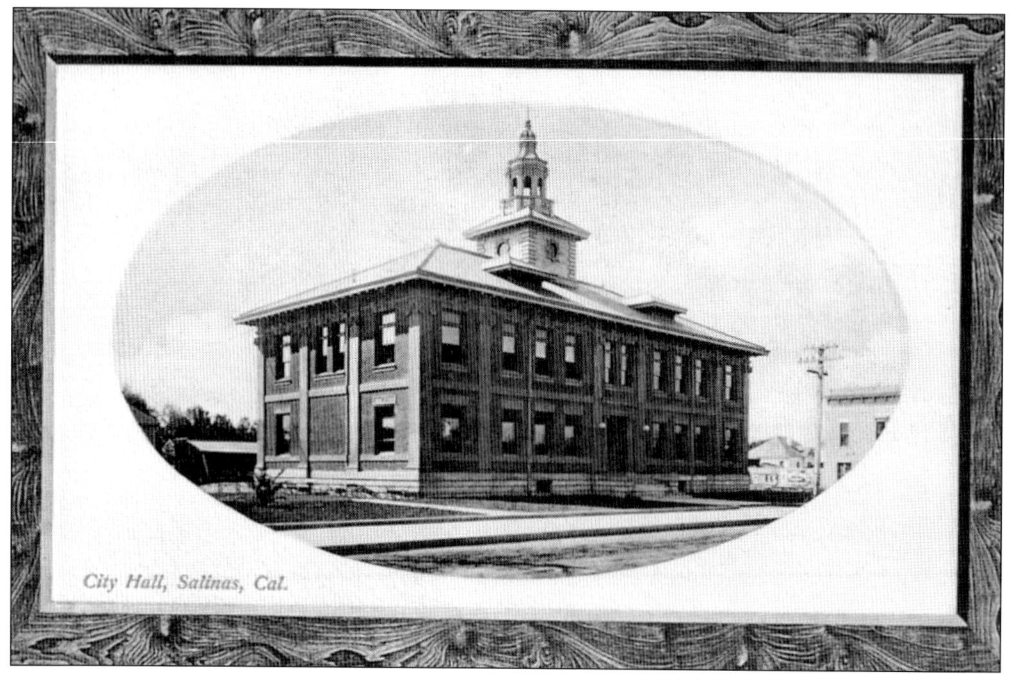

Two views of the original Salinas City Hall appear on these postcards. The view below is from 1906. The earthquake of 1906 damaged the upper story of city hall. The building was torn down and a new one was built to replace it. This building was demolished in the early 1960s to make way for a parking lot.

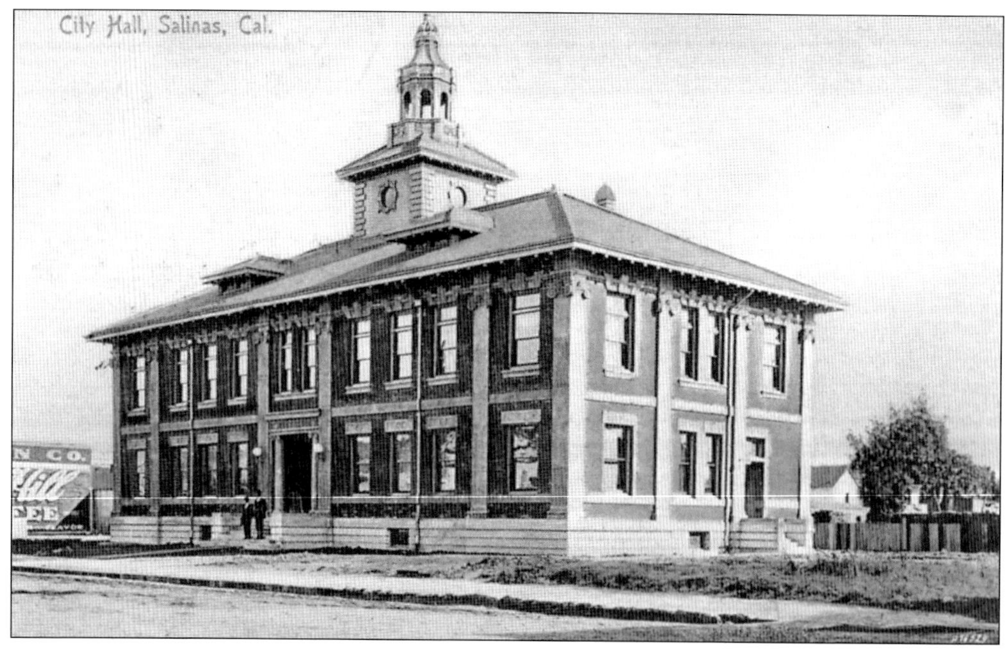

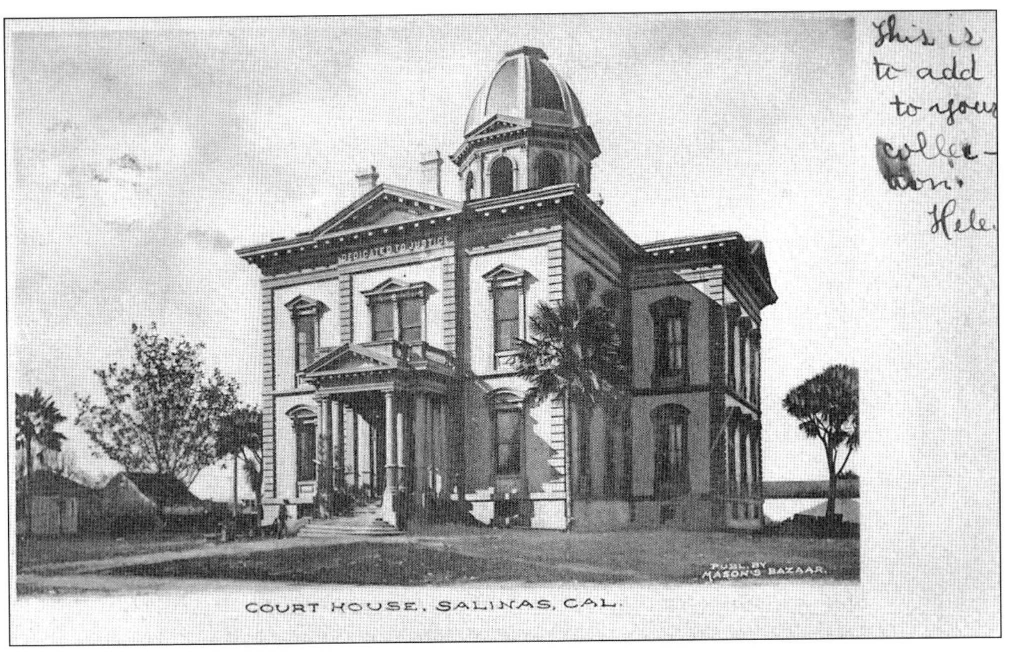

Here are two 1906 views of the original Monterey County Court House on Alisal Street in Salinas. When it came time to build a new courthouse, the new structure was erected right around this building. On completion, the old courthouse was torn down, leaving the new courthouse with a nice courtyard.

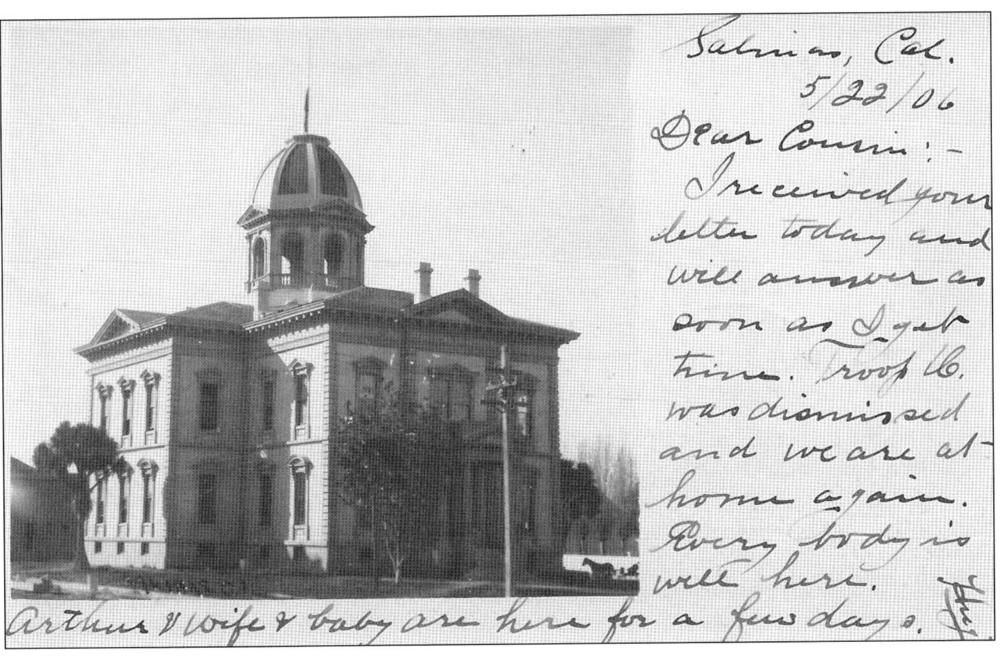

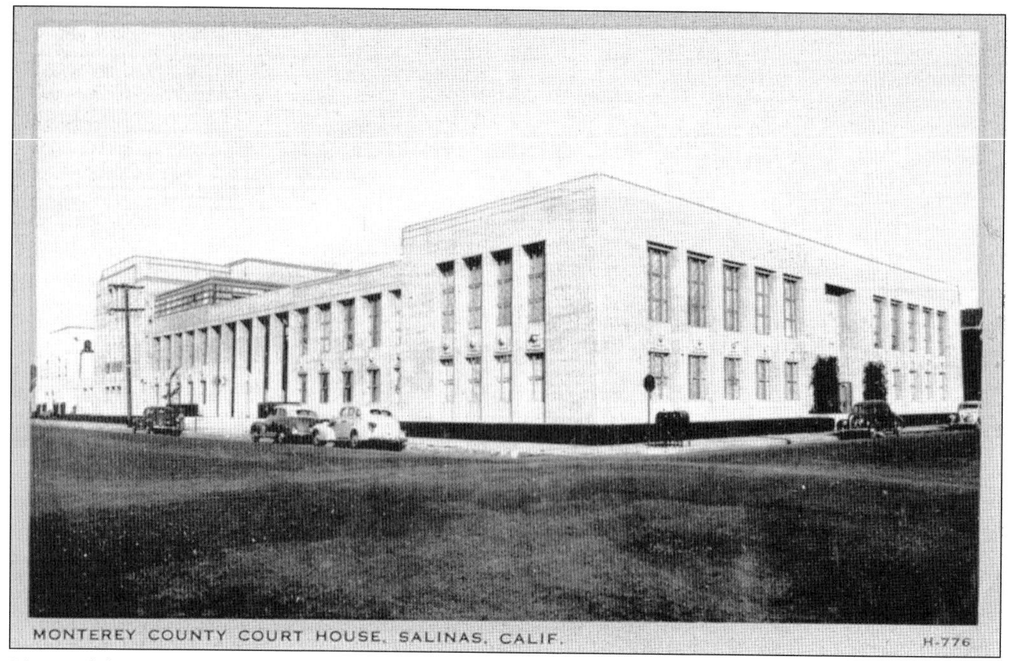

Pictured here is the new Monterey County Court House, as seen in 1940. Designed by local architect Robert Stanton in 1937, the courthouse was built with nearly $500,000 in funds provided by the Work Progress Administration. It was listed in the National Register of Historic Places in 2009.

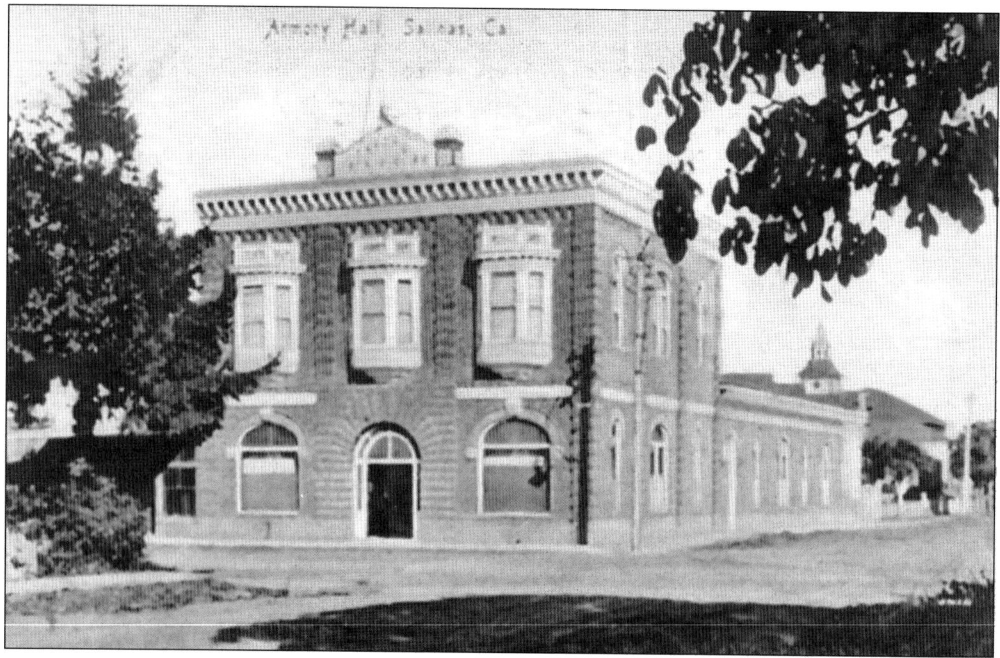

The original National Guard Armory was located at the corner of Alisal and Salinas Streets. When a new armory was built directly behind this structure, it was converted to other uses, including a bowling alley in the 1950s. This building has been beautifully restored and is currently used for offices.

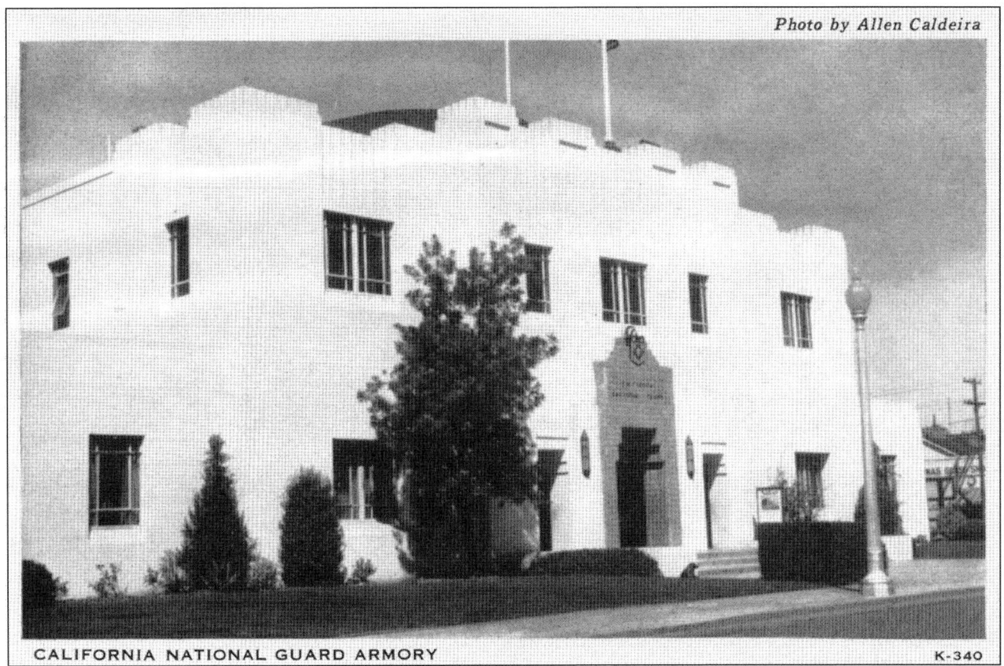

The new California National Guard Armory was built in 1932. During World War II, the local National Guard, Company C, marched from the armory building down Main Street to the train station as the town gathered to bid them farewell. The 107 men and officers were inducted into the Army and ended up being shipped to the Philippines and became a part of the Bataan Death March, with only 47 surviving the ordeal.

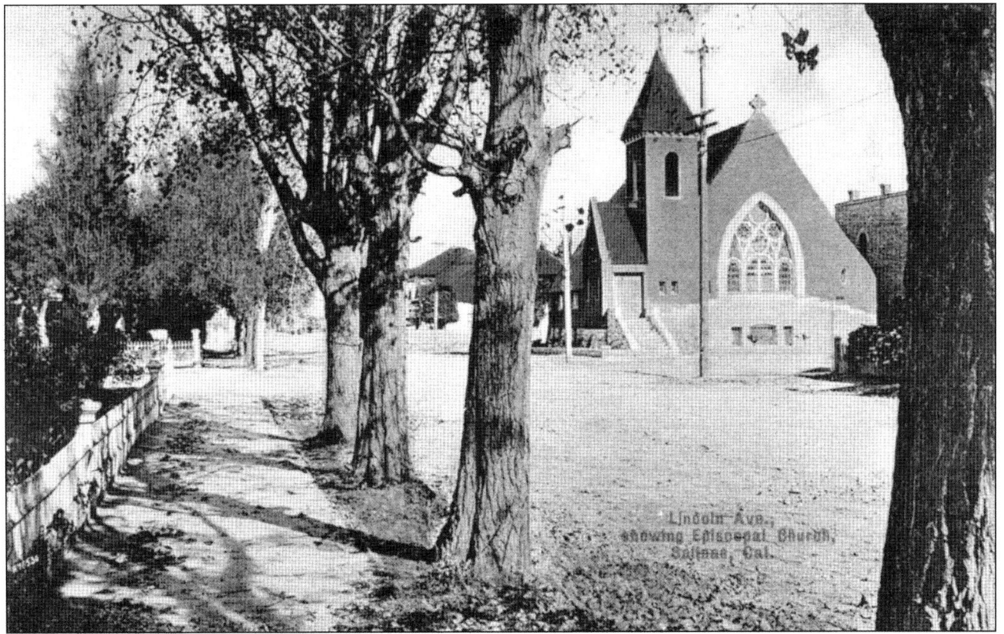

St. Paul's Episcopal Church sat on the corner of Lincoln Avenue and West Alisal Streets. It is seen on this postcard as photographed in 1909. Contractor Lu Grant built the church in 1897 at a cost of $4,515.

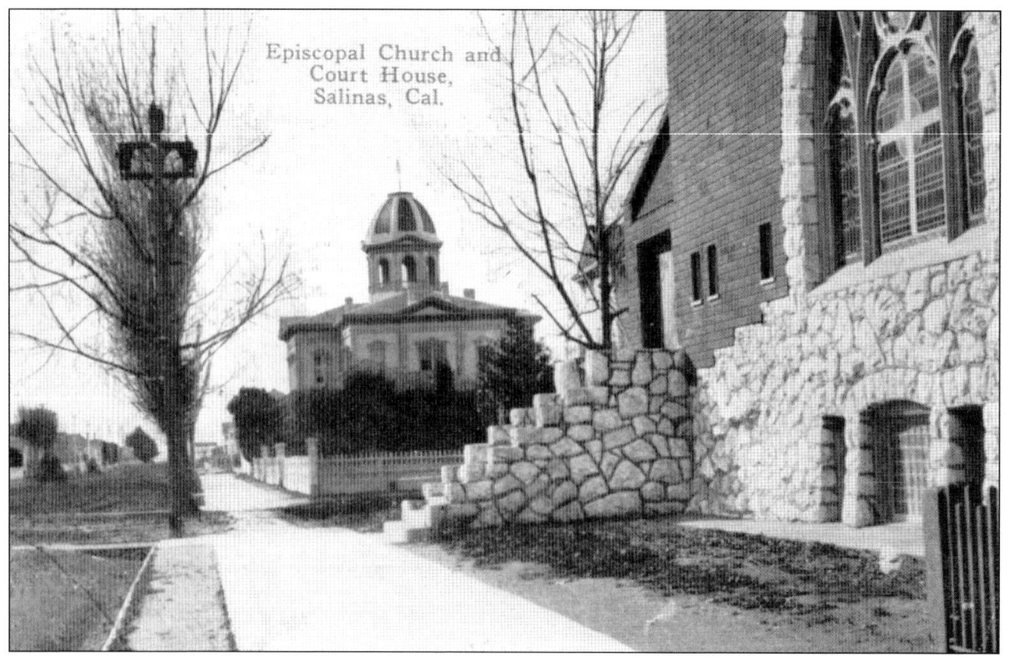

Here is another view of St. Paul's Episcopal Church, with the old courthouse in the background.

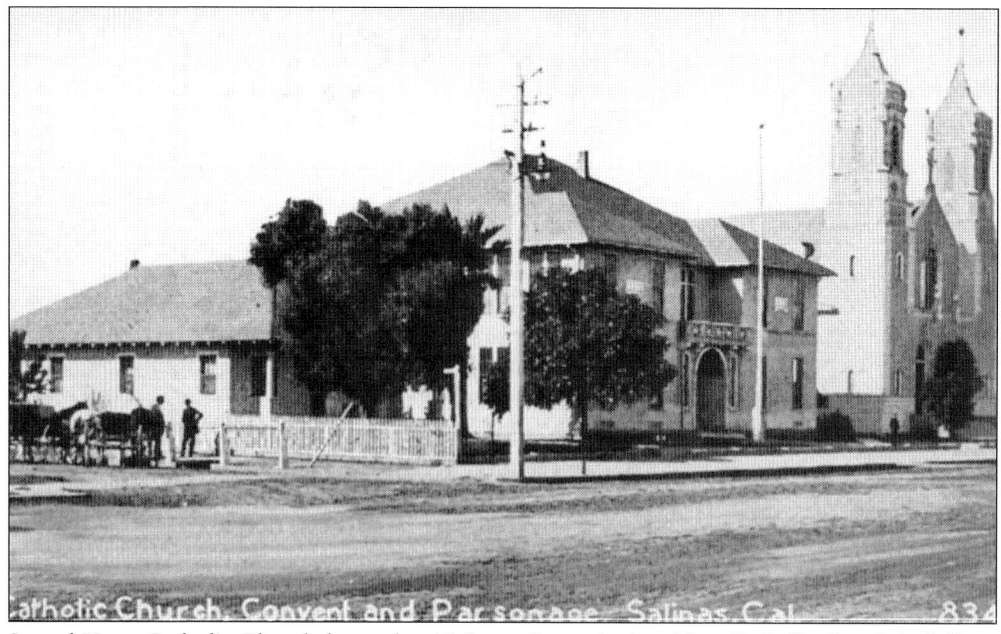

Sacred Heart Catholic Church, located at 10 Stone Street, is the oldest Catholic church in Salinas. The original building was constructed of brick in 1882 for $19,000 but was destroyed in the 1906 earthquake. The church was rebuilt with a wooden frame; however, it burned to the ground on Christmas Eve 1926. The current structure was completed in 1928 at a cost of $90,000. Shown adjacent to the church is the convent and parsonage.

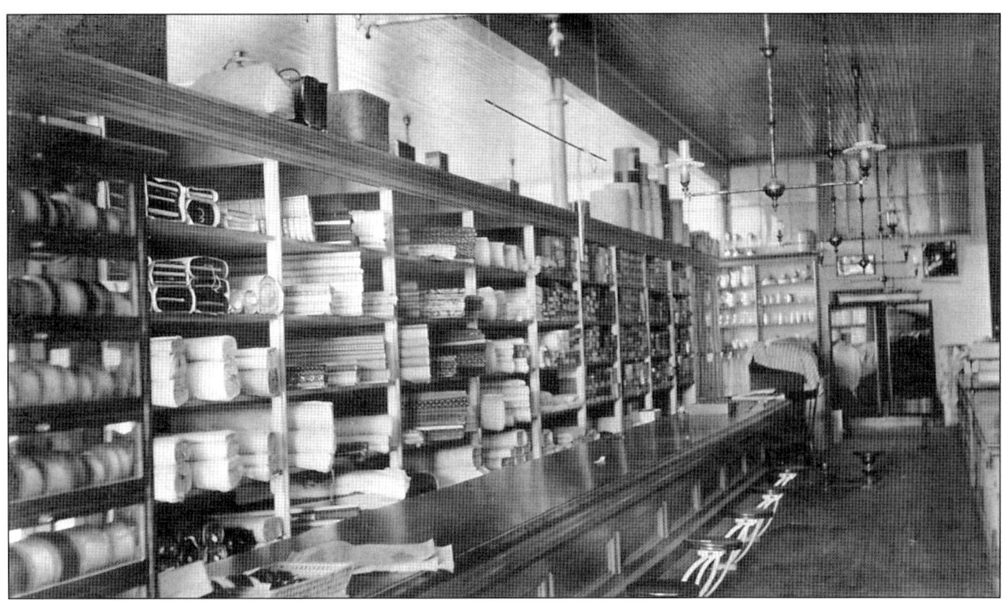

The interior of the Ford and Sanborn store, located at the corner of Main and Gabilan Streets, is seen in these two postcards. This was the building in Salinas most seriously damaged by the earthquake of 1906.

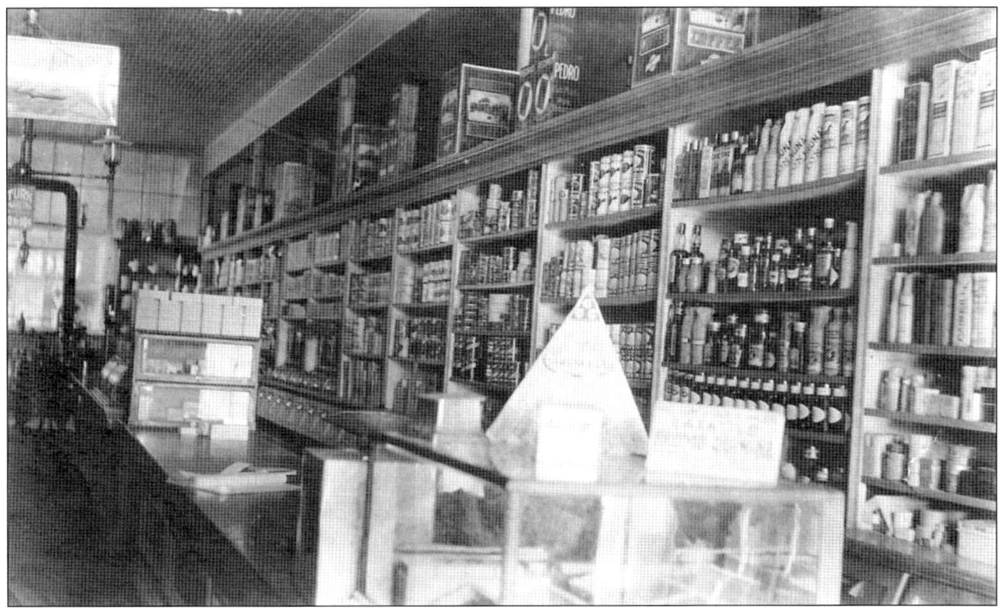

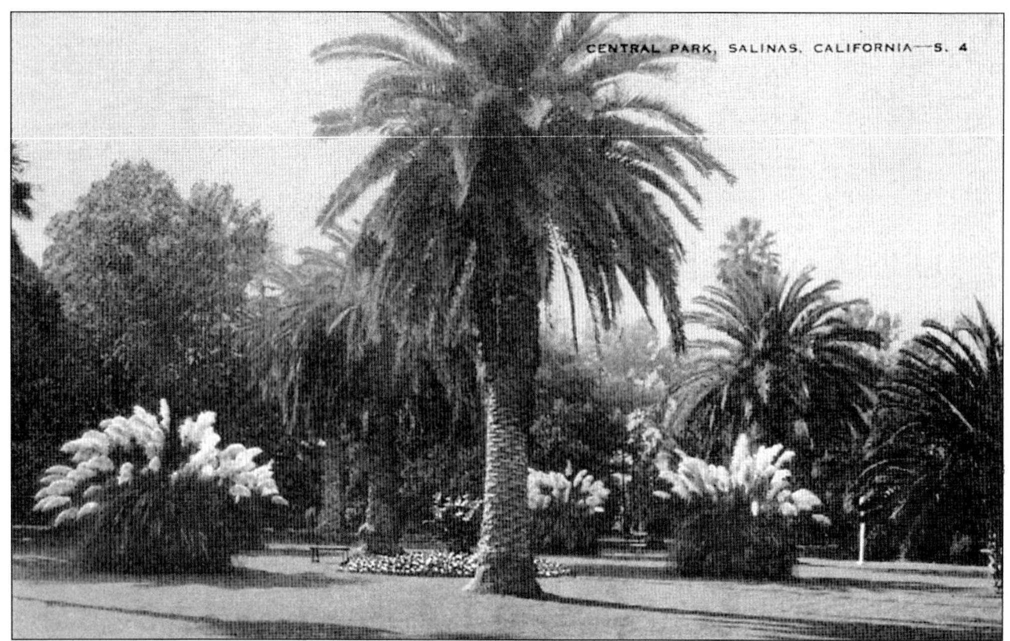

Central Park, located on Central Avenue several blocks west of the downtown area, is the oldest park in Salinas. Created in 1874, the park was gifted to the City of Salinas by W.H. Stone, who set aside a block of land 580 feet square. At one time, it was the site of a zoo. In later years, a children's playground was erected along with tennis, basketball, and volleyball courts. The year 1944 was a time of remembrance, when 57 rose bushes were planted by members of the American Legion Auxiliary Post 31 in honor of 57 Salinas World War II veterans. In time, the Memorial Rose Garden deteriorated, and on Memorial Day, May 30, 2011, it was brought back to life by Post 31 in partnership with the Salinas Valley Leadership Class 29 and rededicated in honor of the veterans.

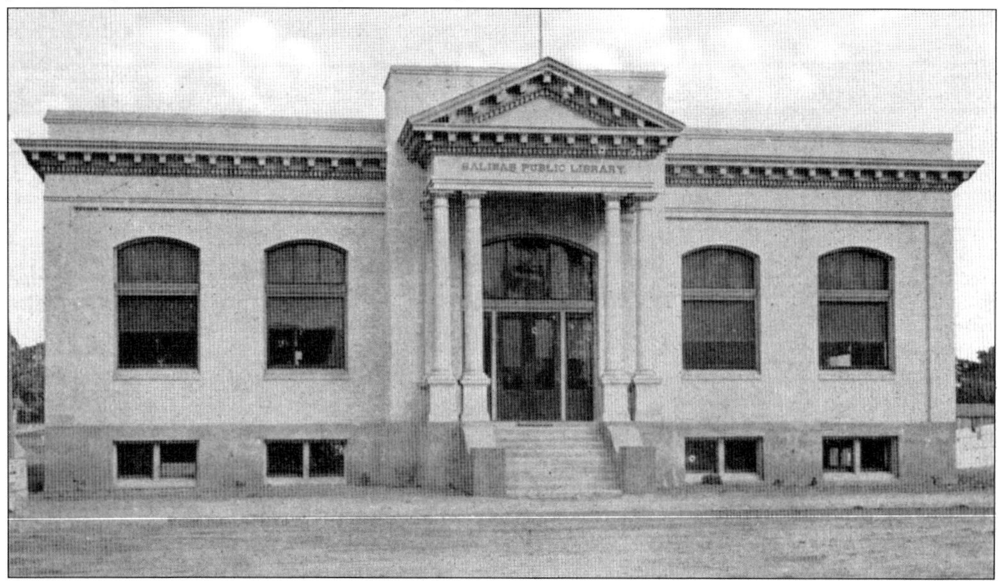

This was the original Salinas Public Library. The Salinas Civic Club (later the Salinas Women's Club) received a $10,000 grant from the Carnegie Foundation and was able to open this library in 1909. It served until 1960 and was demolished in 1961.

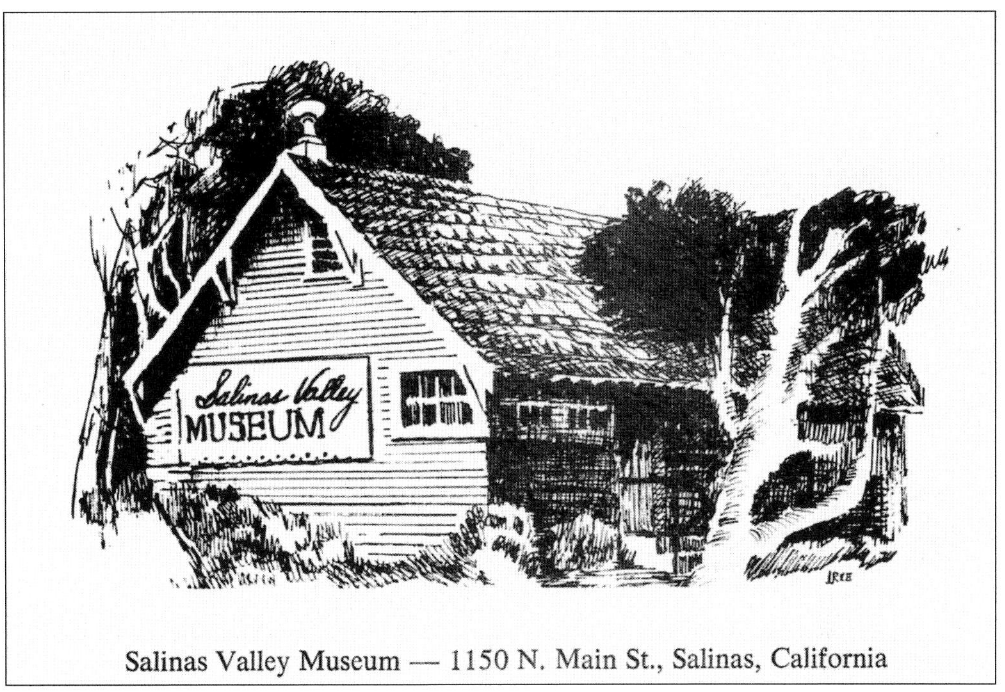

Salinas Valley Museum — 1150 N. Main St., Salinas, California

The Salinas Valley Museum, also known as the "Cottage" museum, was located on the rodeo grounds on North Main Street. It was operated by the Monterey County Historical Society.

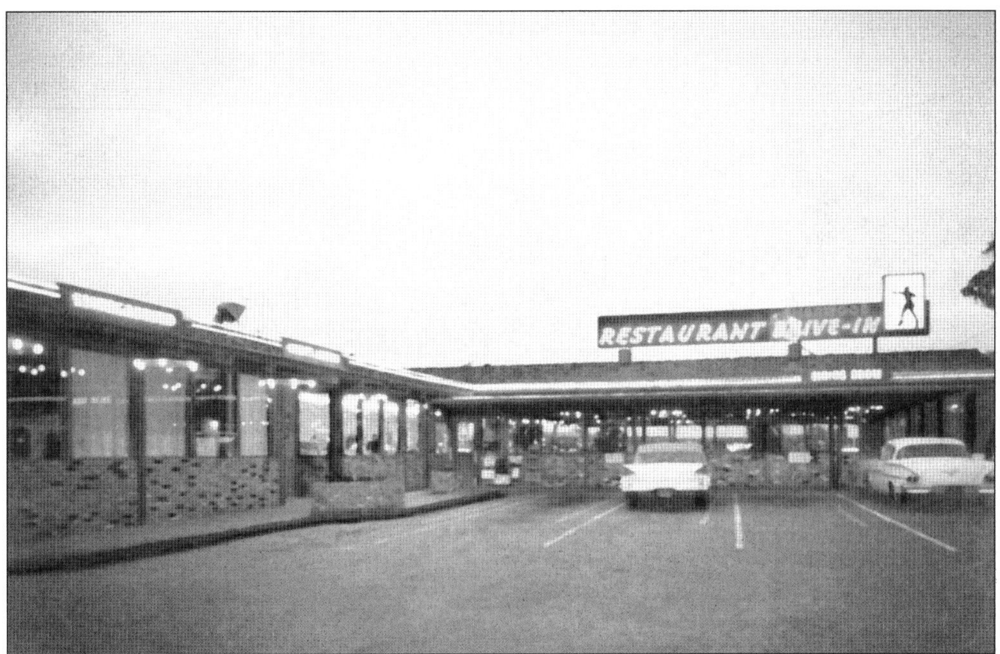

The Sherwood Drive-In Restaurant was located opposite the rodeo grounds on North Main Street. It boasted a complete coffee shop, car service, and two dining rooms featuring chuck wagon–style lunches and smorgasbord dinners. Robin Hood decor was found throughout the restaurant. The cars date this postcard to the late 1950s.

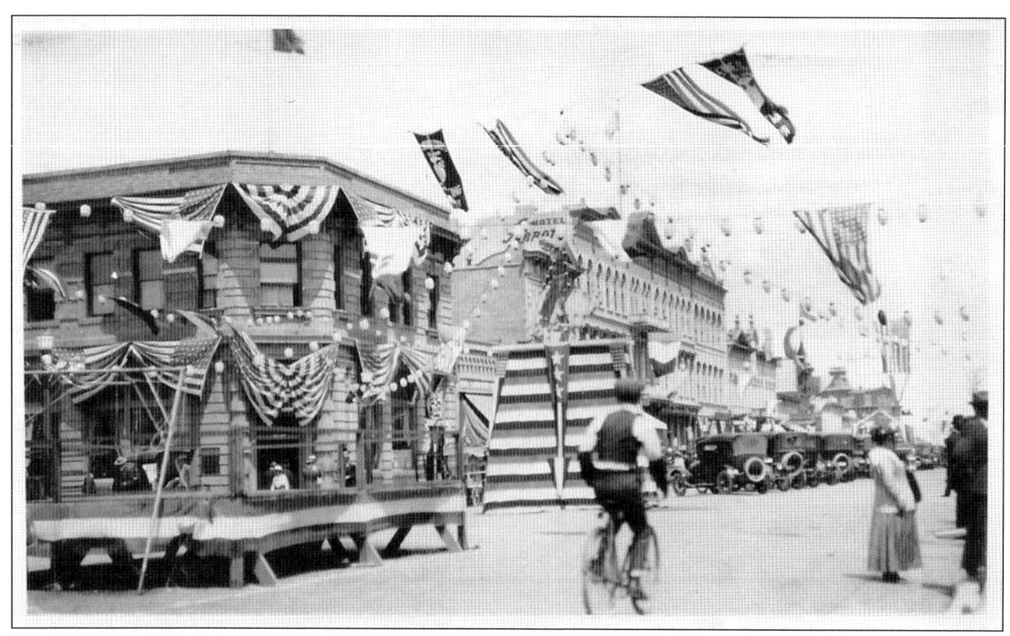

July 19th Salinas is once more celebrating. The weather has been nice for several weeks but is warm to-day. We are getting some good news from France. I didn't get your Jan. card until a week or so ago. Kind regards to both of you From A.B.

Mrs J. P. Besse
47 Buckingham St
Hartford
Conn.

This rodeo parade took place in 1918. The large building in the background is the Abbott House, built in 1873. This property was purchased by George and Mike Cominos in 1919, and it was thereafter known as the Cominos Hotel. At left is the reverse of the above postcard. Note the sender's message, written during the Great War: "We are getting some great news from France."

Four

HAPPENINGS

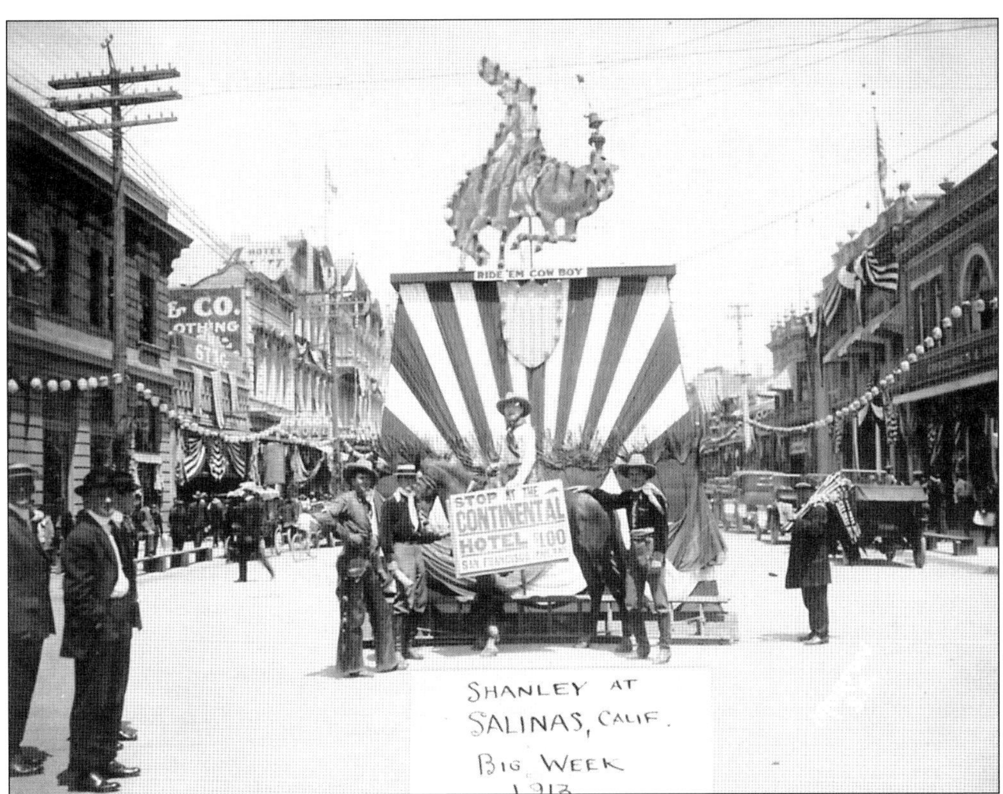

Big Week is rodeo week in Salinas. The first rodeo was held on August 11, 1911, and it has been held ever since; the year 2013 will be the 103rd rodeo. Called the California Rodeo, it has become one of the "Big Four" rodeos of the United States and parts of Canada.

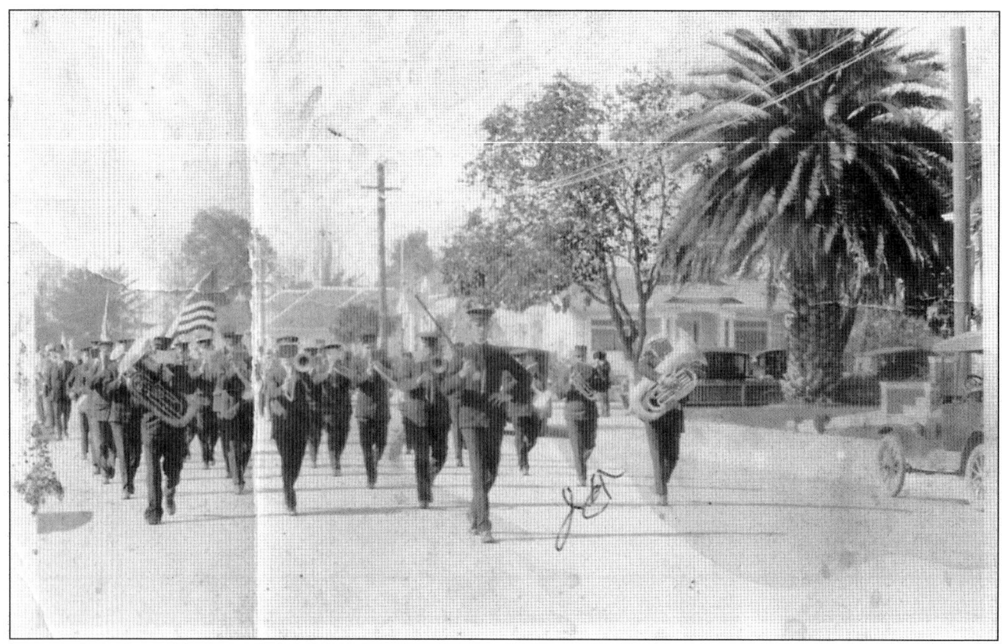

The Salinas City Band performs in 1911. That year marked the beginning of the horse parade down Main Street, led by James R. Hebbron, who became known as the "Grand Old Man of the California Rodeo." He led every parade from 1911 until 1926, when he retired at the age of 97.

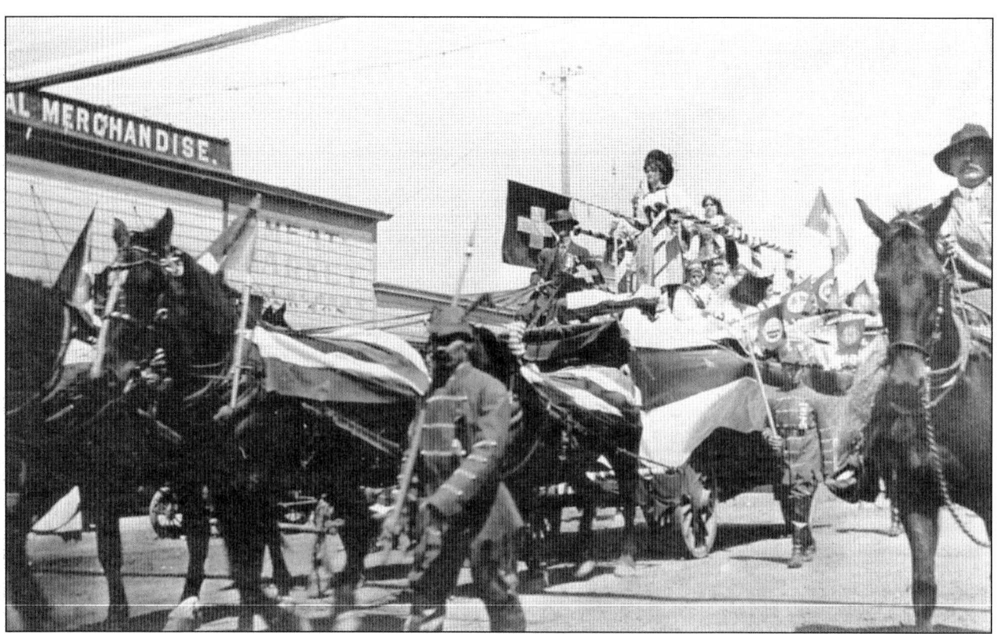

A Red Cross float appeared at the 1911 horse parade. The townsfolk also held an informal night parade at the close of the rodeo. Jim Bardin Sr. led the parade dressed as "King Spud," due to the prominence of the Burbank potato in local agriculture. He rode in a stately chariot pulled by six white horses.

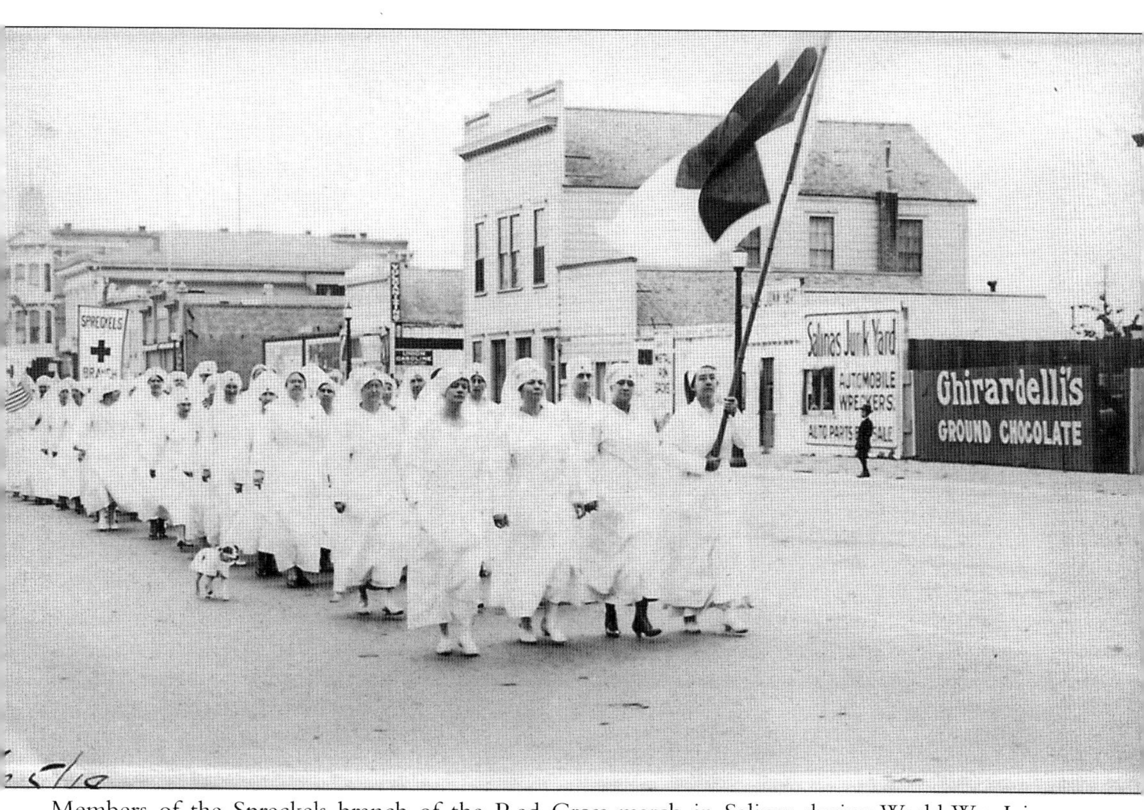

Members of the Spreckels branch of the Red Cross march in Salinas during World War I in support of war bonds.

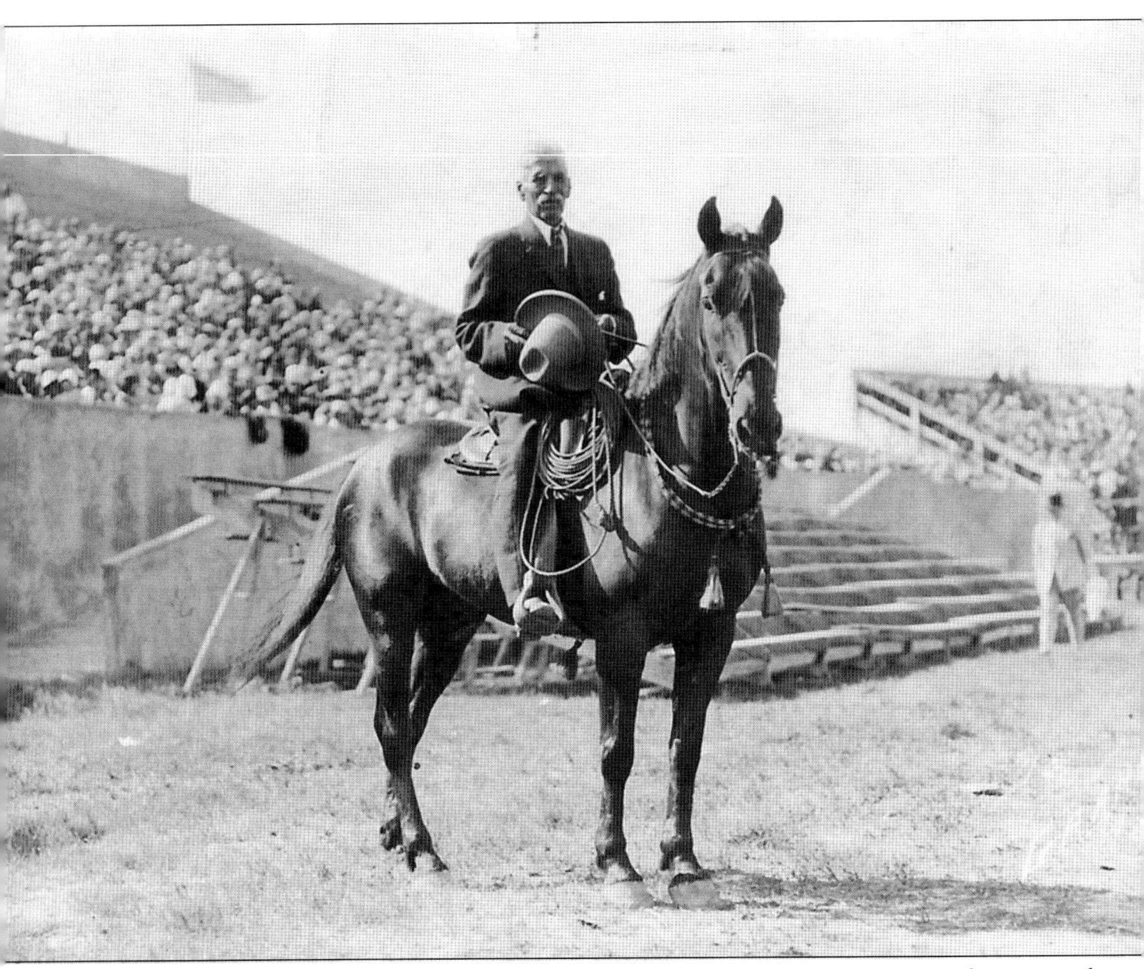

Benito Soberanes poses at the Rodeo in 1914. He owned the B. Soberanes Real Estate and Insurance Office in Salinas, where he was known each day to climb in his buggy and race to the Jeffrey Hotel for lunch with his horse Ben (not shown here). He was a member of the cattlemen who decided that Monterey County should have a rodeo like the San Juan Bautista Fiesta and Rodeo. In 1909, the cattlemen changed the name of the event, initially known as the Wild West Show, to the California Rodeo Salinas. In 1914, they had the rodeo incorporated under the name California Rodeo.

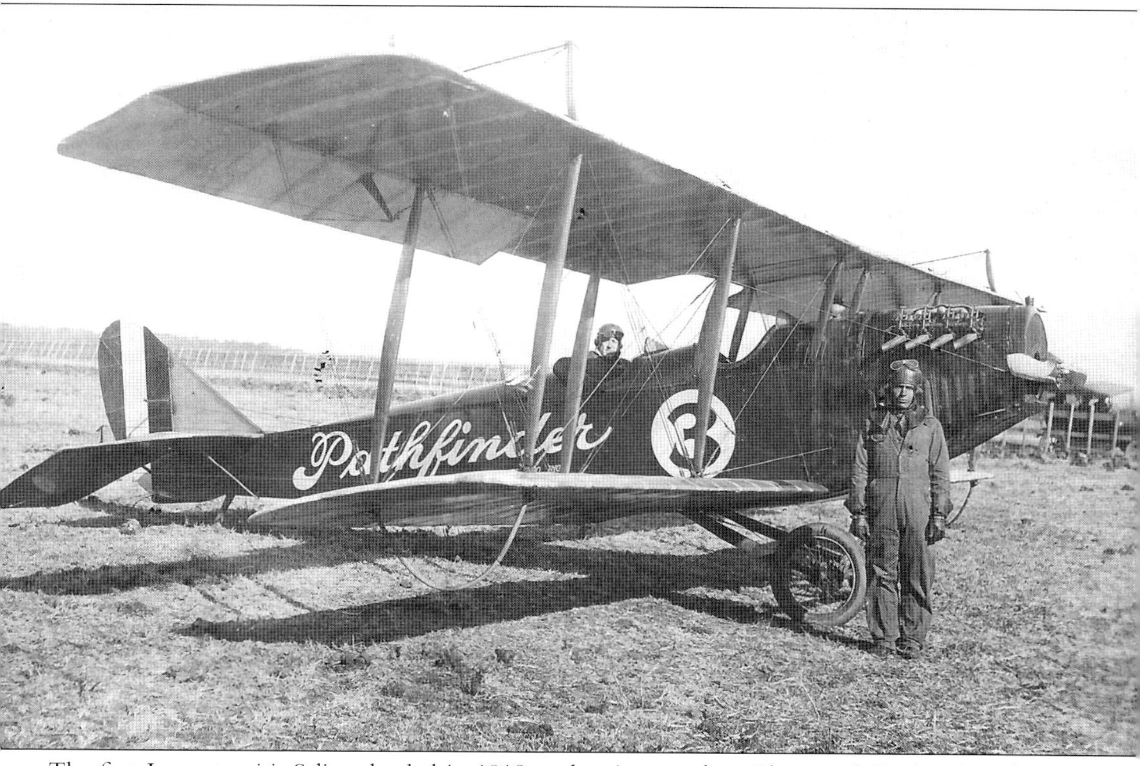

The first Jenny to visit Salinas landed in 1918 at the airport where Sherwood Gardens is today. Large numbers of these planes were sold as surplus after World War I, and they were a popular craft for barnstormers.

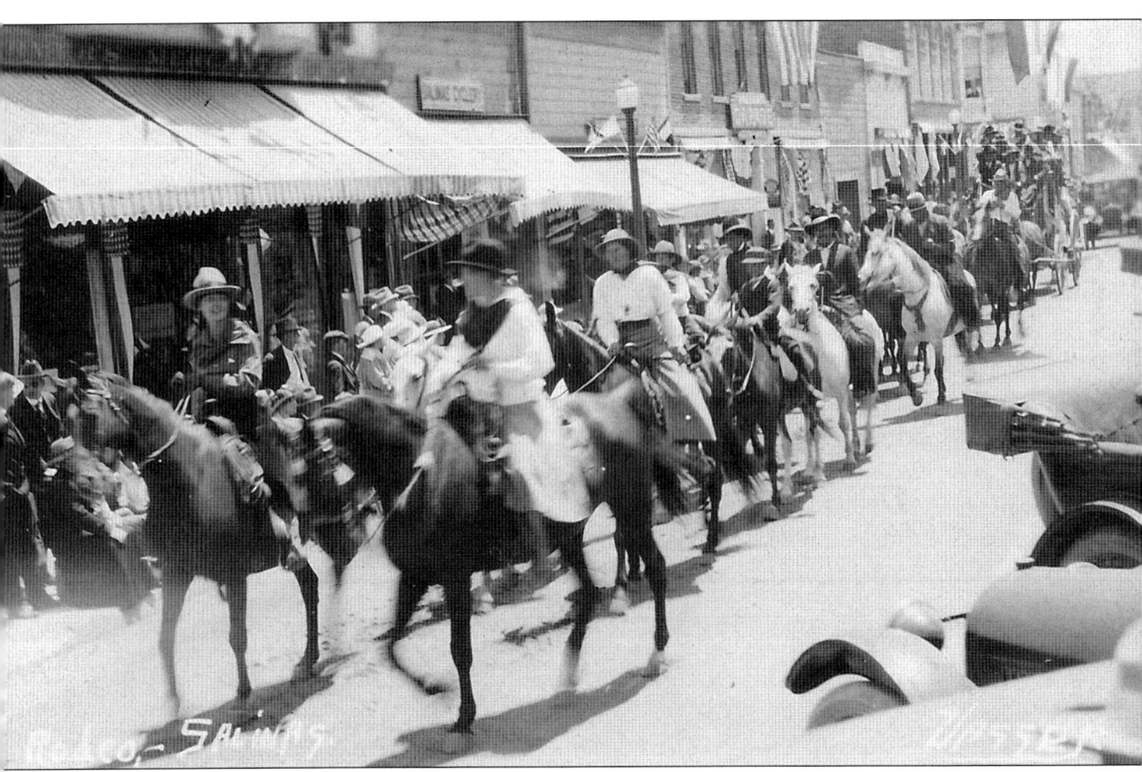

A Big Week horse parade is pictured here in the 1920s. The early horse parades were a family affair. Note the two youngsters at center with a man and woman directly behind them, possibly their parents. The horse parades were held during the day, and the Colmado del Rodeo ("climax of the roundup") parade was an evening affair. In 1921, the Colmado del Rodeo parade was perhaps the first ever dry parade, held due to the enactment of Prohibition.

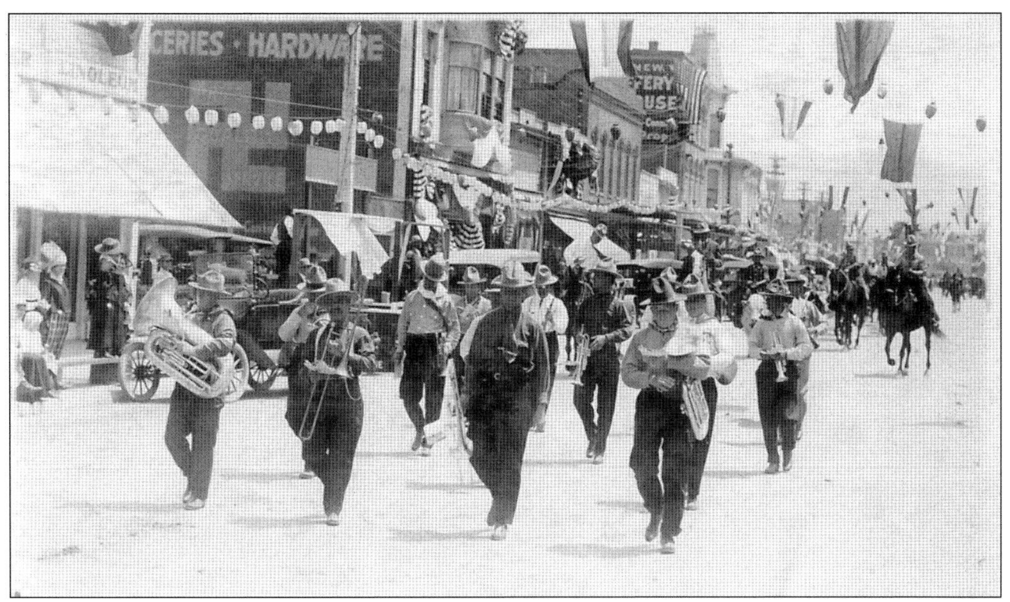

These two postcards convey images of another Big Week horse parade on Main Street. Both took place in the 1920s. The procession, consisting mostly of local cowboys and cowgirls, was over a mile long; by 1929, the local cowboys began to be outnumbered by professionals in the competition.

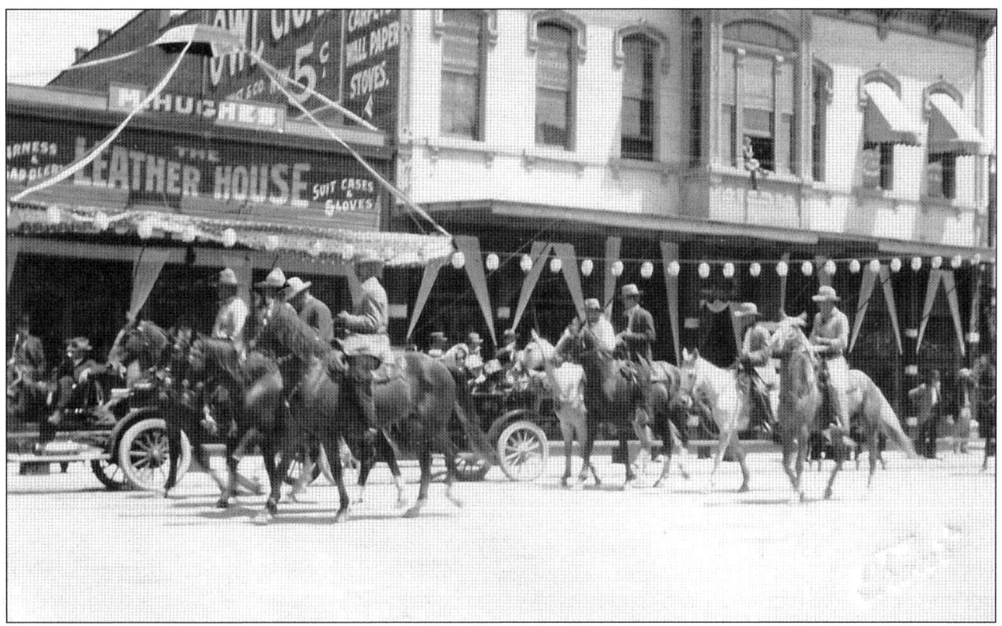

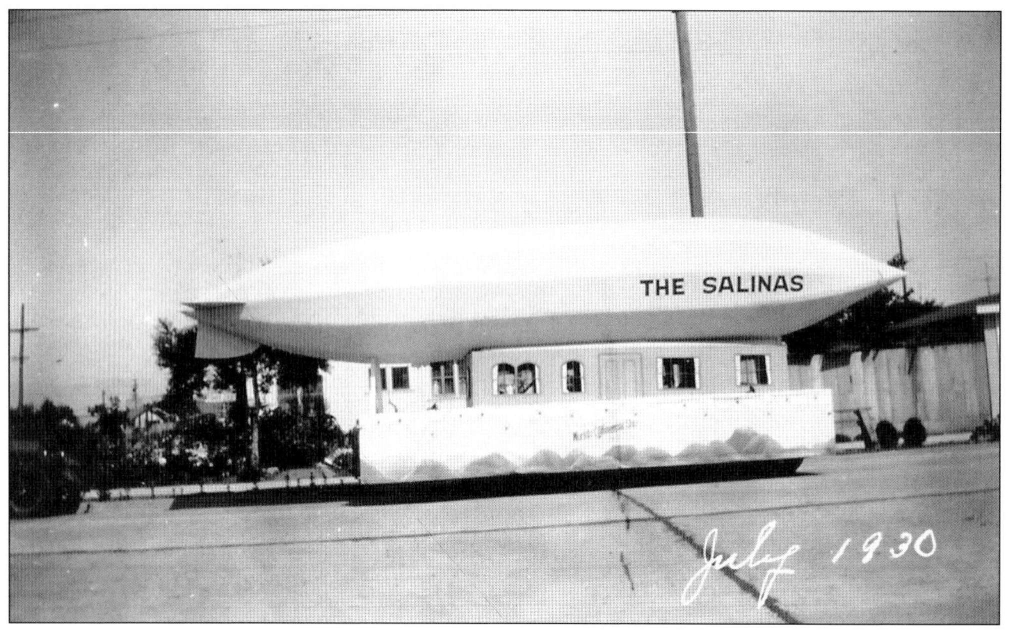

Pictured here is a float featuring a blimp named after Salinas in the 1930 Big Week parade. The banner reads, "Worlds Commercial Shop featuring fine furniture."

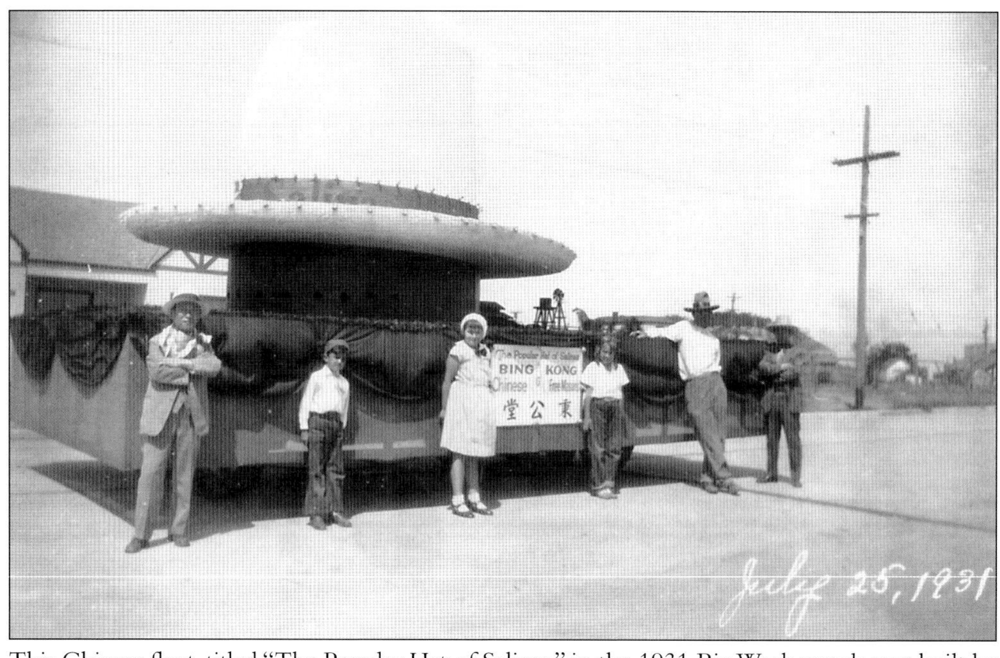

This Chinese float, titled "The Popular Hat of Salinas," in the 1931 Big Week parade was built by the Chinese Free Masons and was the theme for the nighttime parade, the Colmado del Rodeo. Pictured at far left is Shorty Lee, unofficial mayor of Chinatown. The others are unidentified.

This famous California stock horse, Chiquito, was a champ. He was owned by William Jeffery, proprietor of the Jeffrey Hotel in Salinas. Below is the reverse of the postcard at right. It definitely sings the praises of Chiquito.

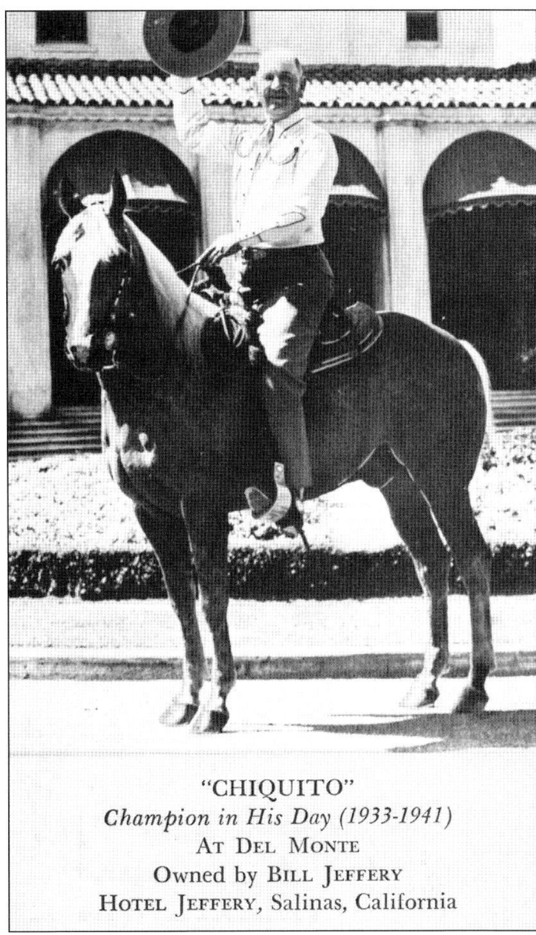

"CHIQUITO"
Champion in His Day (1933-1941)
AT DEL MONTE
Owned by BILL JEFFERY
HOTEL JEFFERY, Salinas, California

Post Card

PLACE
STAMP
HERE

Testimonial of the State Agricultural Society
to
"CHIQUITO"

Famous California Stock Horse Owned by
William Jeffery of Salinas

"CHIQUITO, OUR FRIEND": For many summers you have delighted the old and young by your ever cheerful and generous performances at every gathering in California where horse lovers congregate. You demonstrate by your performance the fact that a smaller horse can, and perhaps does more easily than those larger in stature, carry a large man. This rugged quality is due to your perfect symmetry, rhythm of movement, and perfect coordination with your rider. Ever immediately obedient and most efficient, you perfectly typify what the California stock horse should be, that is, immediately and quickly responsive to the thought and will of your rider, answering his signals with great speed and with a minimum of effort.

The California State Fair, always recognizing perfection, is proud to do you the honor of presenting you its highest token of appreciation—the Gold Medal of California and a Special Award Gold Ribbon.

Here's to you: A gallant, stouthearted, kindly affectionate gentleman, and to William Jeffery of Hotel Jeffery, Salinas, your owner, trainer and rider.

EL Camino PRESS

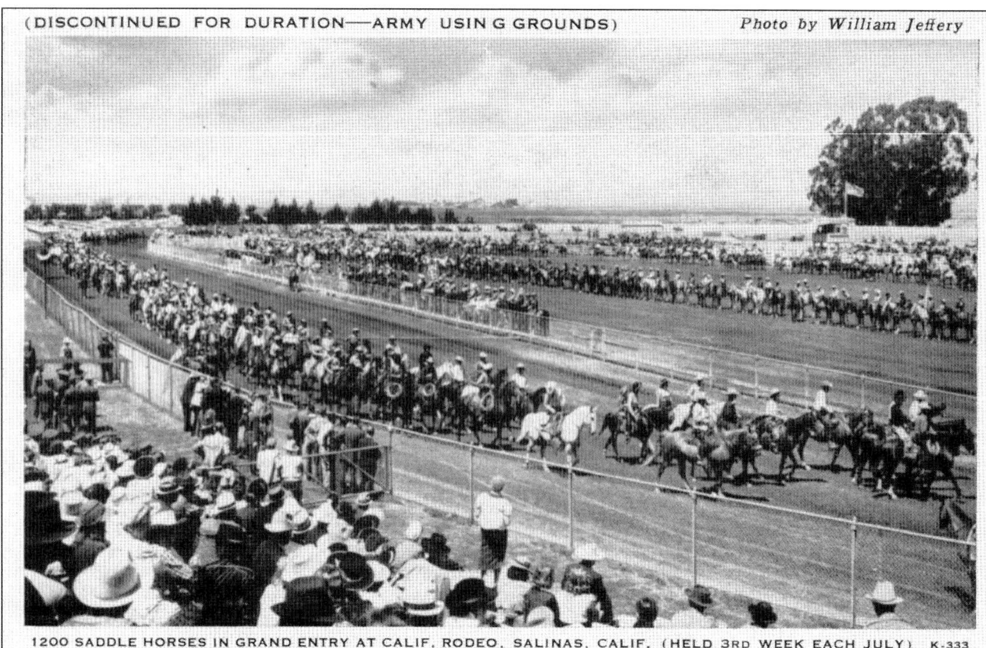

The California Rodeo is truly one of the Big Four. One difference from other rodeos, however, is the pronunciation. Salinas traces its roots back to a local Spanish and Mexican tradition and pronounces the word as "roh-*dey*-oh," rather than the more traditional pronunciation, "*roh*-dee-oh," used elsewhere. Below is the reverse of the above postcard. It is difficult to discern the entire message, but the sender seems excited. He wrote, in part, "The big week is over and everybody seems glad. I am sure glad."

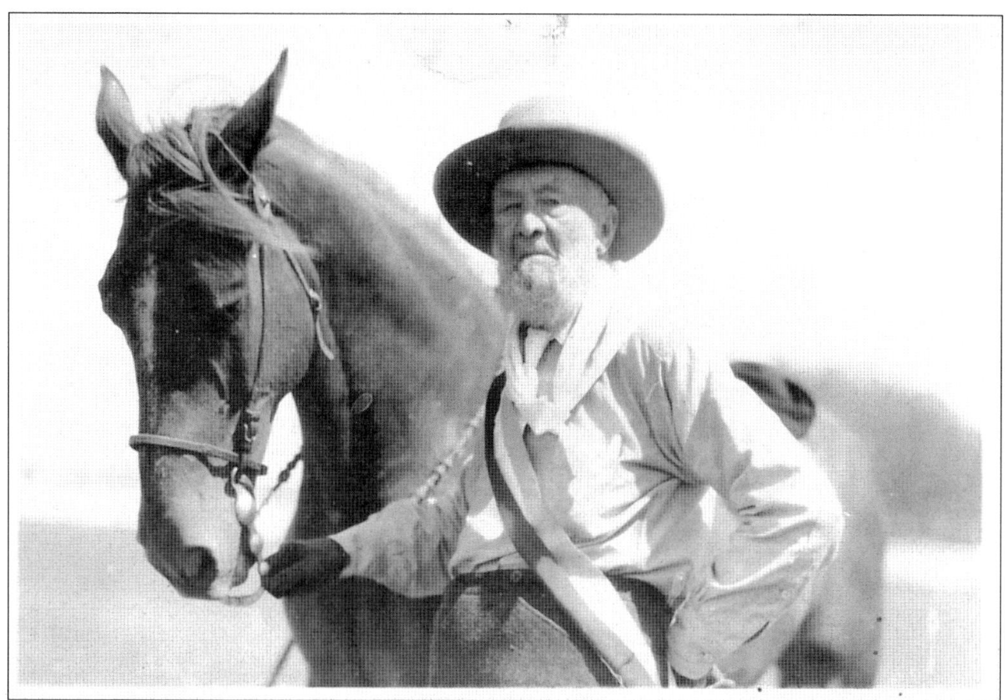

James R. Hebbron was known as "the grand old man of the California Rodeo." He led the parade each year between 1911 and 1926, when he retired at age 97. He was instrumental in the organization of the first agricultural association in Monterey County in 1875, and became its first vice president.

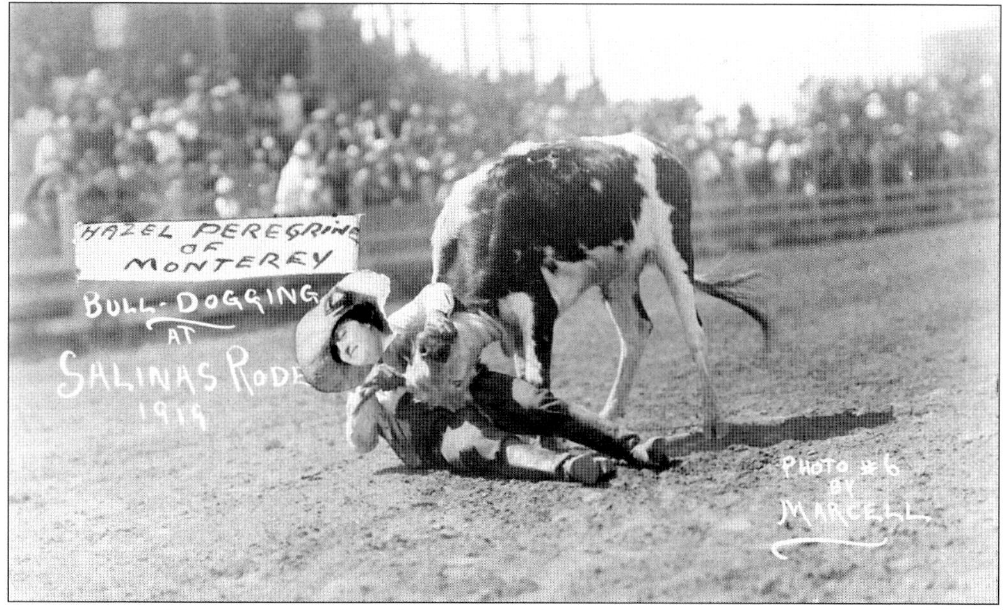

Seen here is bulldogging action from the California Rodeo in 1919. The postcard appears to have been altered.

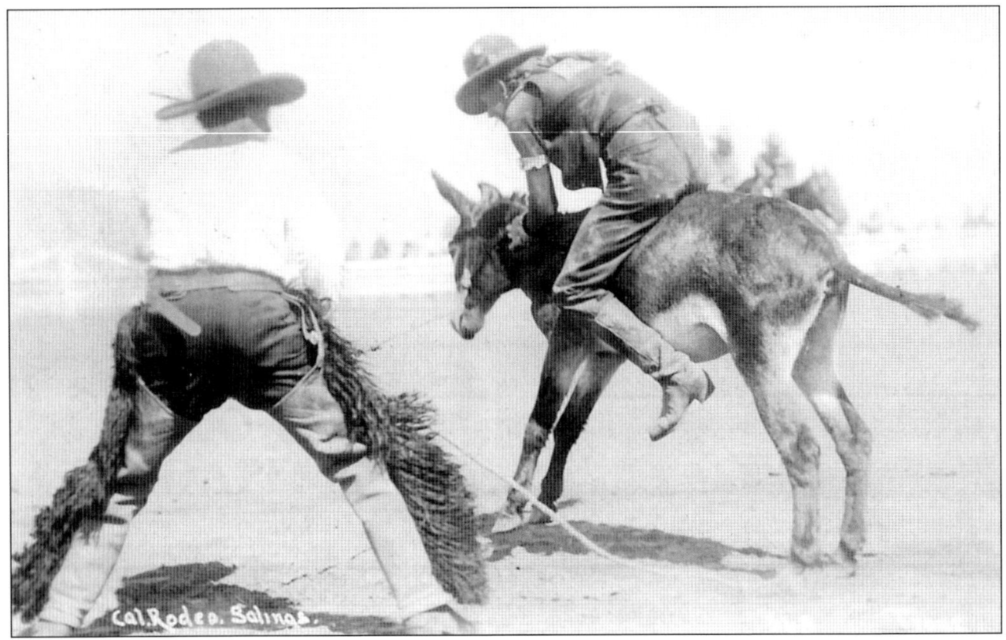

This postcard shows trick rider Rose Stadtler Walker "horsing" around at the California Rodeo.

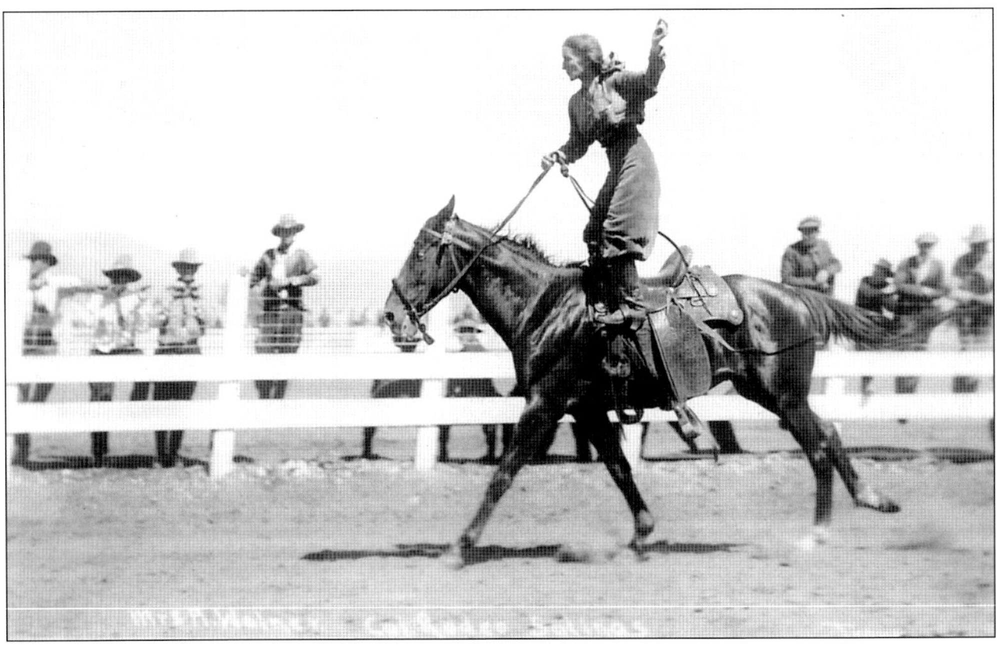

In 1912, the Wild West Show was repeated and was even more successful than the first year. One of the highlights was the inclusion of cowgirls for the first time, competing in a cowgirls' bucking-horse contest. Pictured here is Rose Stadtler Walker, a trick rider at the California Rodeo. Women trick riders were very rare in the early years. Walker was one of the few and the best.

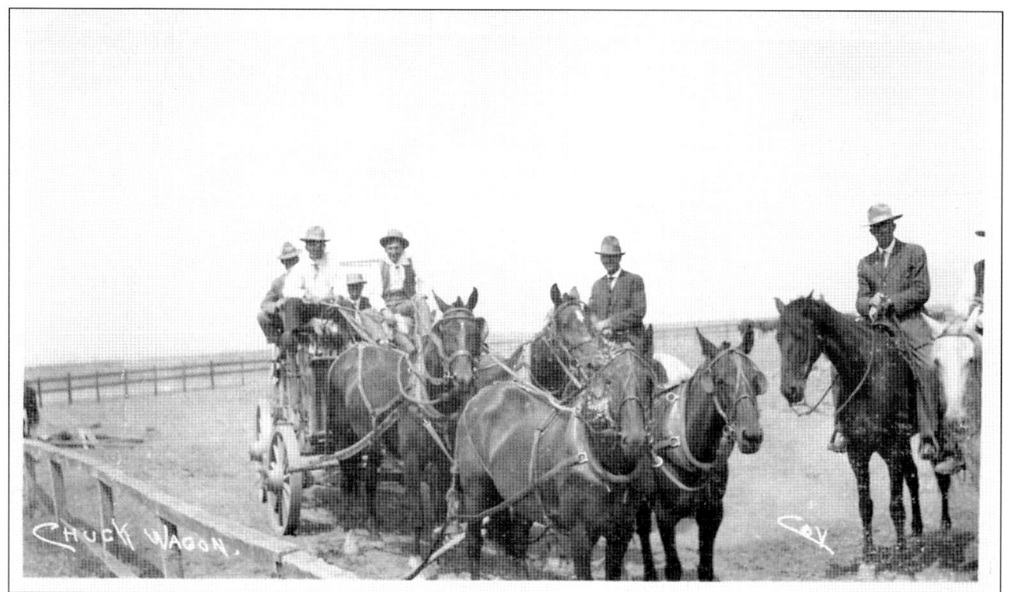

The chuck wagon made an appearance at the first rodeo in 1911.

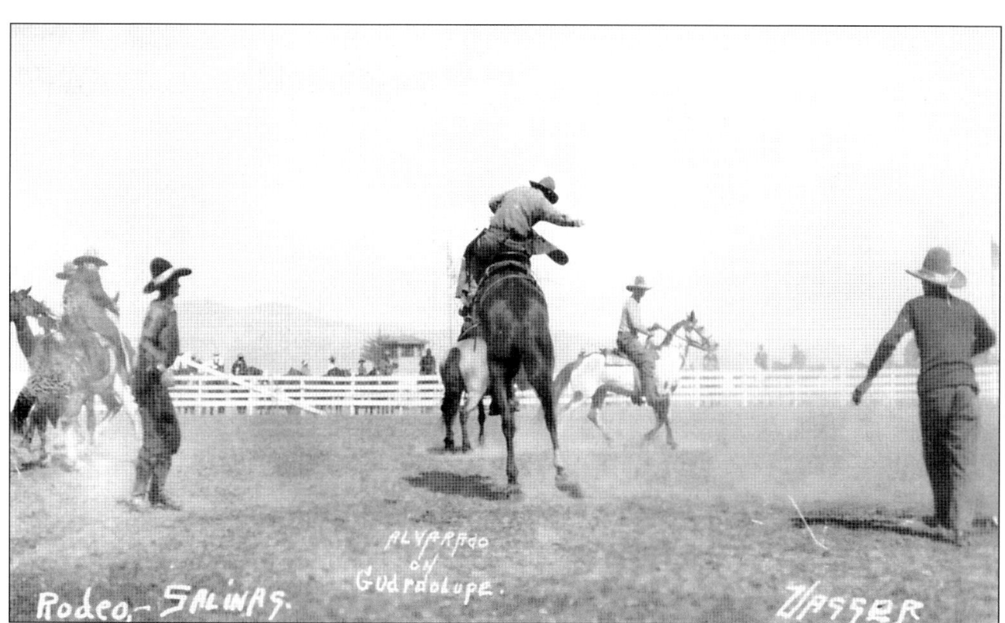

Bucking bronco action is pictured here at the California Rodeo. Bucking broncos were one of the highlights of the rodeo, as seen here with Alvarado riding Guadalupe. The horses were brought by train from King City.

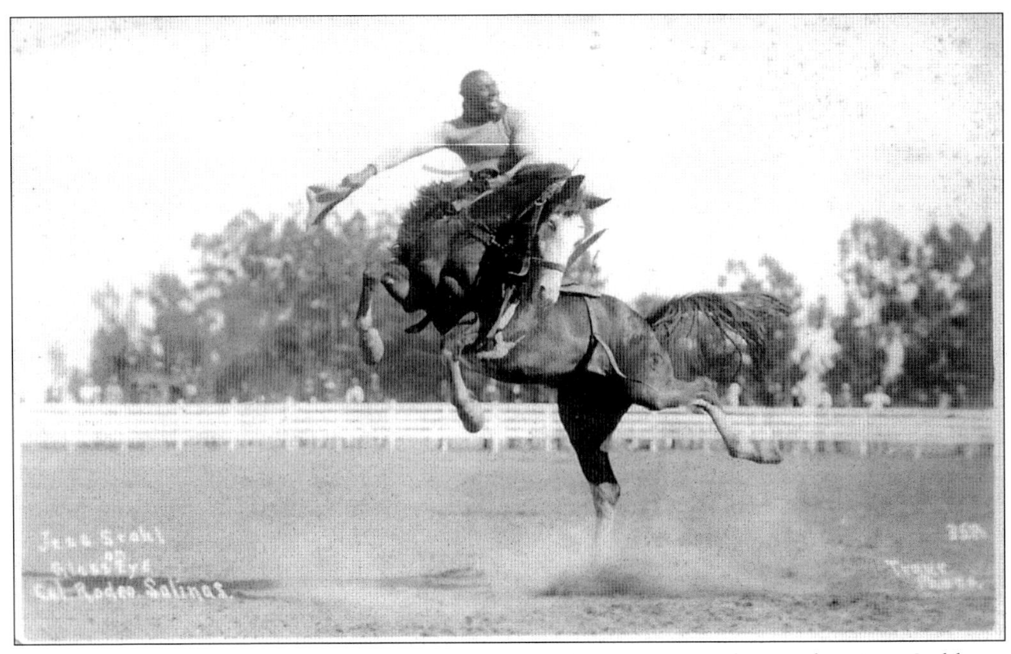

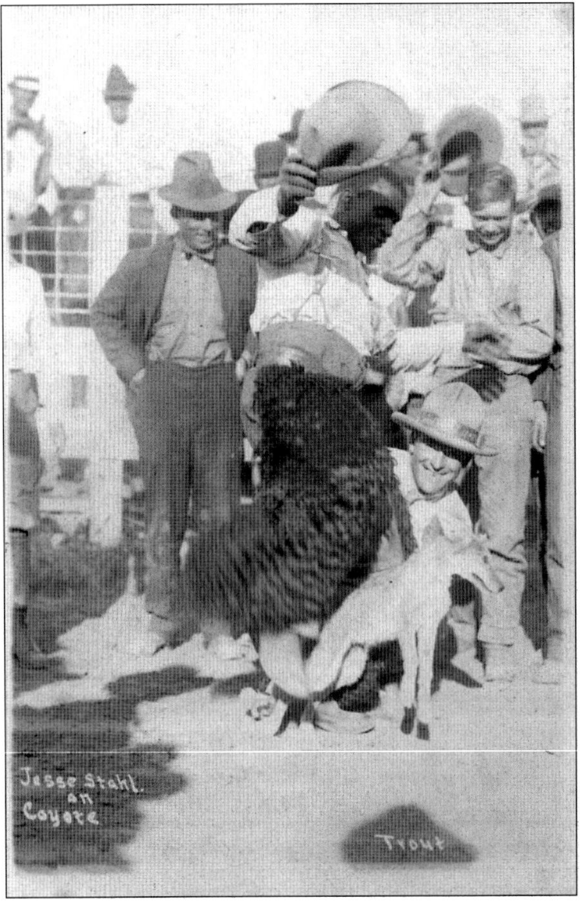

Famous rodeo cowboy Jesse Stahl rides a previously unridden bucking horse called Glass Eye; this was one of the highlights of the show. Stahl also rode a horse named Coyote. As a jest, members of the rodeo captured a coyote that Stahl rode for the photograph at left. Stahl retired in 1929 and rode a bucking horse backwards, bidding farewell. He was one of the most famous black cowboys of his time and is enshrined in the Cowboy Hall of Fame.

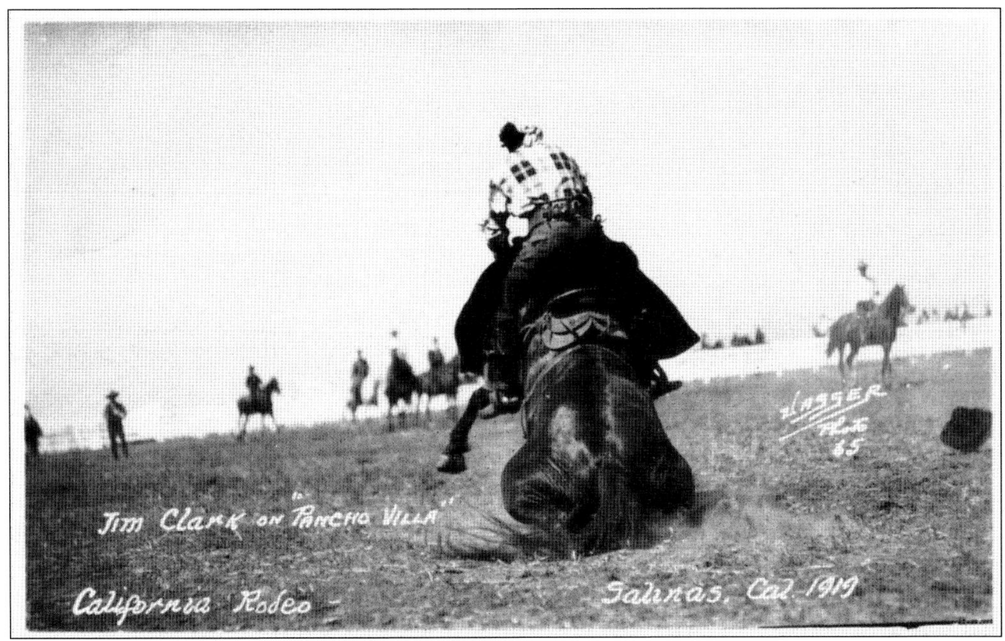

Jim Clark rides Poncho Villa, named for the infamous Mexican bandito, in 1919.

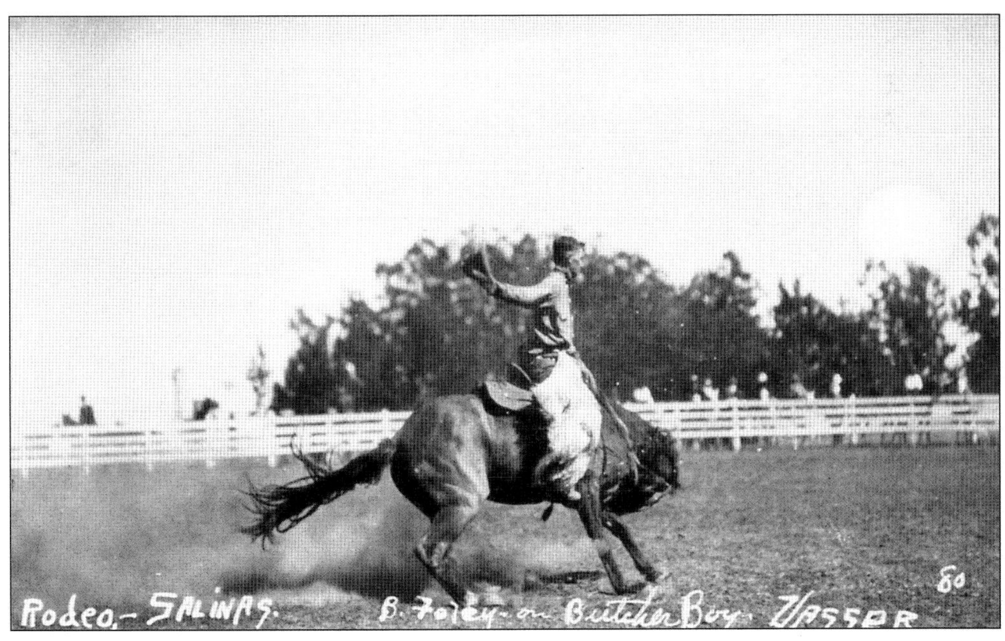

B. Foley rides the daunting Butcher Boy.

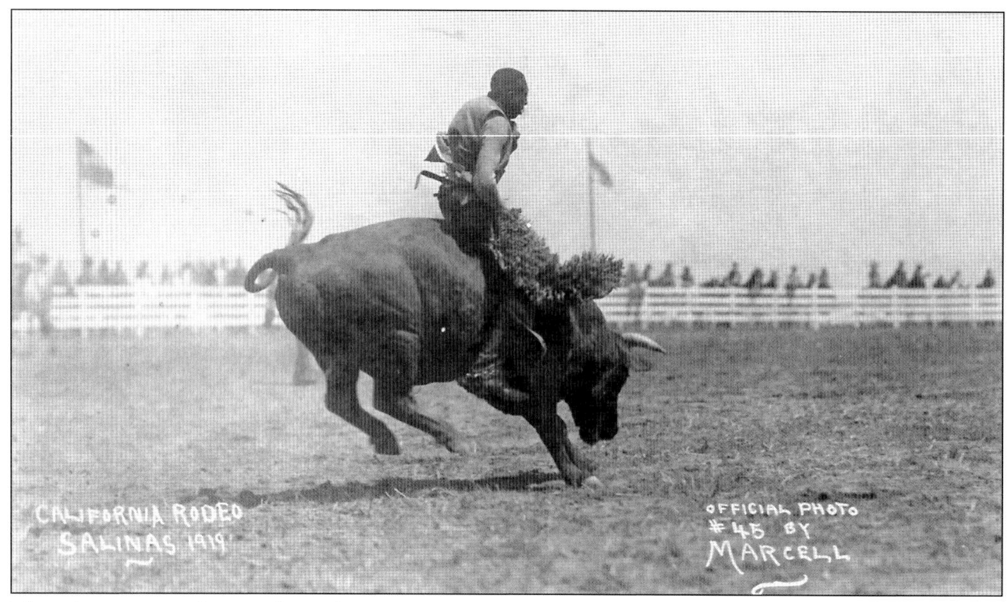

The picture was taken at the rodeo in 1919. The rider is most likely Jesse Stahl.

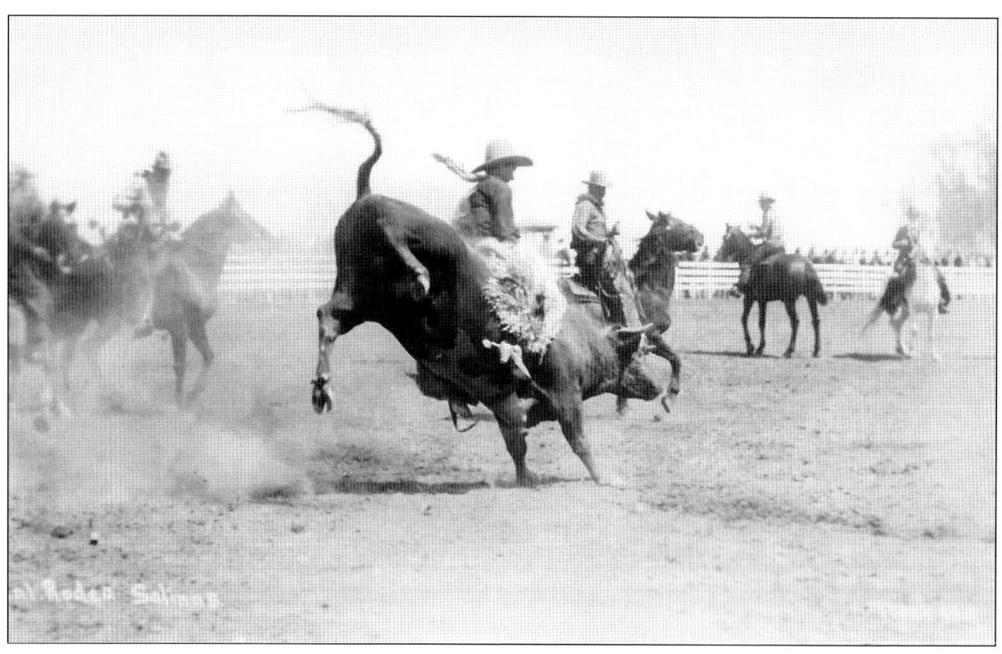

This postcard features another great image of bull riding at the California Rodeo. Cowboys on horses surround the bull rider, ready to come to his aide if he is thrown. A great deal of skill is required to perform such a ride. Bull riding was and is a dangerous event. Those on horses must be alert and ready to pick up the rider if he should be thrown, or when he dismounts, for fear of him being gorged or trampled.

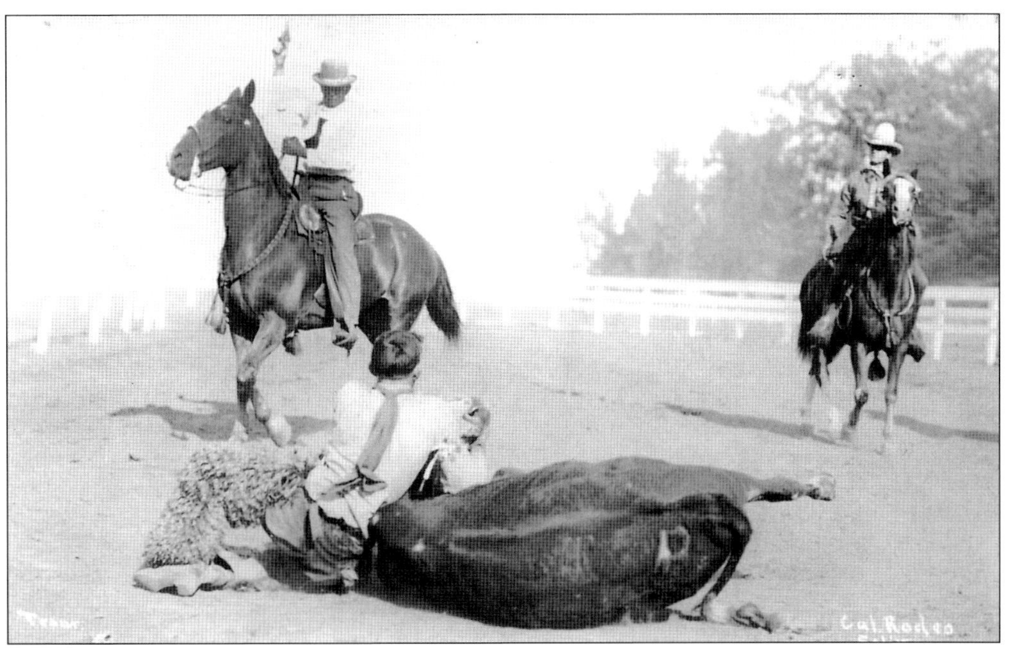

Bulldogging takes great skill and teamwork. These cowboys show off their talent at the California Rodeo in 1919.

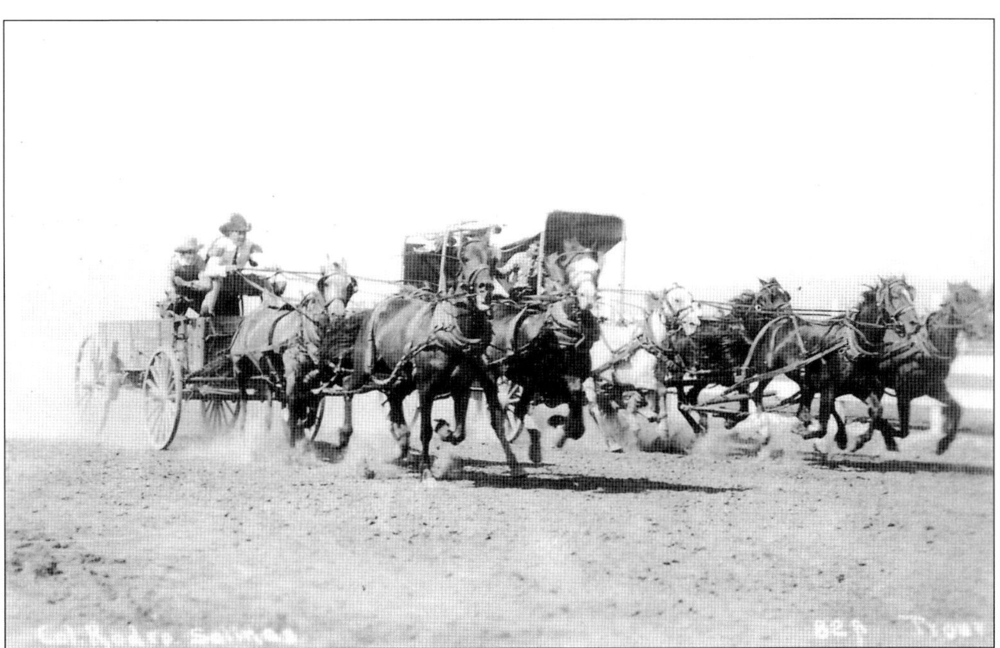

Buggy racing was another popular event at the rodeo, and in Salinas, it goes back to the time when stagecoach races were held to see who would be first to reach the stage stop at the Half Way House, Salinas's first structure.

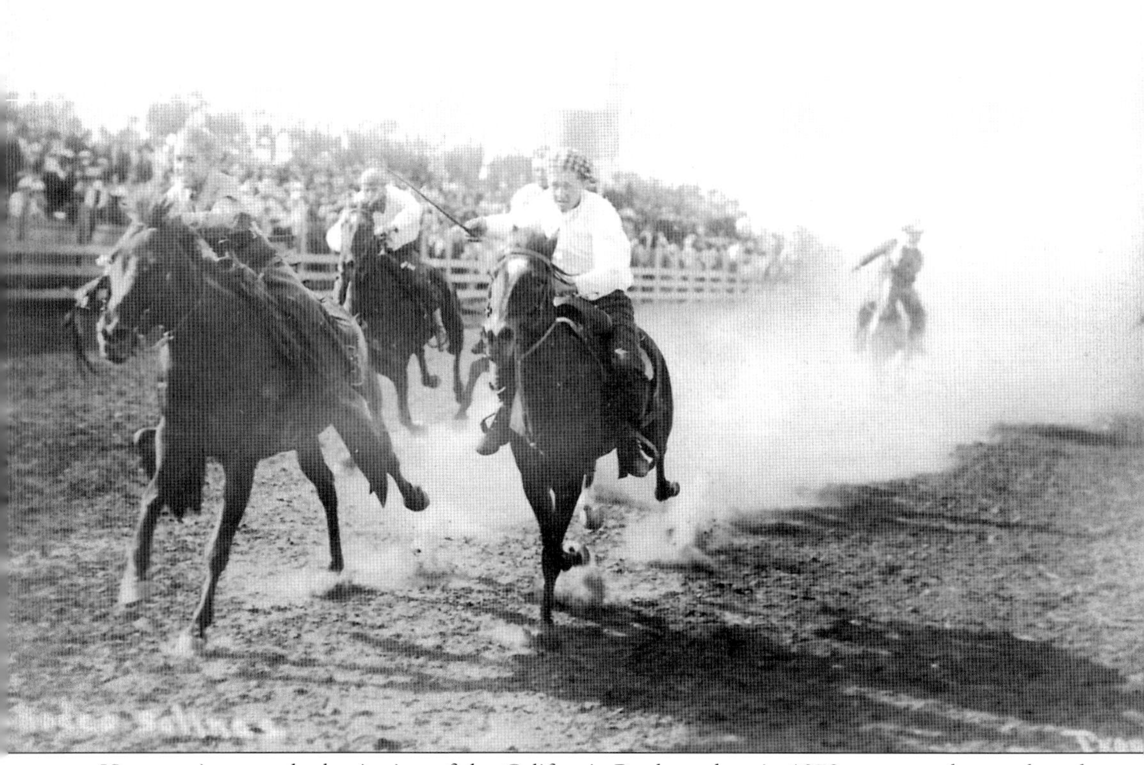

Horse racing was the beginning of the California Rodeo when in 1872, a racetrack, grandstand, stables, bar, and restaurant were built on 69.4 acres donated to the city of Salinas by Eugene Sherwood and Richard Hellman. In 1875, the park hosted three days of horse racing. In 1878, the name of the park was changed to Sherwood Park.

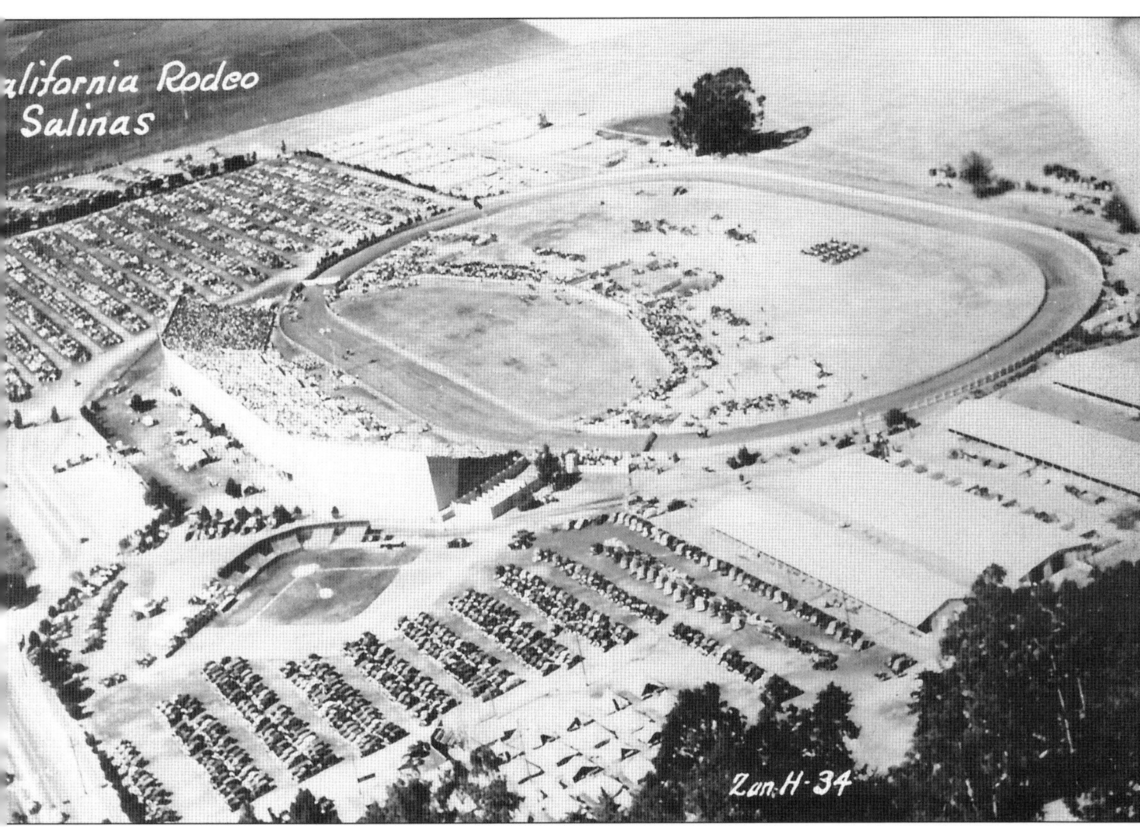

This aerial view of the rodeo grounds shows the old grandstands built in 1924 along with a racetrack and barns. In 1996, the grandstands were condemned, and the rodeo association raised over $9 million to not only rebuild the stands, but also build a facility that could be used all year long for concerts, football games, soccer games, motor events, festivals, and graduations; this resulted in the Salinas Sports Complex of today. The complex is operated by the California Rodeo Association in partnership with the city of Salinas.

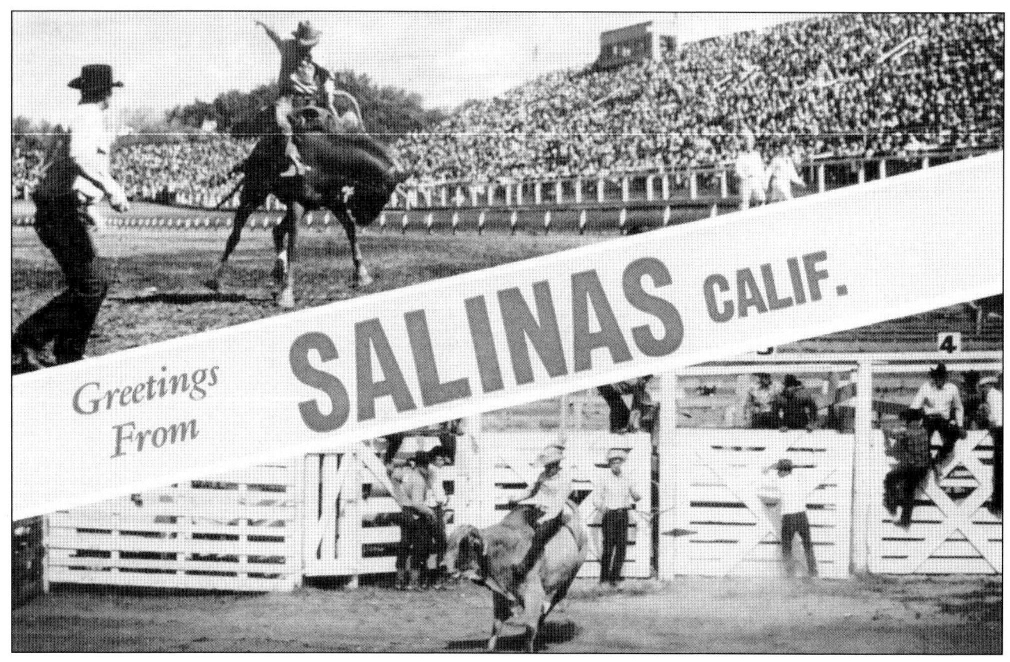

Pictured here are two postcards promoting the rodeo. The Salinas Sports Complex is located on land owned by the city and situated on 80 acres in Sherwood Park. The California Rodeo Association holds a 50-year lease with the city to run and maintain the facilities for not only the California Rodeo, but also a year-round center for activities.

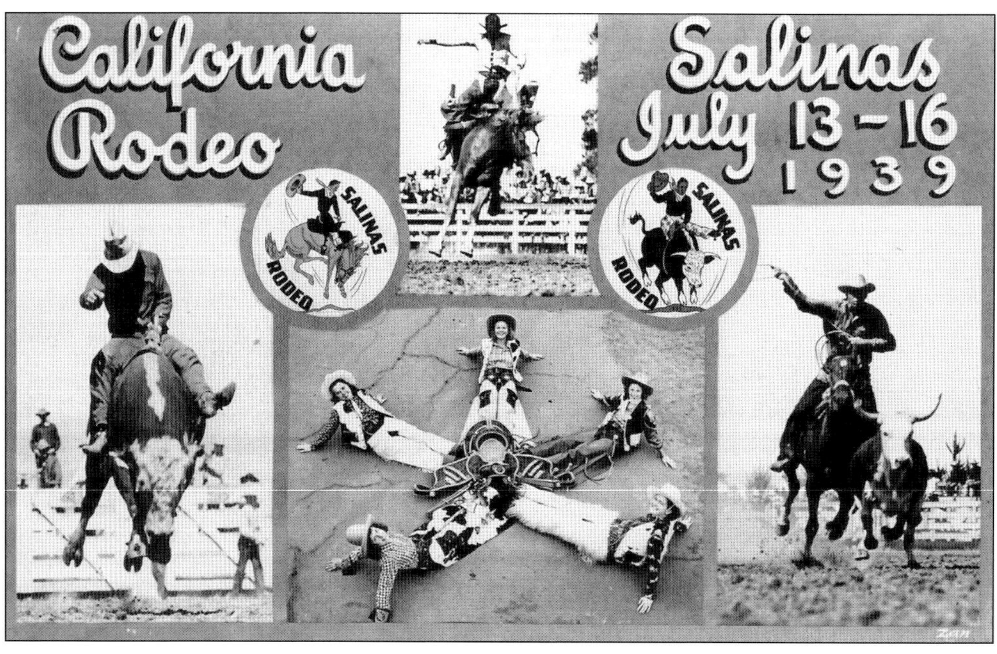

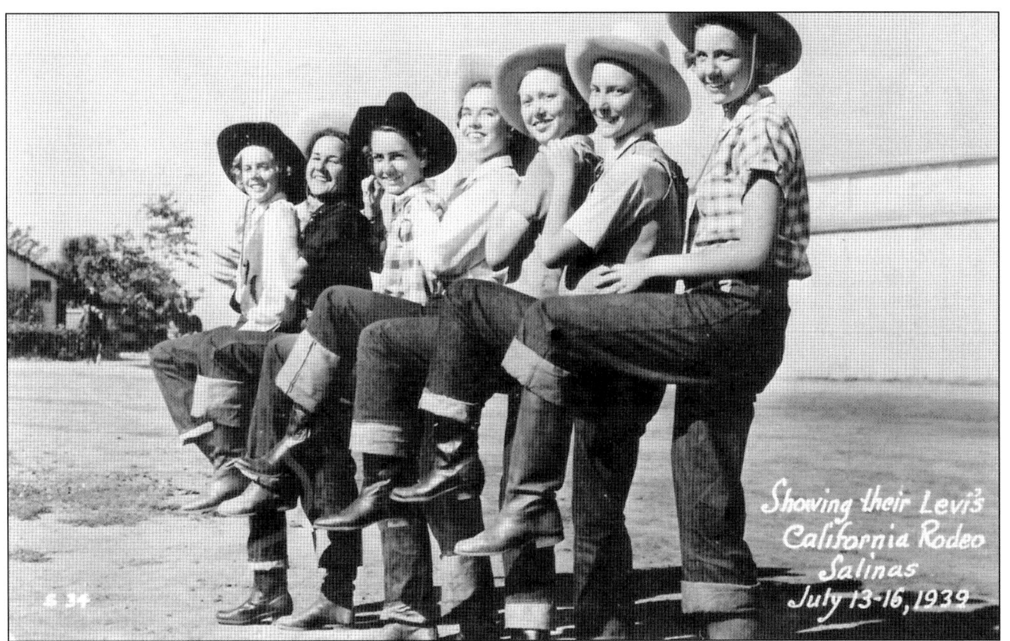

Here is another promotional postcard, this one dating from 1939, with a group of ladies showing off their Levis.

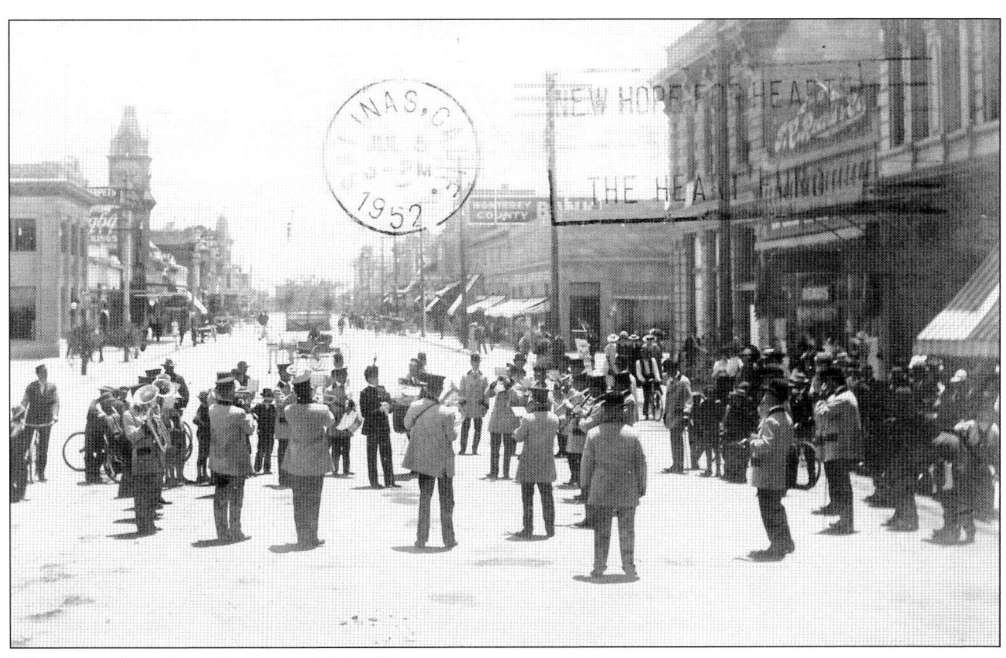

This street band performs on Main Street.

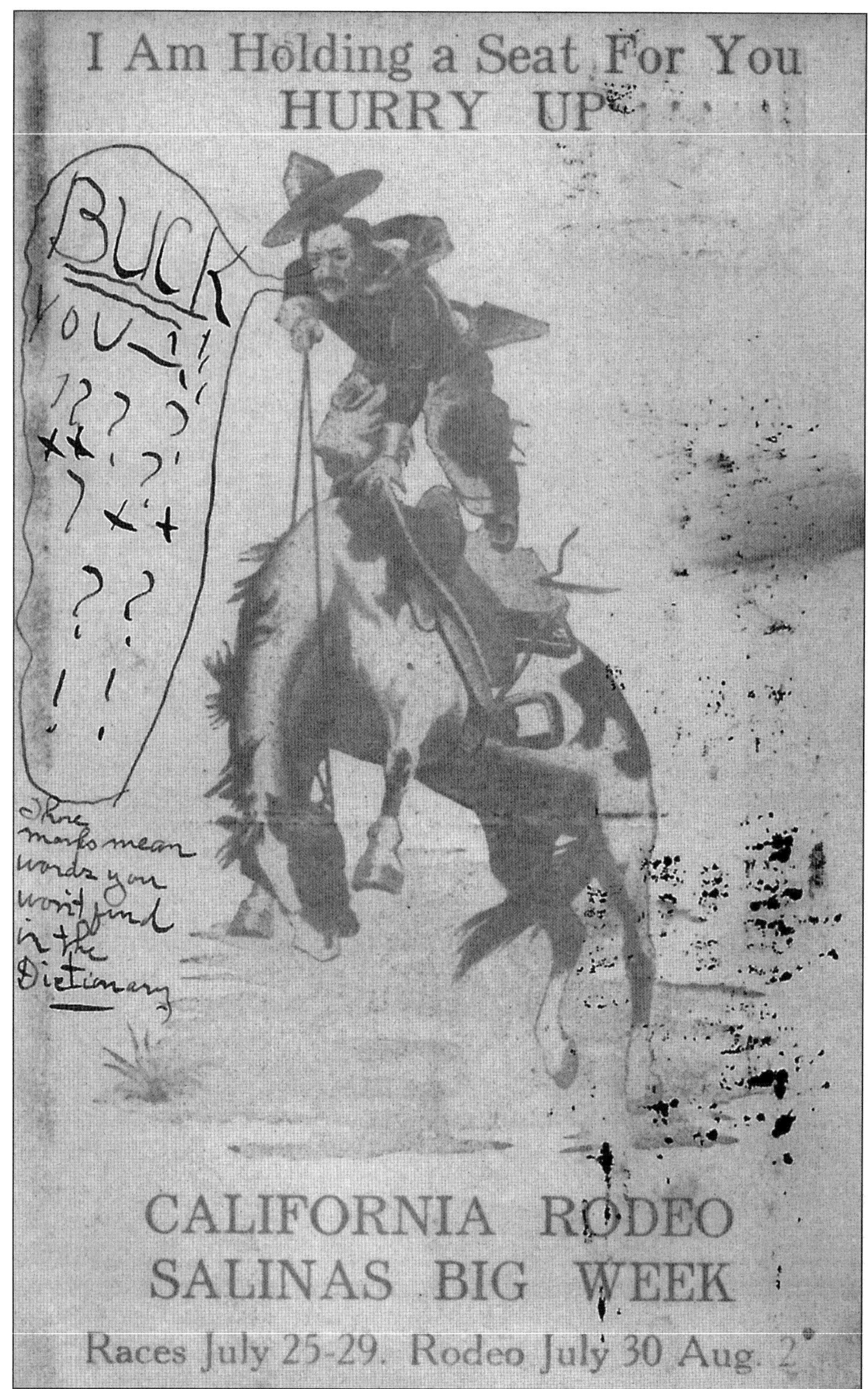

The original board of directors of the California Rodeo consisted of 11 men. Due to the size of the present-day rodeo, there are 52 board members and hundreds of volunteers who are dedicated to carrying on the 102 years of early California and American West traditions.

Five

The War Years

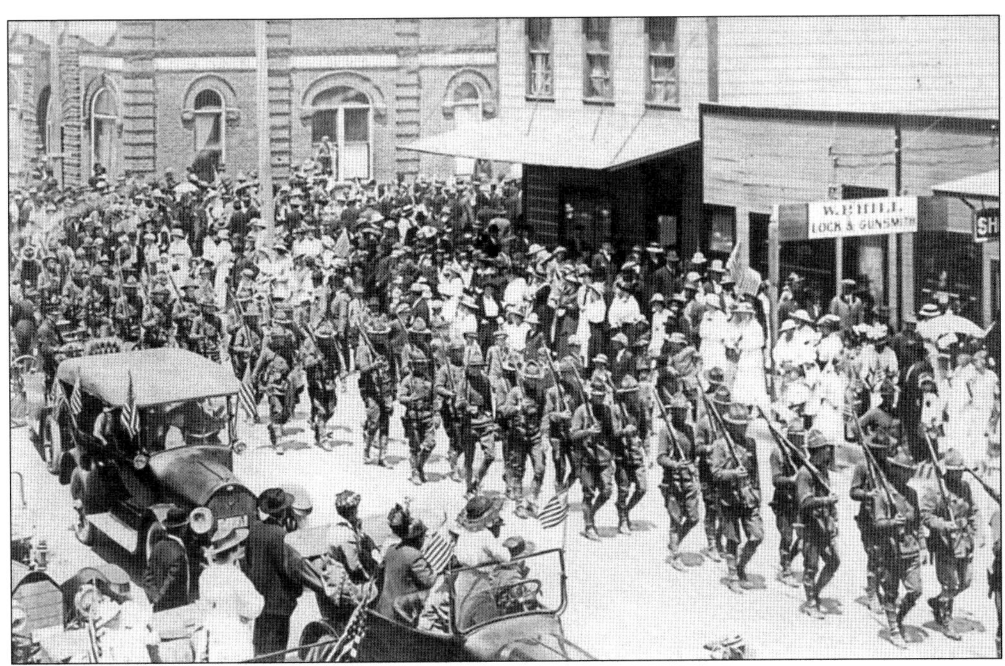

Troop C Cavalry, National Guard of California was organized on August 5, 1895. Based in Salinas, the troop saw its first real action in 1916 when it was sent to the Mexican border to protect that area from Pancho Villa.

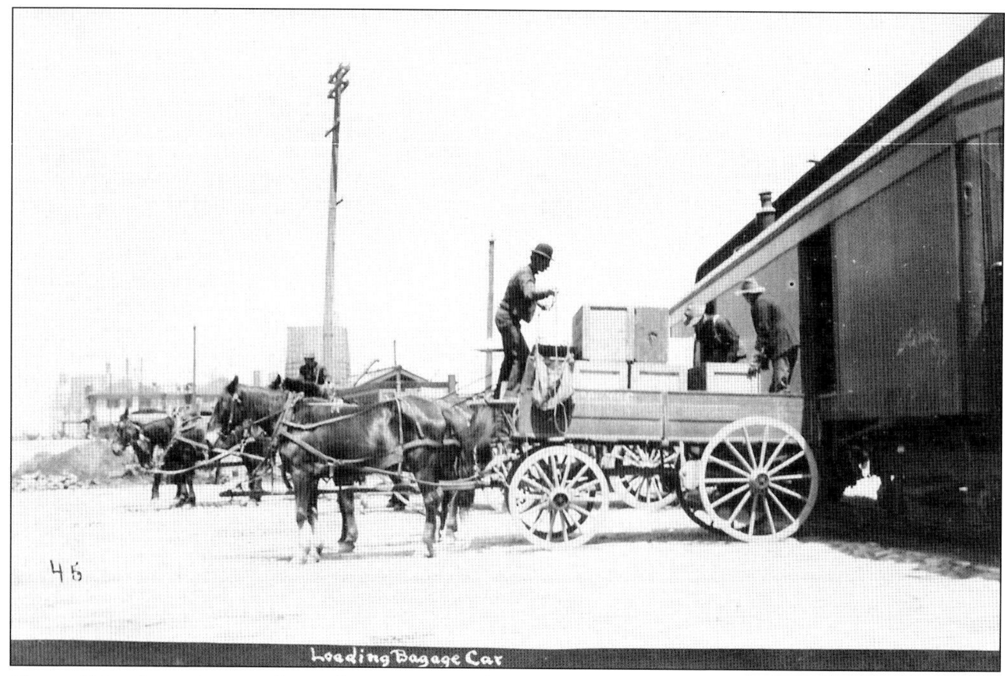

Troop C loads equipment into a baggage car. The date of this image is uncertain, but it could have been captured in 1906 when the troop was sent to San Francisco following the earthquake.

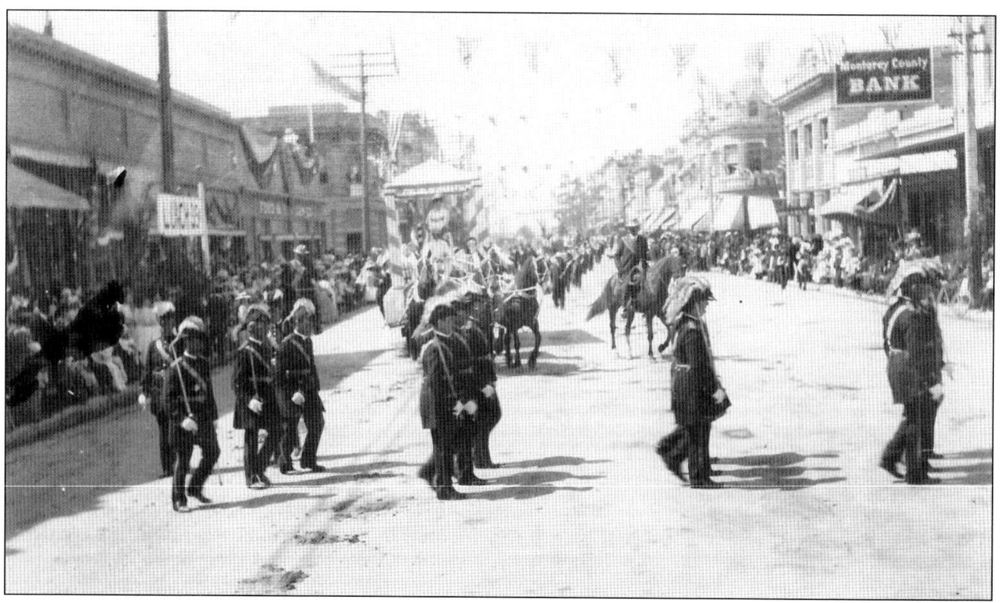

This drill team is outfitted for the rodeo parade.

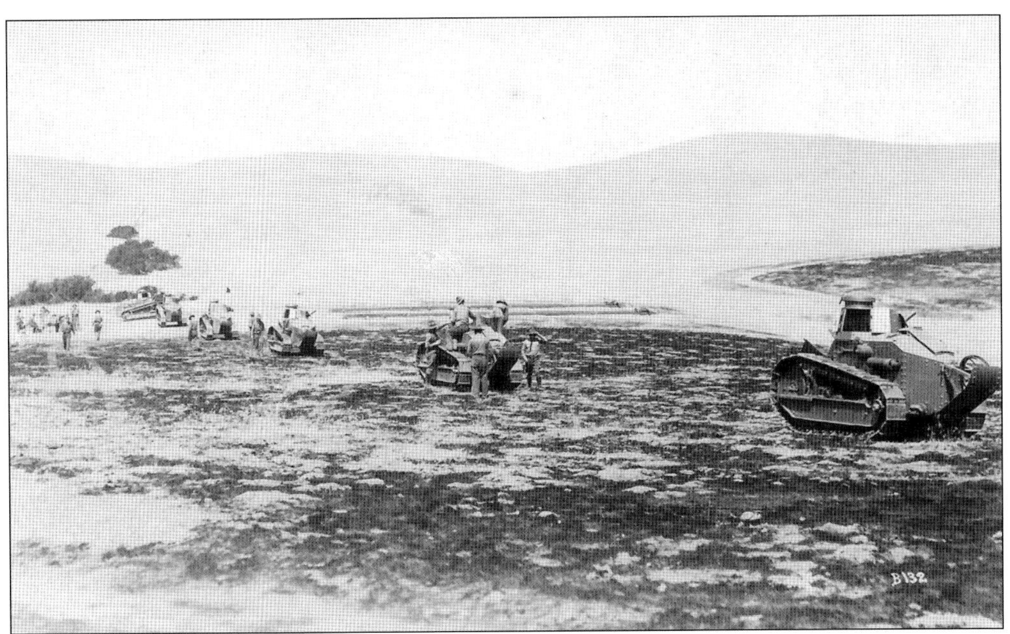

In 1924, Troop C was reorganized as the 40th Tank Company and equipped with eight light tanks of French Renault design left over from World War I. This photograph shows training exercises.

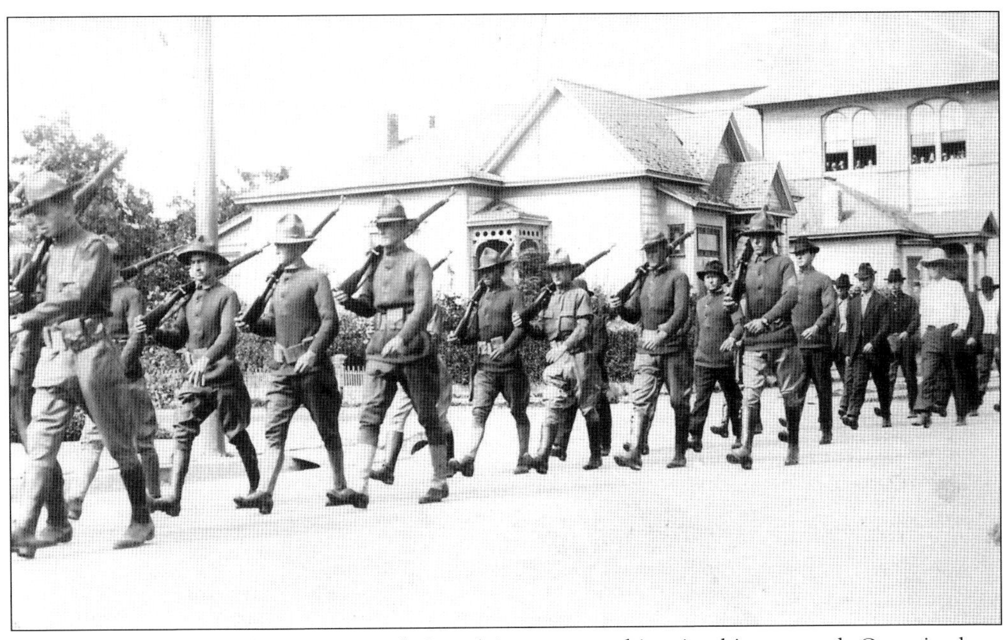

Troop C Cavalry, California National Guard is seen marching in this postcard. Organized on August 5, 1895, the troop was the first guard unit formed in the central coast. Their headquarters was the new brick armory at the corner of Salinas and Alisal Streets in Salinas. The commanding officer was Capt. Michael J. Burke, first lieutenant was J.L. Matthews, and second lieutenant was E.W. Winham.

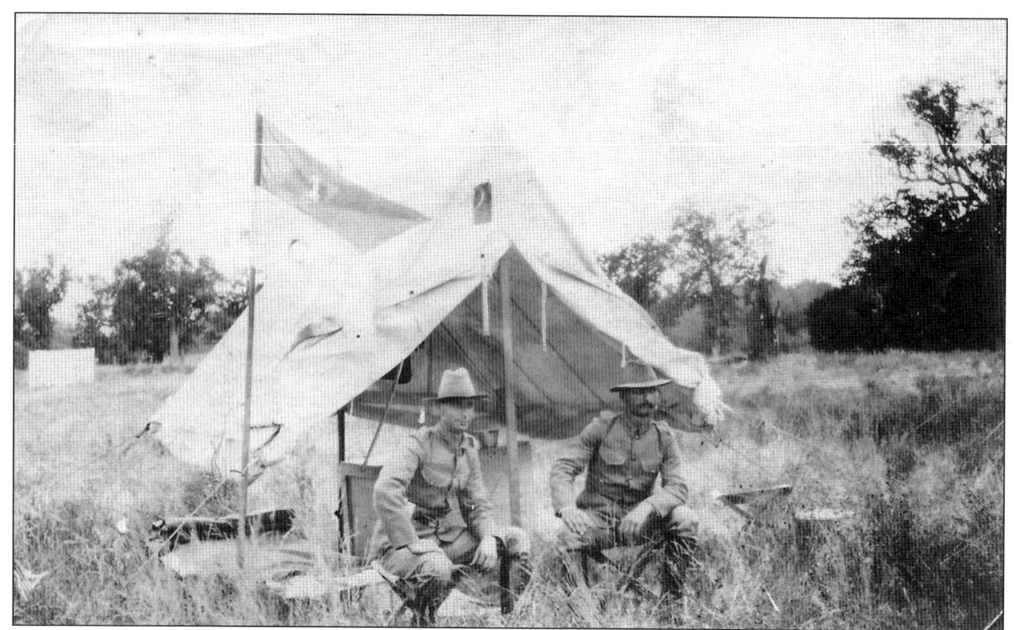

Captain Vierra and Lieutenant Fulle of Troop C pose in a bivouac shelter.

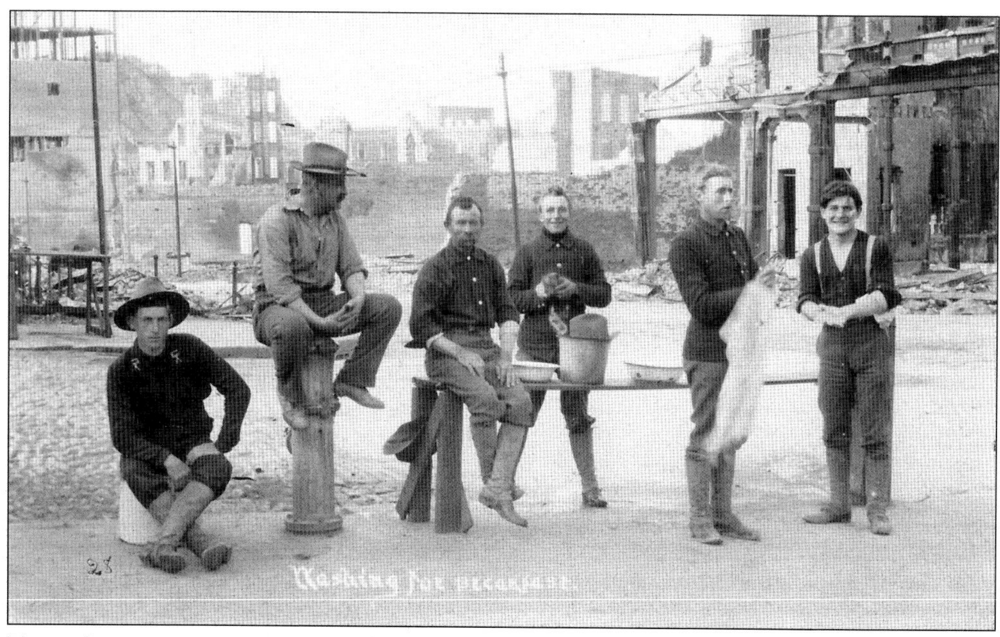

Troop C was sent to San Francisco for just over a month following the great earthquake of 1906. The individuals in this postcard, with rubble in the background, are identified from left to right, as Clarence McDougall, Jack O'Malley, Louie Schneider, Grover Tholcke, Dave Anderson, and Harry Muller.

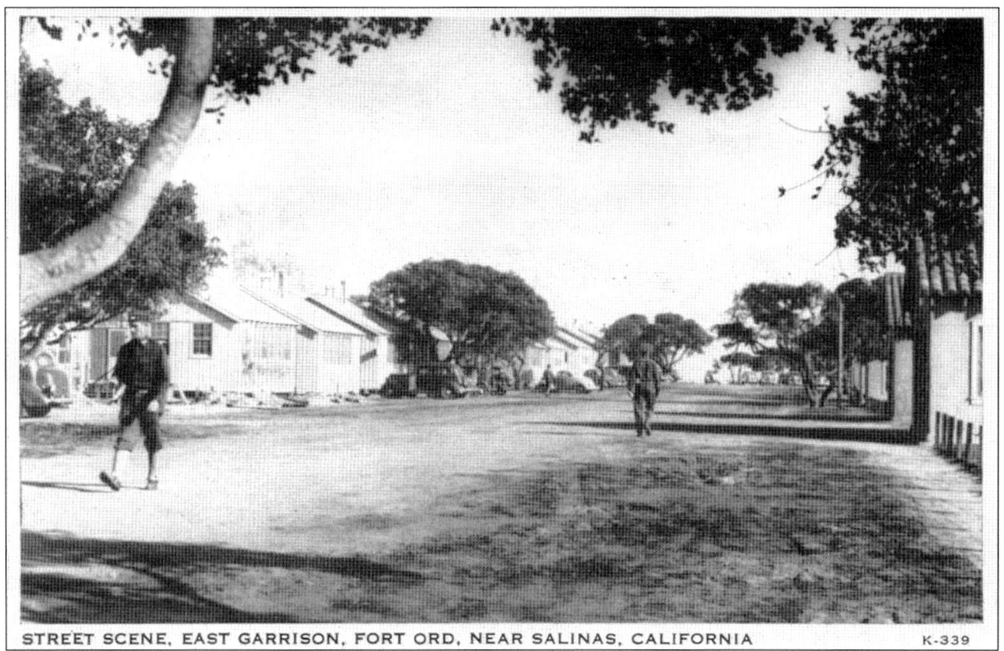

East Garrison, the easternmost part of Fort Ord, overlooked the town of Salinas and the Salinas River.

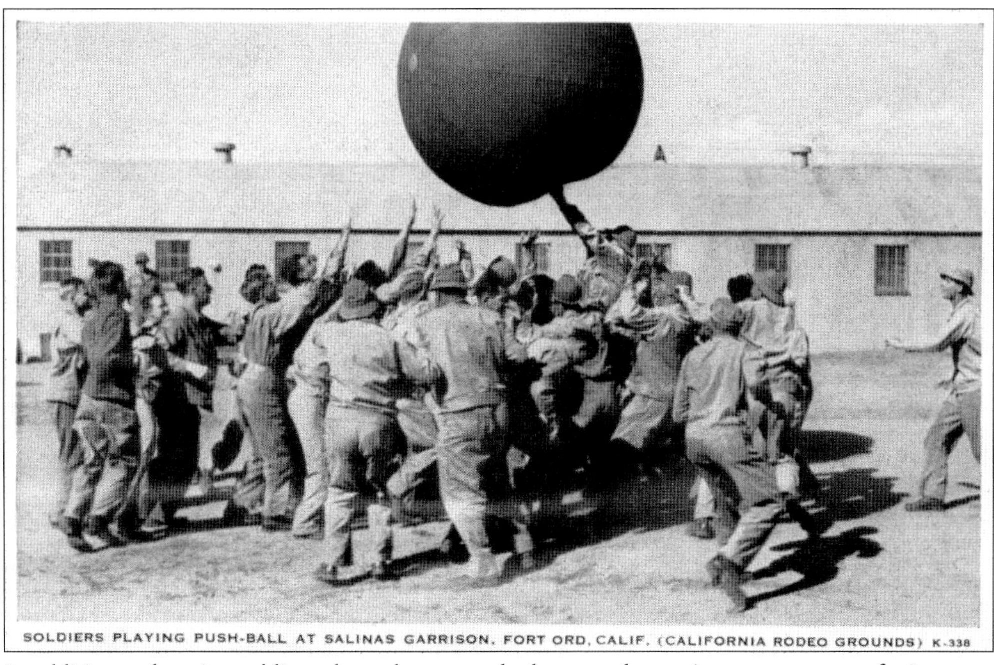

In addition to housing soldiers, the rodeo grounds also served as an internment camp for Japanese Americans during the early part of World War II.

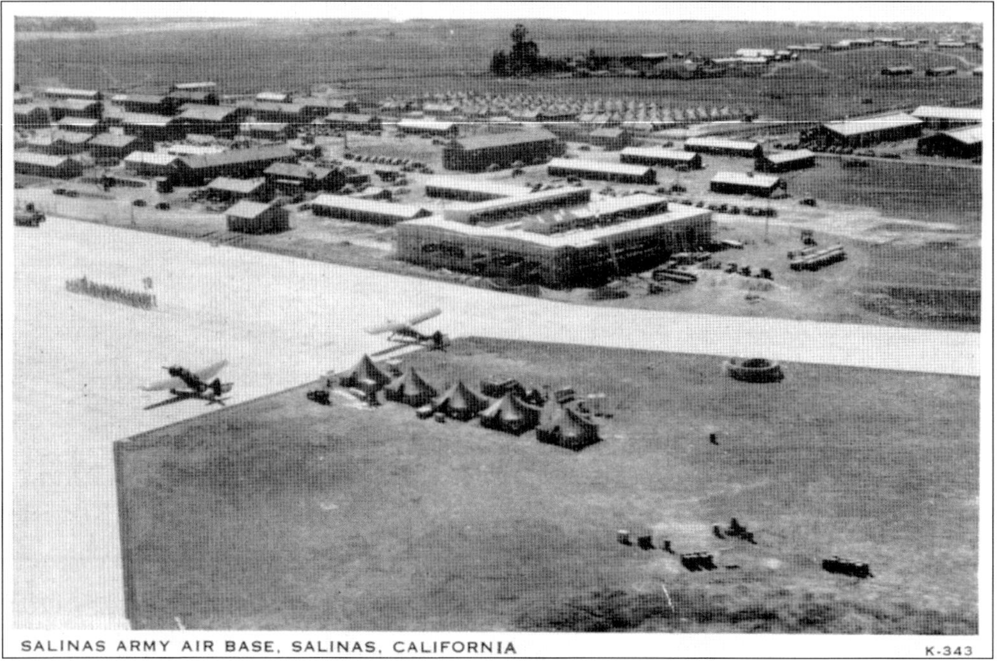

During World War II, Salinas was home to an Army air base. It was located at the site of the current Salinas Municipal Airport.

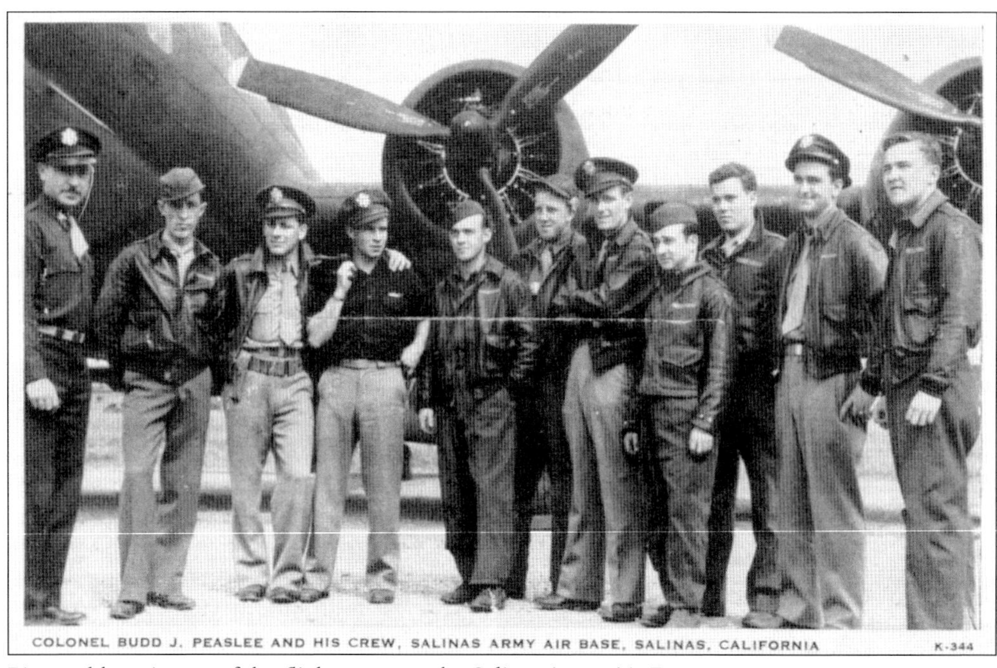

Pictured here is one of the flight crews at the Salinas Army Air Base.

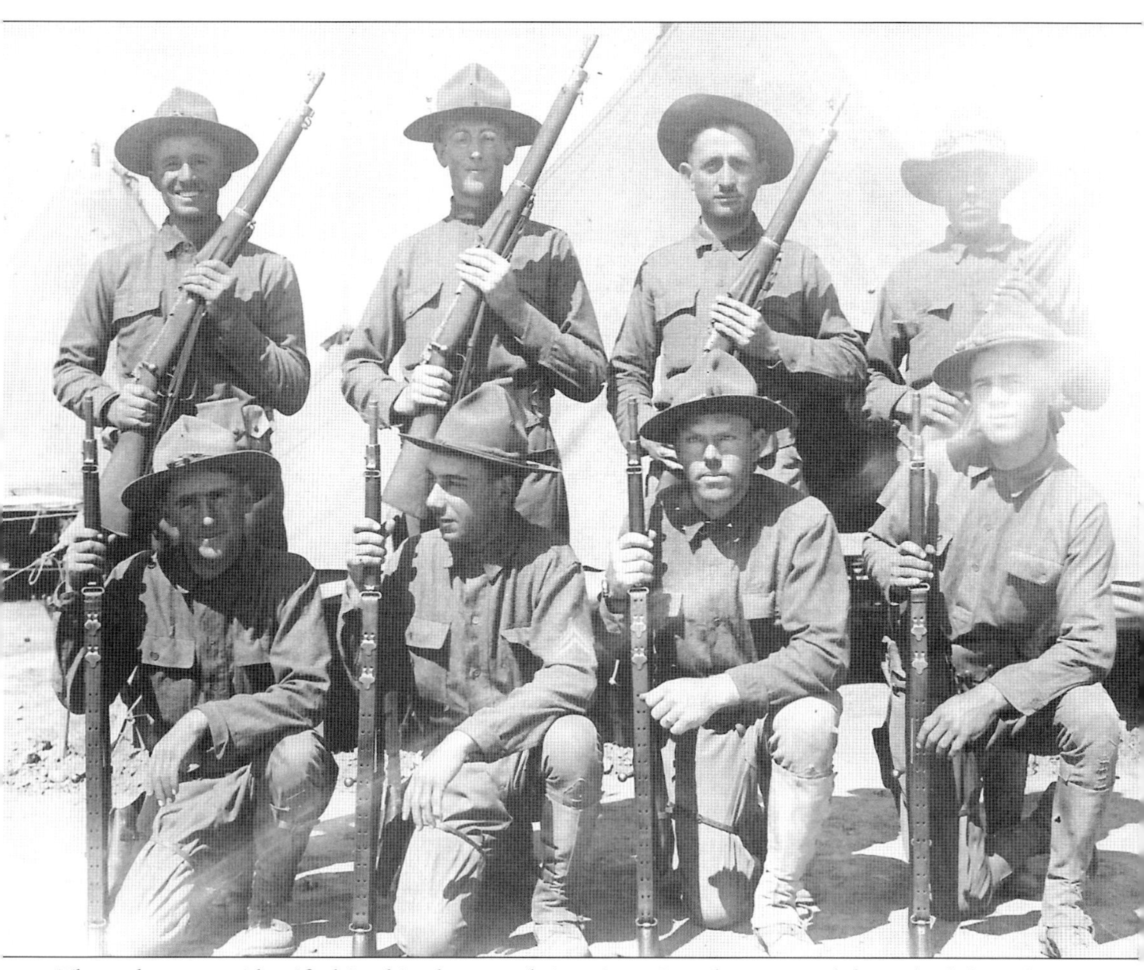

The only person identified in this photograph is Minor C. Bolton, second from the left in the second row.

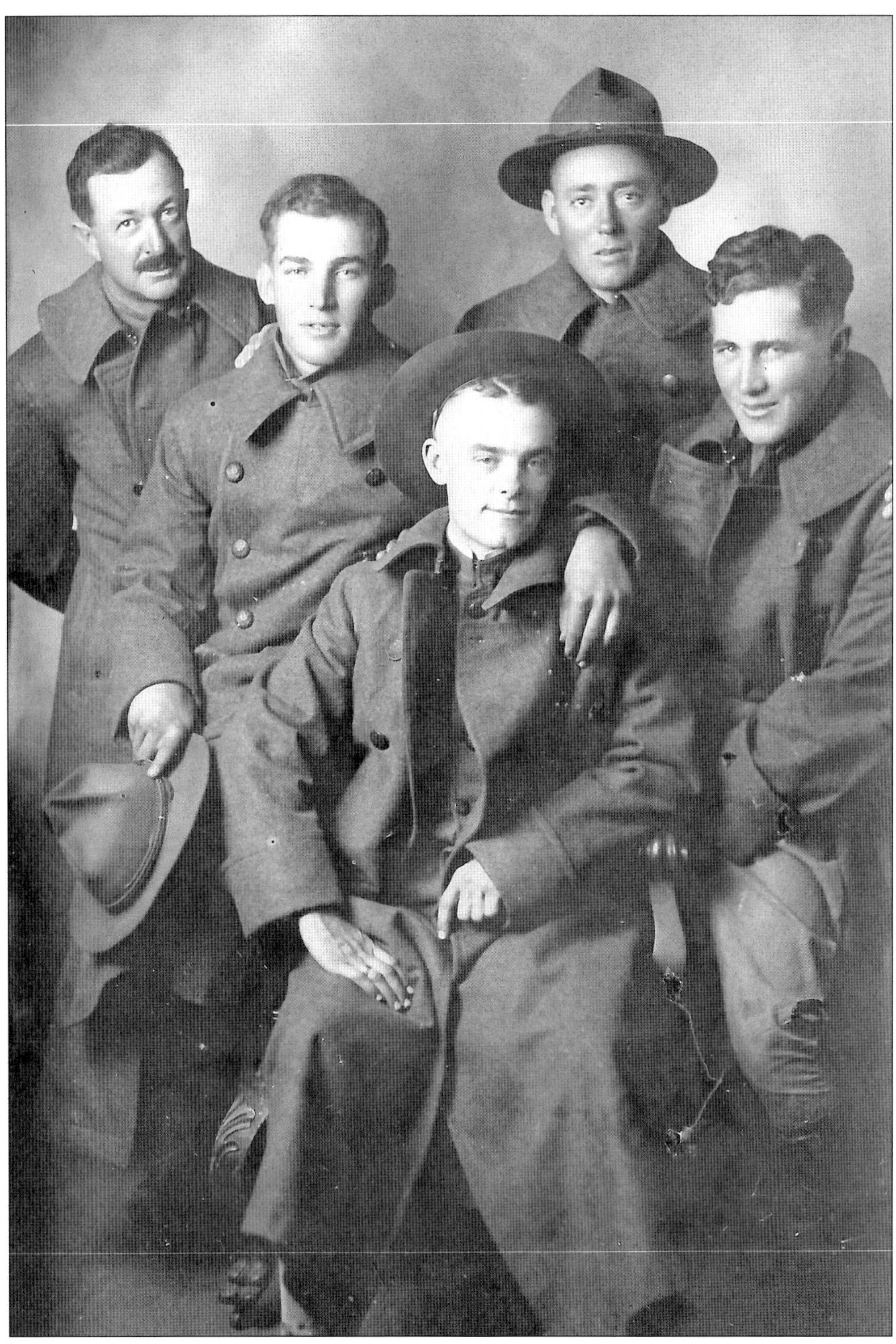

Identified in this image are (top left, third row) Bill Hitchcock, (far right, second row) Raymond Frye, and (center, first row) George Hunter.

Six

Disasters

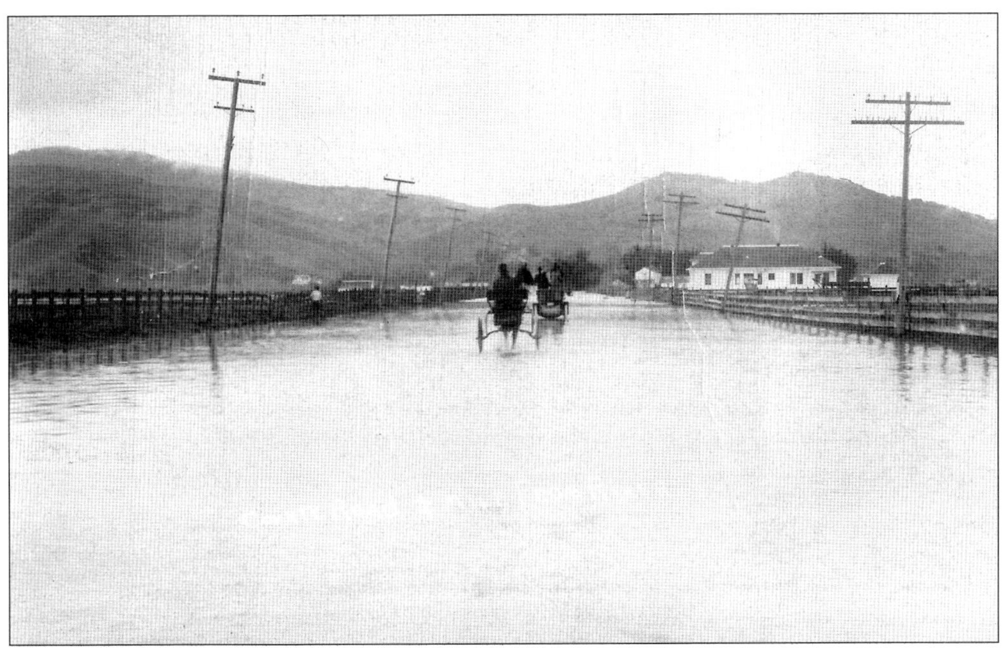

Seen here is the flooding of the Salinas River south of town in 1903. This area has flooded numerous times, but the house shown on the right is still standing. In 1995, flooding reached the outskirts of Salinas, a mile from the river, when a levee broke.

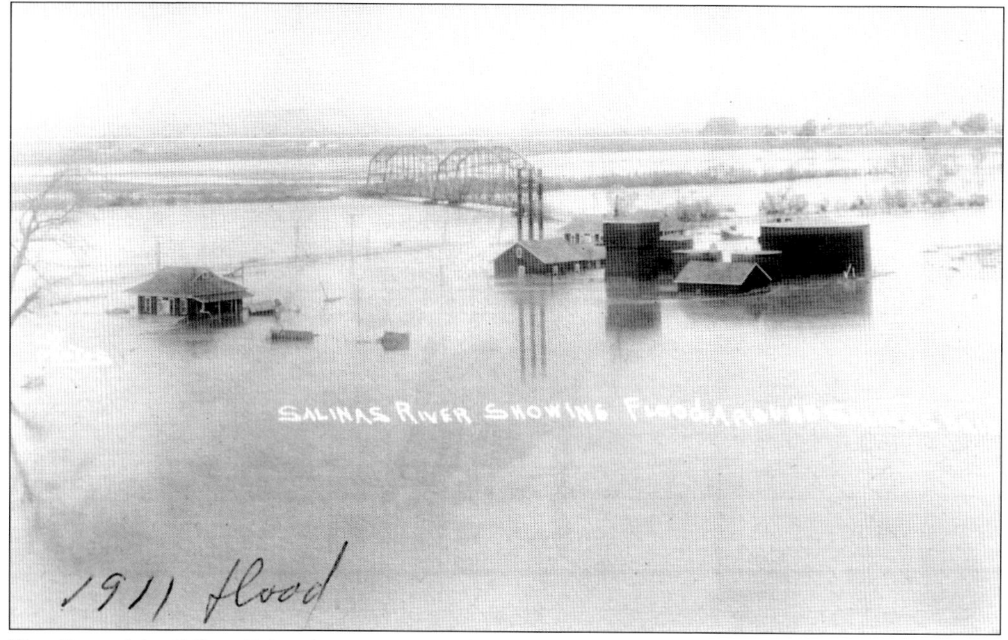

Flooding of the Salinas River is again pictured south of town in 1911. This postcard shows the old bridge spanning the Salinas River.

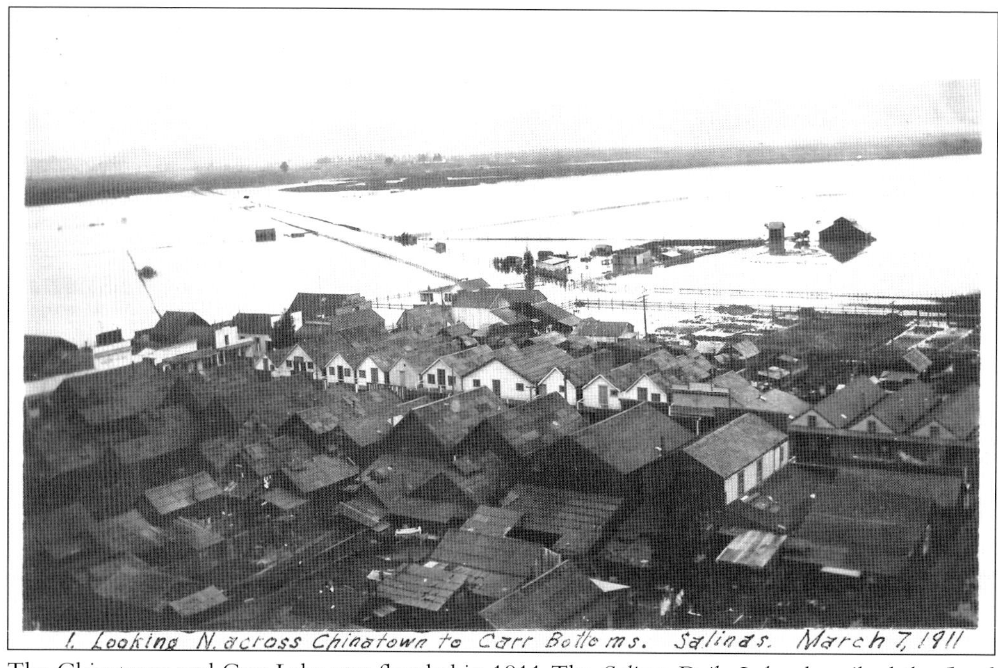

The Chinatown and Carr Lake area flooded in 1911. The *Salinas Daily Index* described the flood as "the most disastrous in the history of Monterey County" and said that "the damaged property is unprecedented. It is reported that more than 2,000 acres of valuable farming land has been destroyed along the course of the Salinas River."

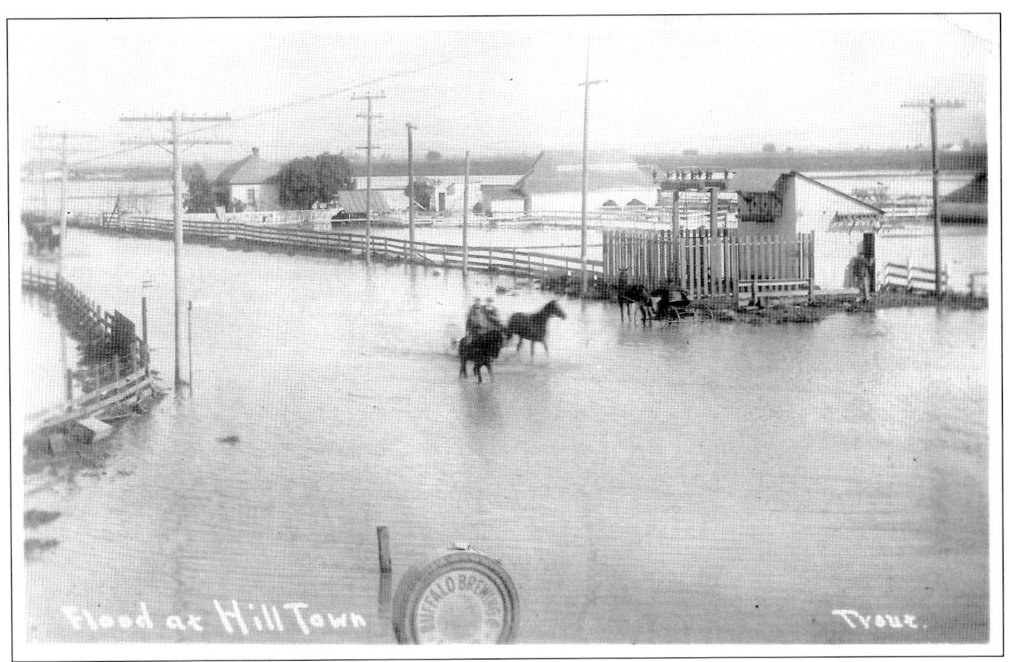

Another flood south of town is pictured here, this one in 1914. The *Index* described the damage to local bridges: "Monterey County has suffered an enormous loss through the damage and destruction of bridges. Passengers arriving from Soledad and Gonzales . . . indicate the loss of all the bridges south of Chualar. The Bradley, San Ardo, San Lucas, King City, Soledad bridges are gone. Two spans of the Gonzales bridge have gone out." Below is the reverse of the above postcard. The sender maintains a sense of humor about the flooding, even ending his message with "ha! ha!"

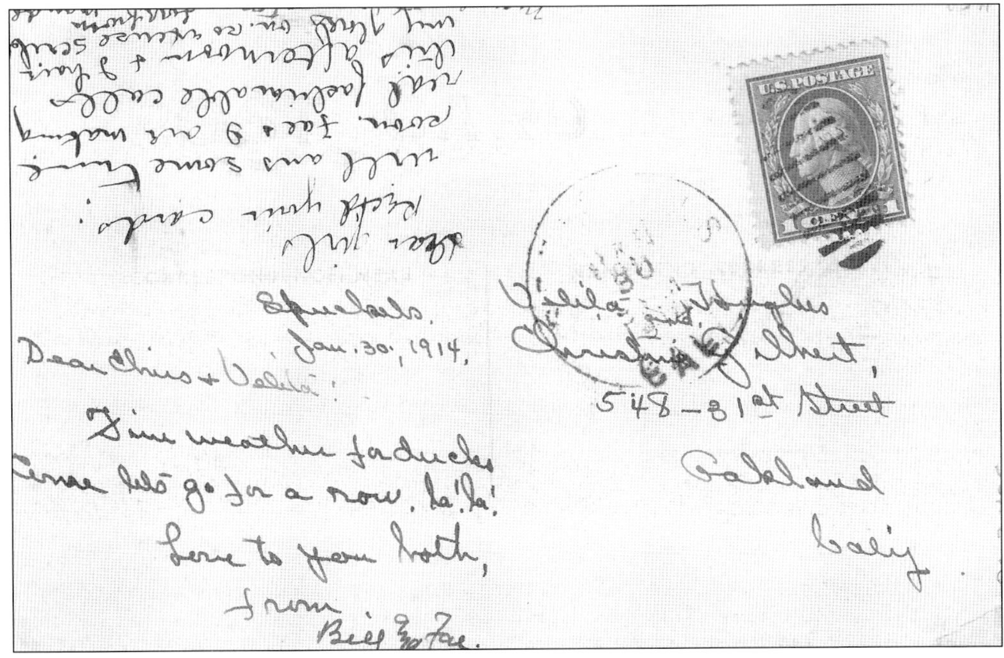
Spreckels.
Jan. 30, 1914.
Dear Chris + Velda!
Fine weather for ducks
[illegible] go for a row. ha! ha!
Love to you both,
from
Bill & Fae.

548 – 81st Street
Oakland
Calif

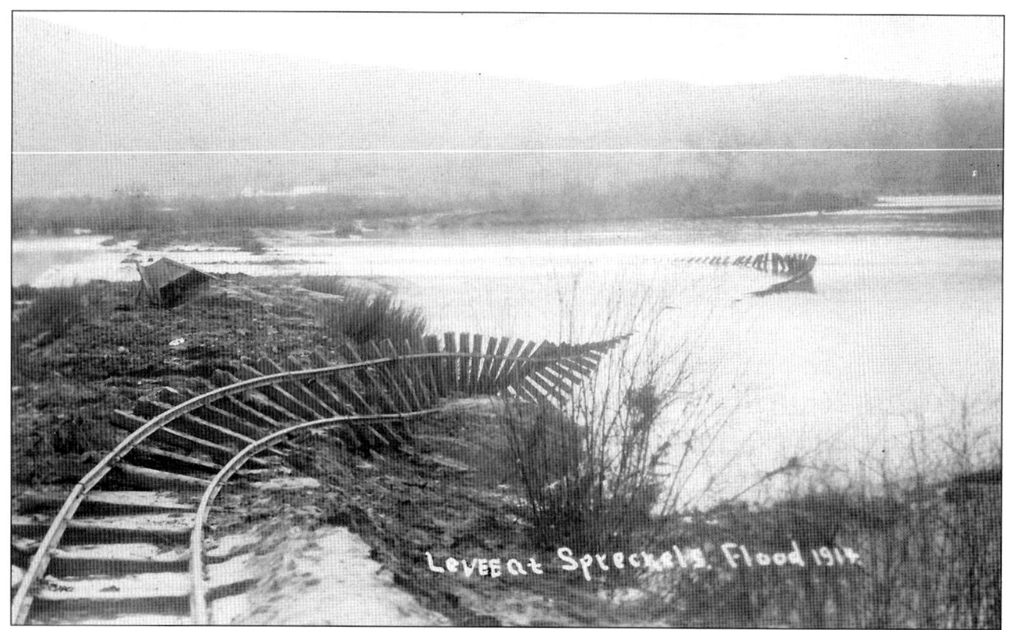

Flooding destroyed a Spreckels levee and railroad tracks spanning the Salinas River in 1914. Spreckels's original wooden bridge had been destroyed by the flood of 1911.

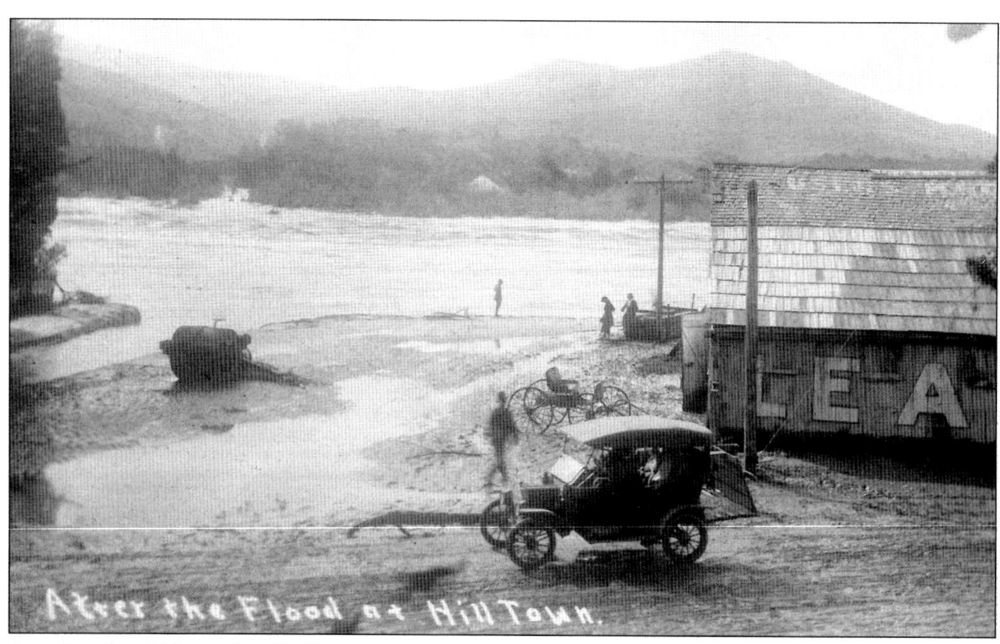

Another flood hit south of Salinas in 1916.

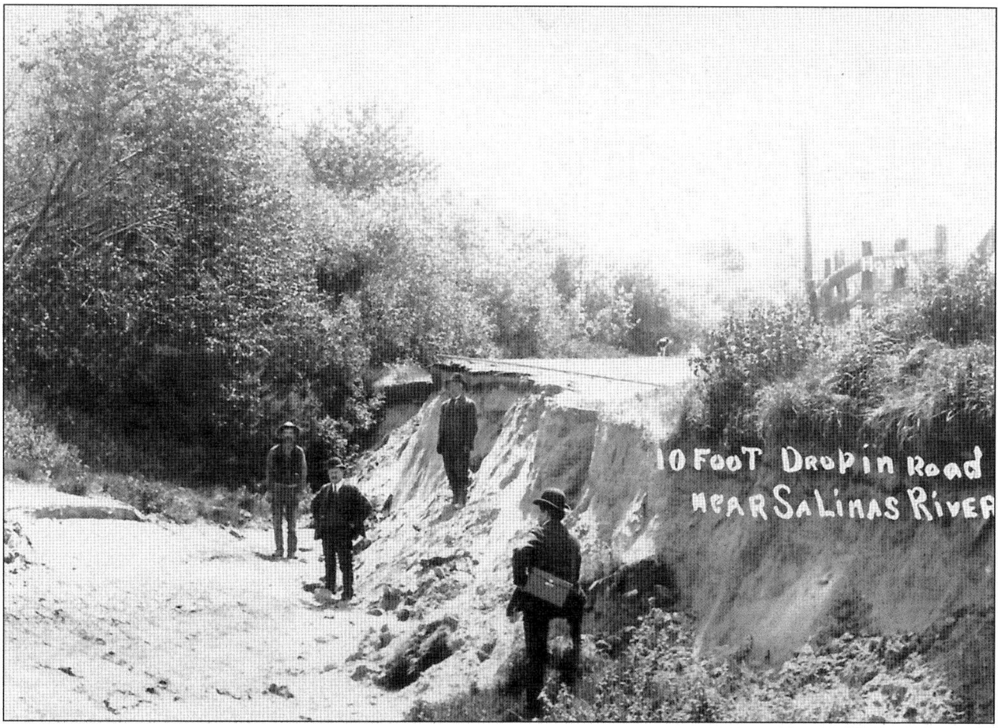

These two views show the damage following the 1906 earthquake. South of Salinas, a number of fissures appeared, and in one place, the ground dropped about 10 feet and gas was reported to have escaped.

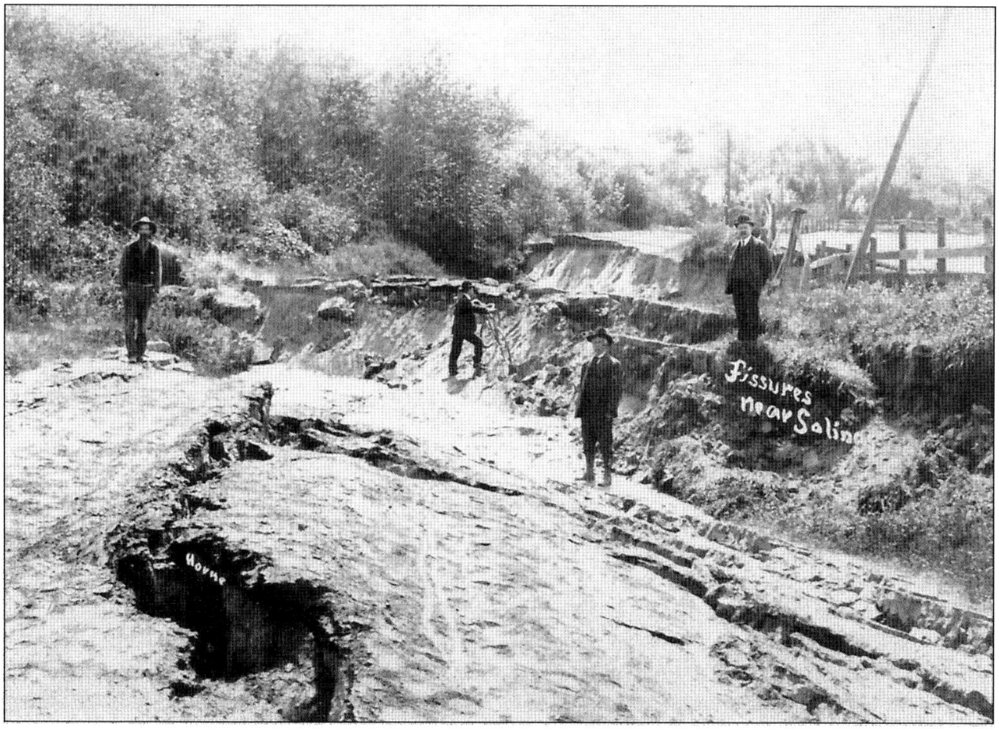

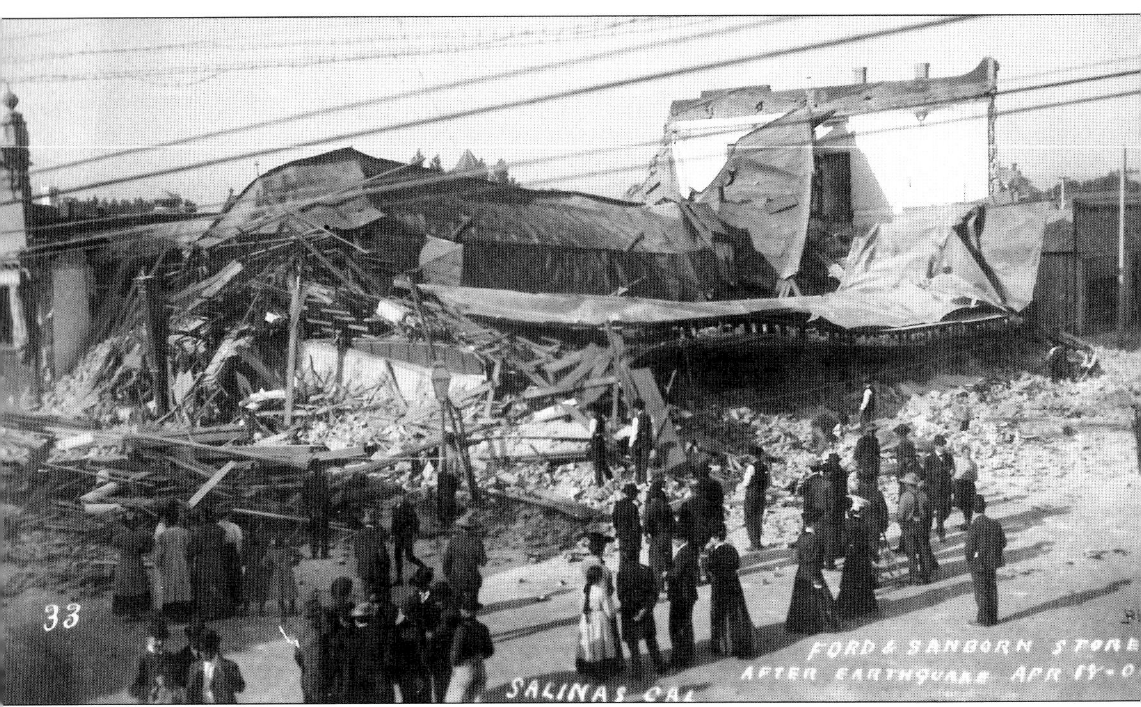

The most serious damage in Salinas from the 1906 earthquake was to the city's largest store, Ford & Sanborn on Main Street, which was totally destroyed. Ford's second store across the street remained standing. Under the leadership of Mayor Thomas Renison, all of the debris in the town was removed within three days, while business went on as usual.

Seven

People and Fun

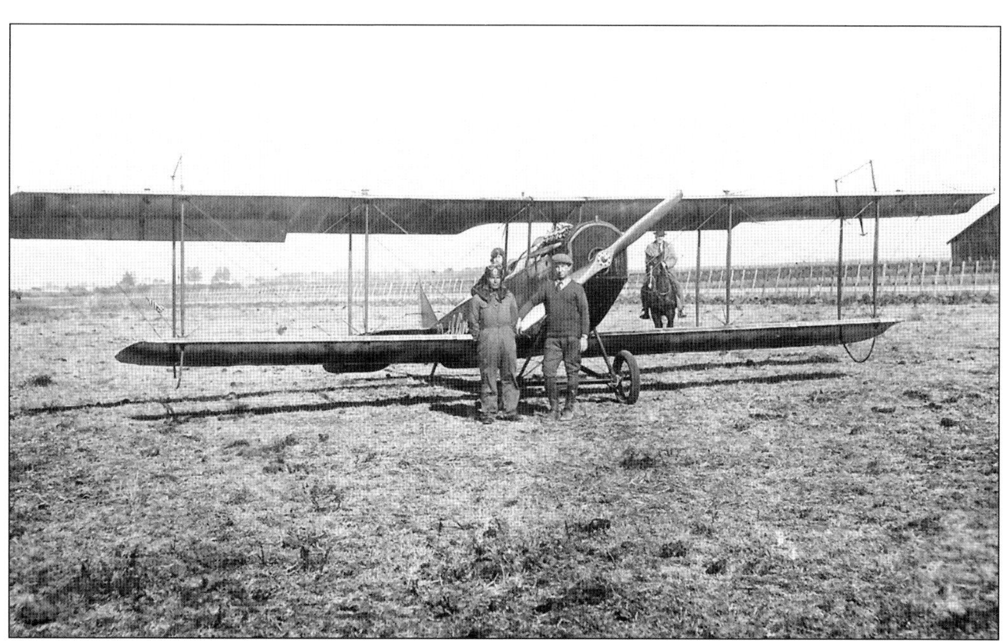

Pictured here is another view of the early Jenny airplane to visit Salinas in 1918.

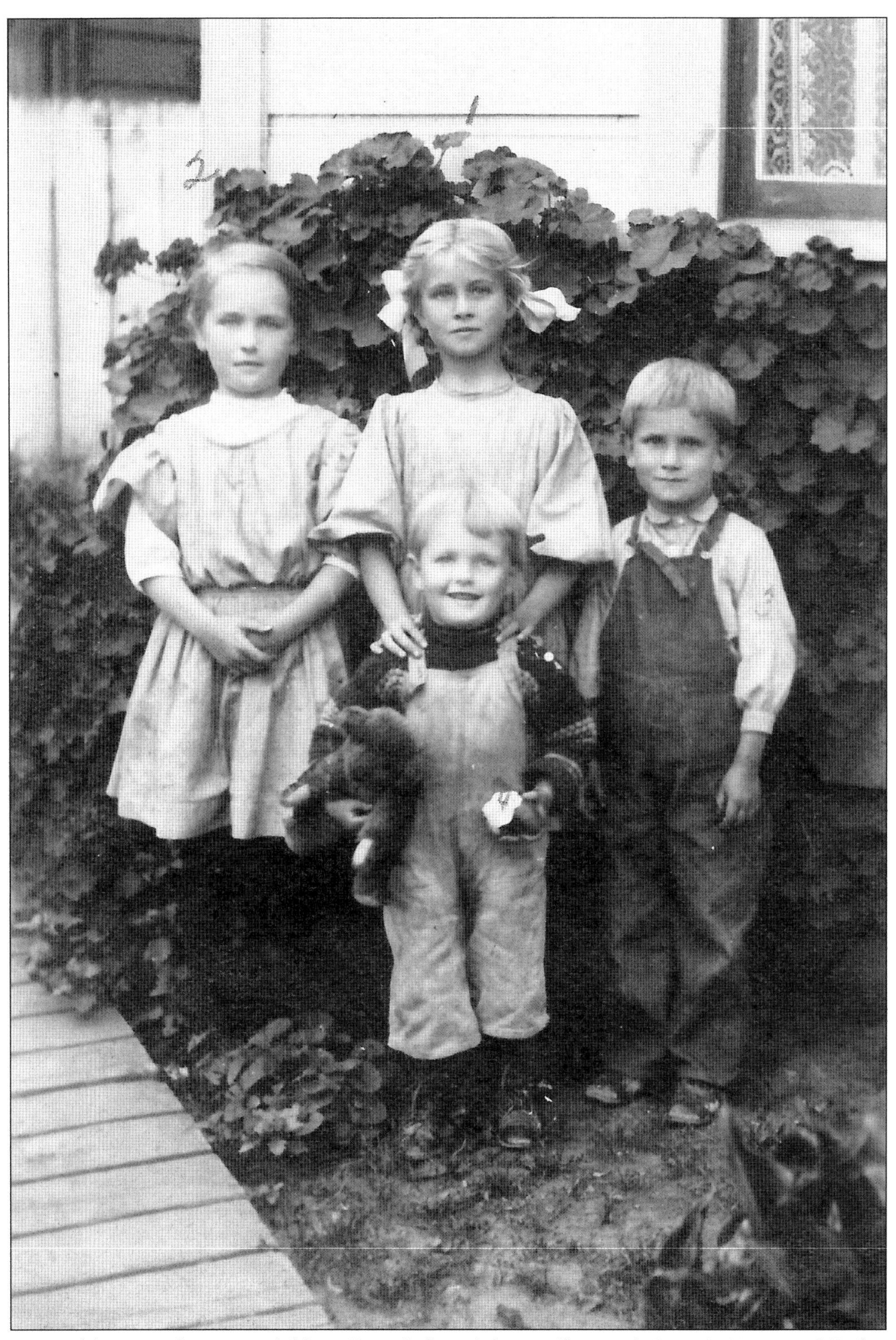

Pictured here are the Hayes children. From left to right are (first row) Georgie Hayes and Earley Hayes; (second row) Jessie Ruth Hayes and Cecil Luetta Hayes.

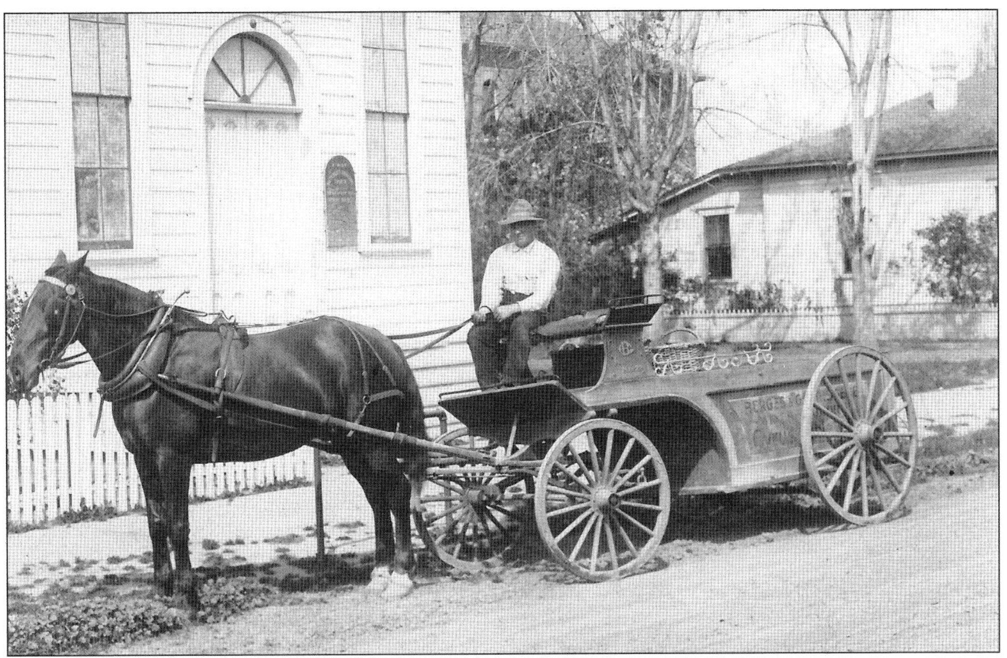

Berges & Garrissere was located on the 100 block of Main Street. This delivery wagon carried wholesale wine and liquors to customers.

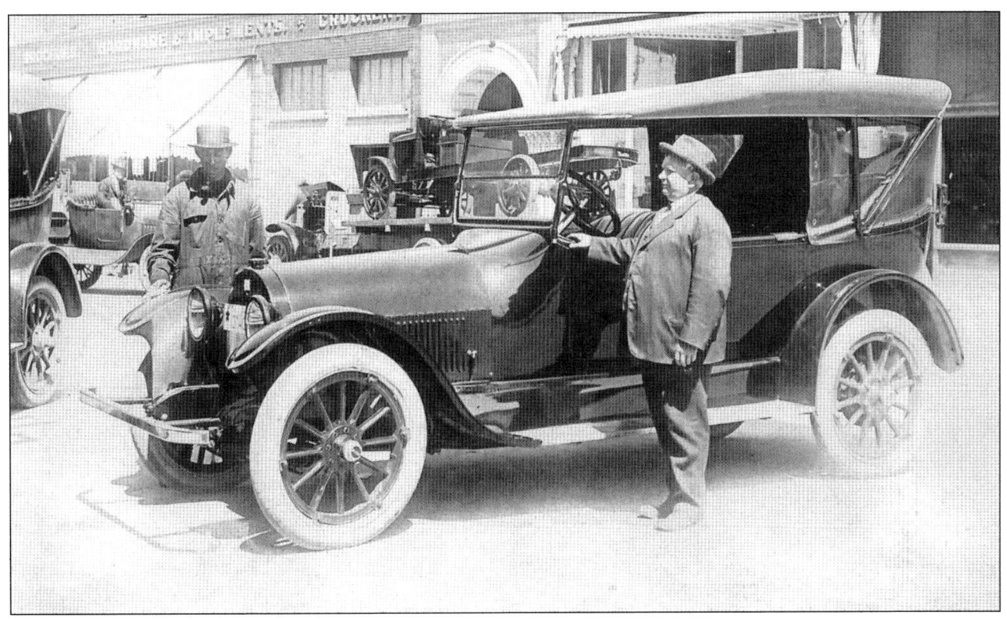

Bill Voss stands beside a new car. Voss ran an auto dealership for many years on Monterey Street.

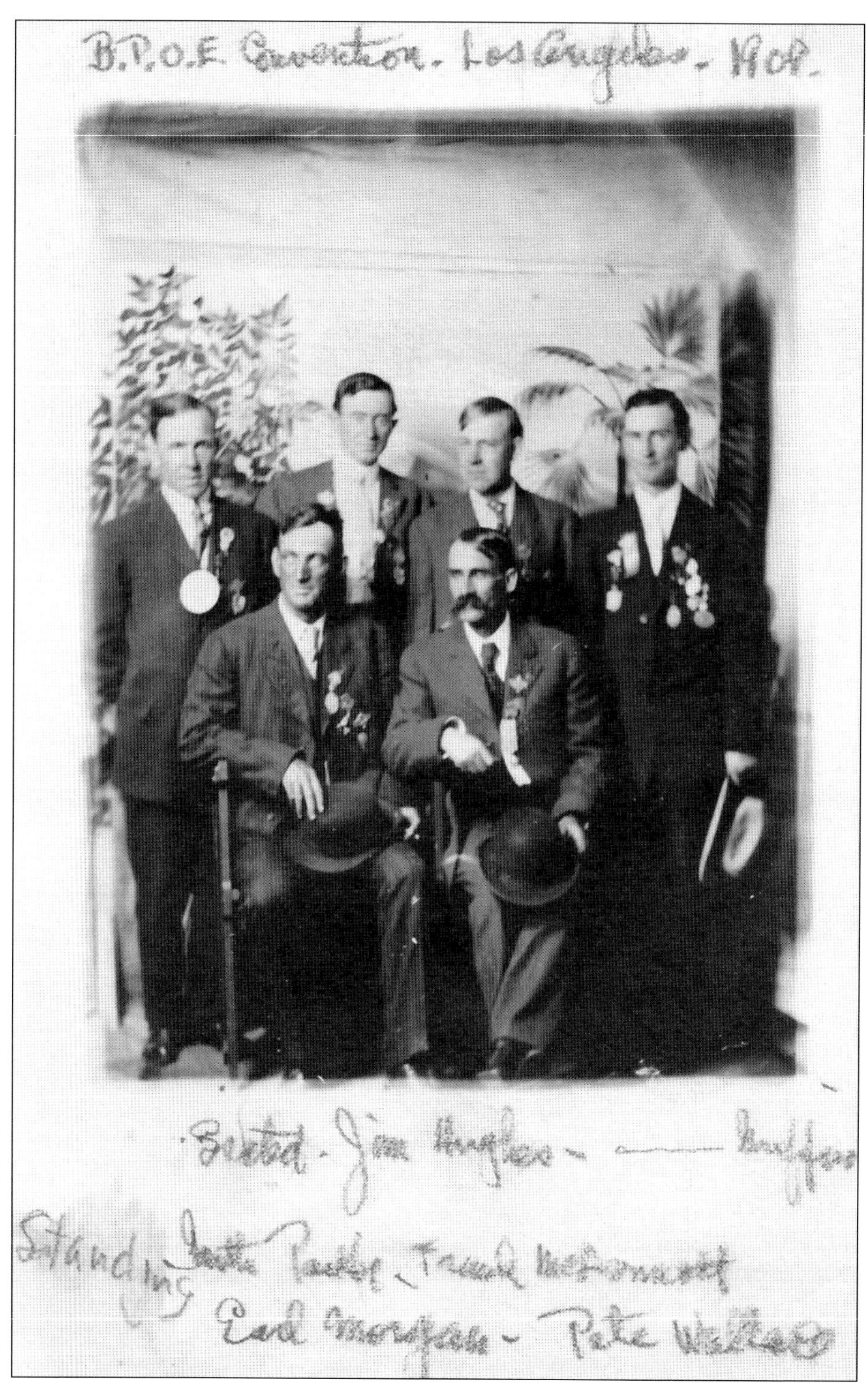

These Salinas men pose at the Benevolent and Protective Order of Elks convention in Los Angeles in 1908. Seated is Jim Hughes on the left. The other name is unreadable, but it may be Griffin. Standing from left to right are Garth Parker, Fred McDermott, Earl Morgan, and Pete Walker.

Pictured are Buster and Rachel Worthington, who do not appear to want their picture taken.

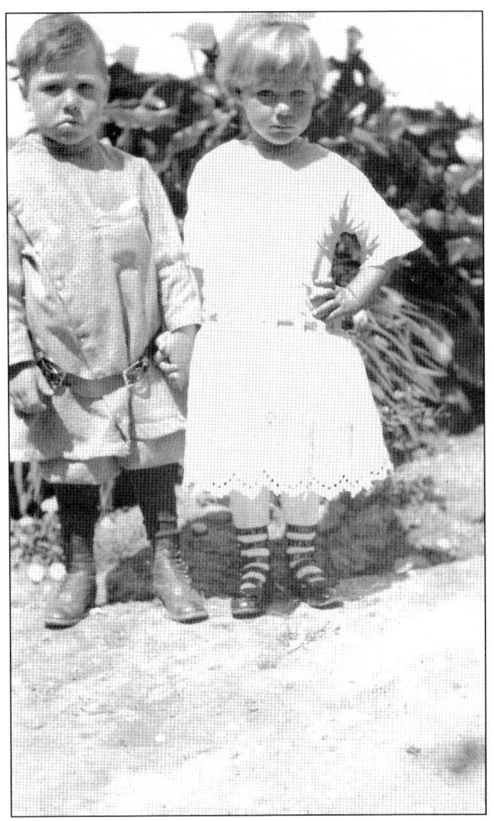

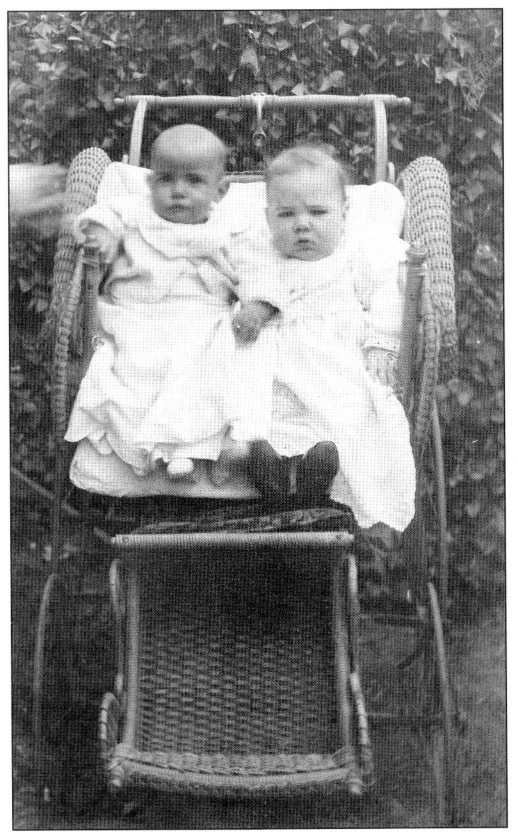

Pictured here are Leslie Worthington and Eleanor Hewston.

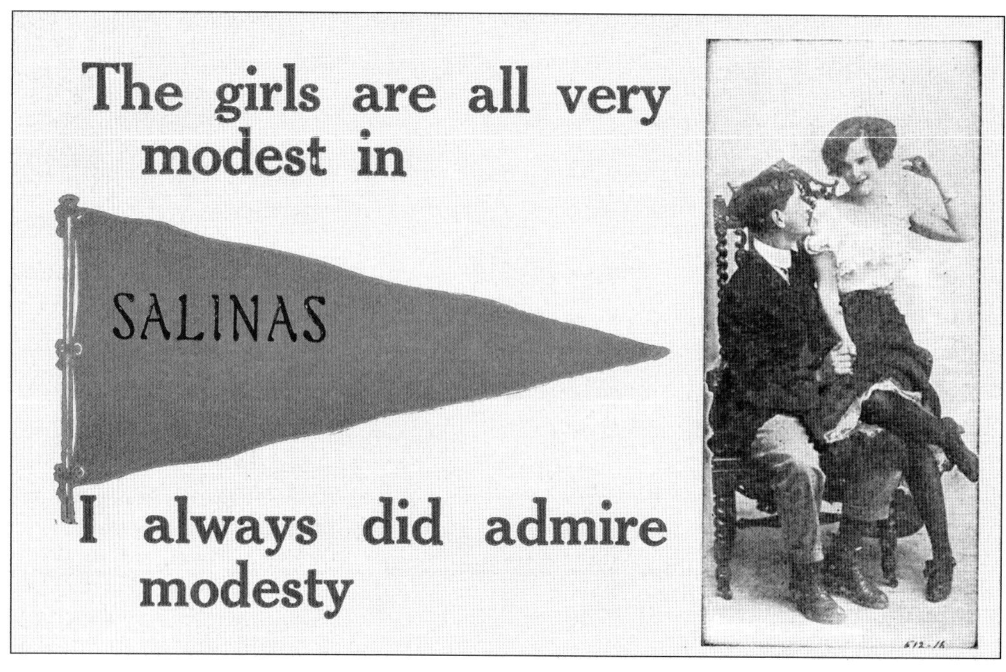

These are two template-designed postcards that promoted the fun town that was Salinas.

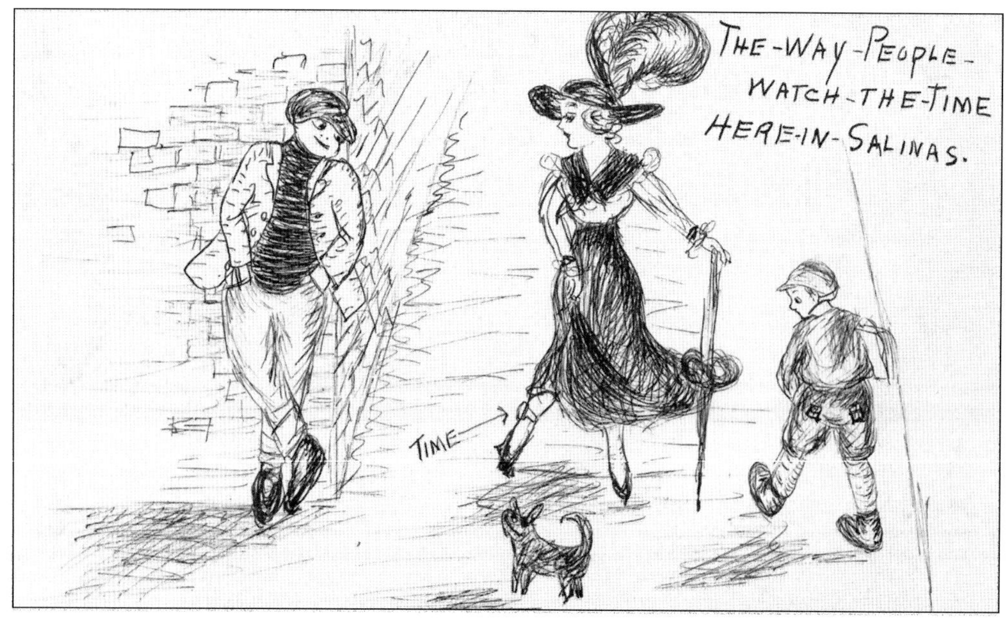

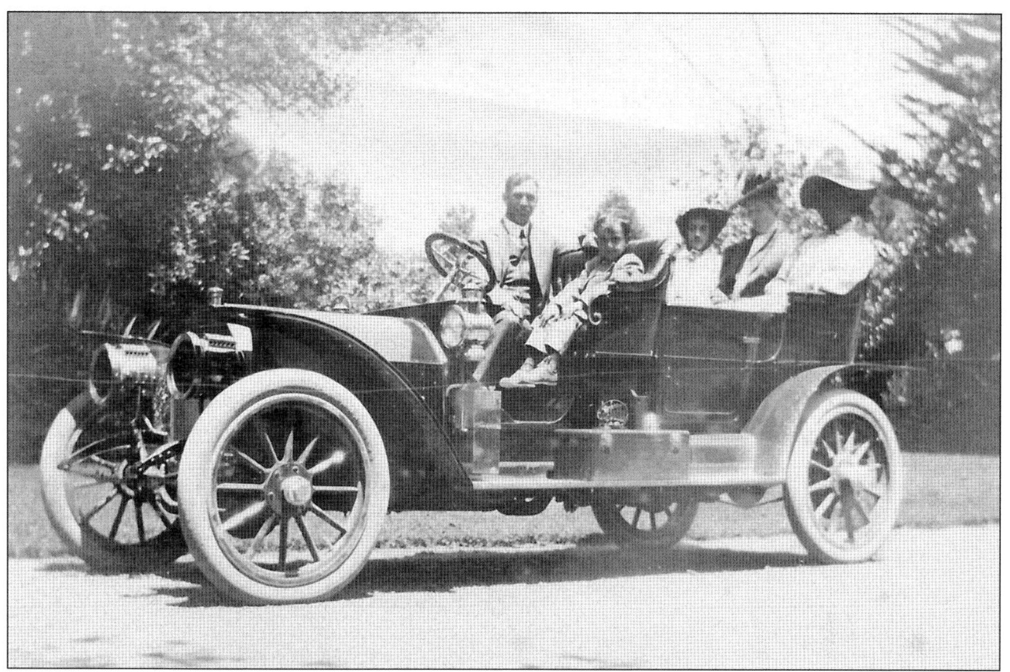

In attendance at the Bullene wedding are, from left to right, Fred Jackson and his son Foster, Louise Bullene, Mrs. Jackson, and Florence (Clem) Tynan in 1909. By this date, the horse-drawn carriage was beginning to be replaced by automobiles.

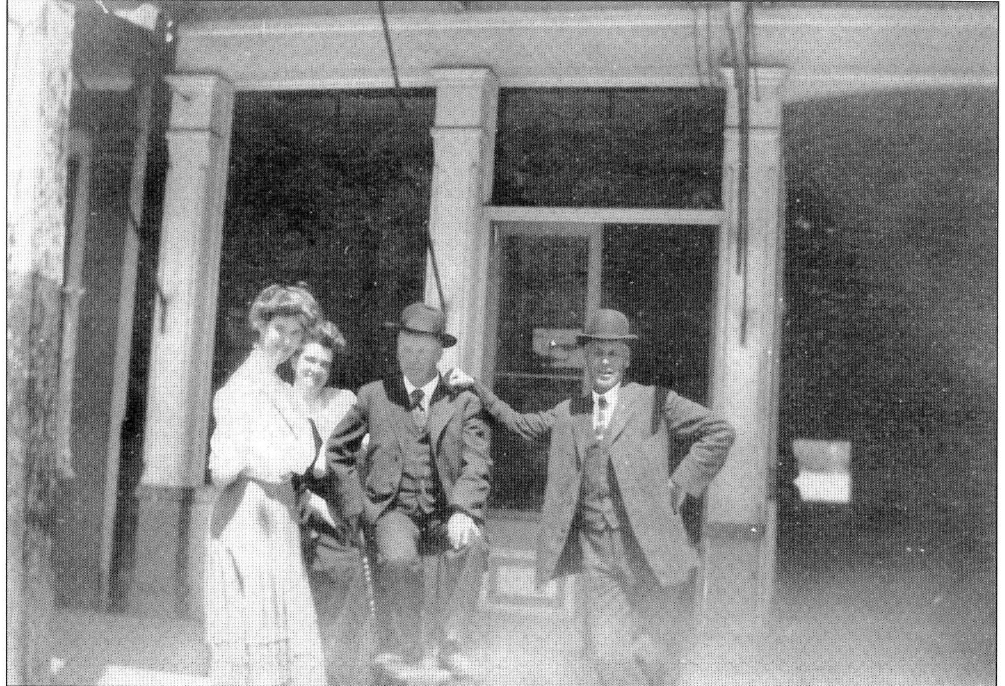

Here is another picture from the Bullene wedding. The two men are Molander (center) and Bullene. The two ladies are identified as friends of Mrs. Bullene from San Diego. This photograph was taken in front of the livery stable on Main Street, north of the Jeffery Hotel at Main and Alisal Streets.

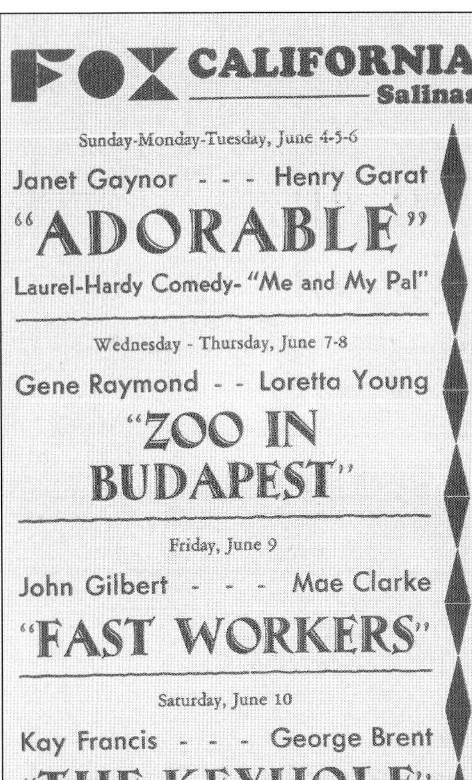

These advertising postcards date from 1933. These popular shows had some intriguing names. In 1930, Twentieth Century Fox bought the T&D Theater and changed its name to Fox California Theater. Completely remodeled in 1936, it was the first in the United States to install and test out a new acoustical plaster, which would have a worldwide future in the treatment of sound.

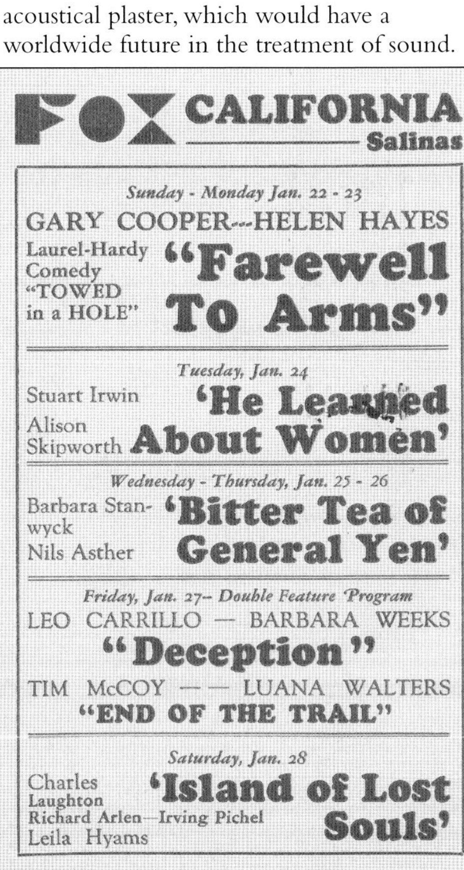

These advertising postcards from 1932 are promoting the Fox California theater in Salinas.

FOX CALIFORNIA
SALINAS, CALIFORNIA

SUNDAY-MONDAY, JULY 31-AUGUST 1
Constance Bennett
'What Price Hollywood'

TUESDAY, AUGUST 2
Renate Muller — Jack Hulbert
"The Office Girl"

WEDNESDAY-THURSDAY, AUGUST 3-4
James Cagney
"Winner Take All"

FRIDAY, AUGUST 5
Big Double Bill
RALPH BELLAMY
"Almost Married"
Also
TOM MIX
"Rider of Death Valley"

SATURDAY, AUGUST 6
Adolphe Menjou — Joan Marsh
"Bachelor's Affairs"
Also
CHIC SALES—"Ex Rooster"

FOX CALIFORNIA
SALINAS, CALIFORNIA

SUNDAY, MONDAY, SEPT. 18-19
WILL ROGERS
"Down To Earth"
With IRENE RICH

TUESDAY, SEPT. 20
Peggy Shannon - Spencer Tracy
"PAINTED WOMAN"

WEDNESDAY, THURSDAY, SEPT. 21-22
LEE TRACY
"Blessed Event"
With MARY BRIAN

FRIDAY, SEPT. 23
JOAN BLONDELL
"Miss Pinkerton"
With GEORGE BRENT
—Also—
SHOWER OF GOLD NITE

SATURDAY, SEPT. 24
JACKIE COOPER
"Divorce in the Family"

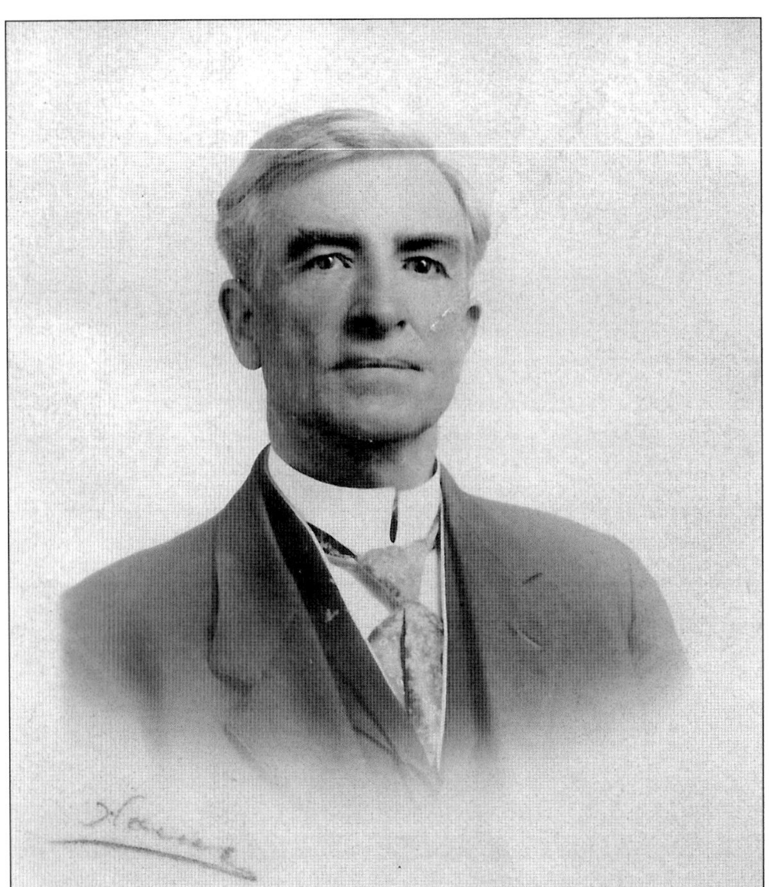

Miguel Smith was the interpreter at the courthouse and teacher of Spanish, French, and German.

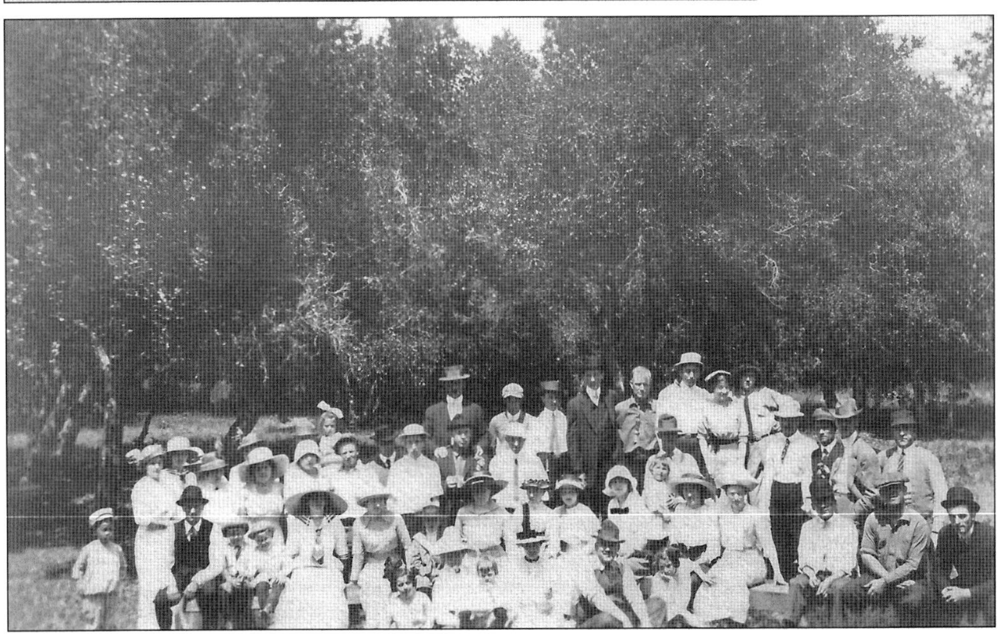

The staff of the Ford & Sanborn store pose in this postcard at a company family picnic.

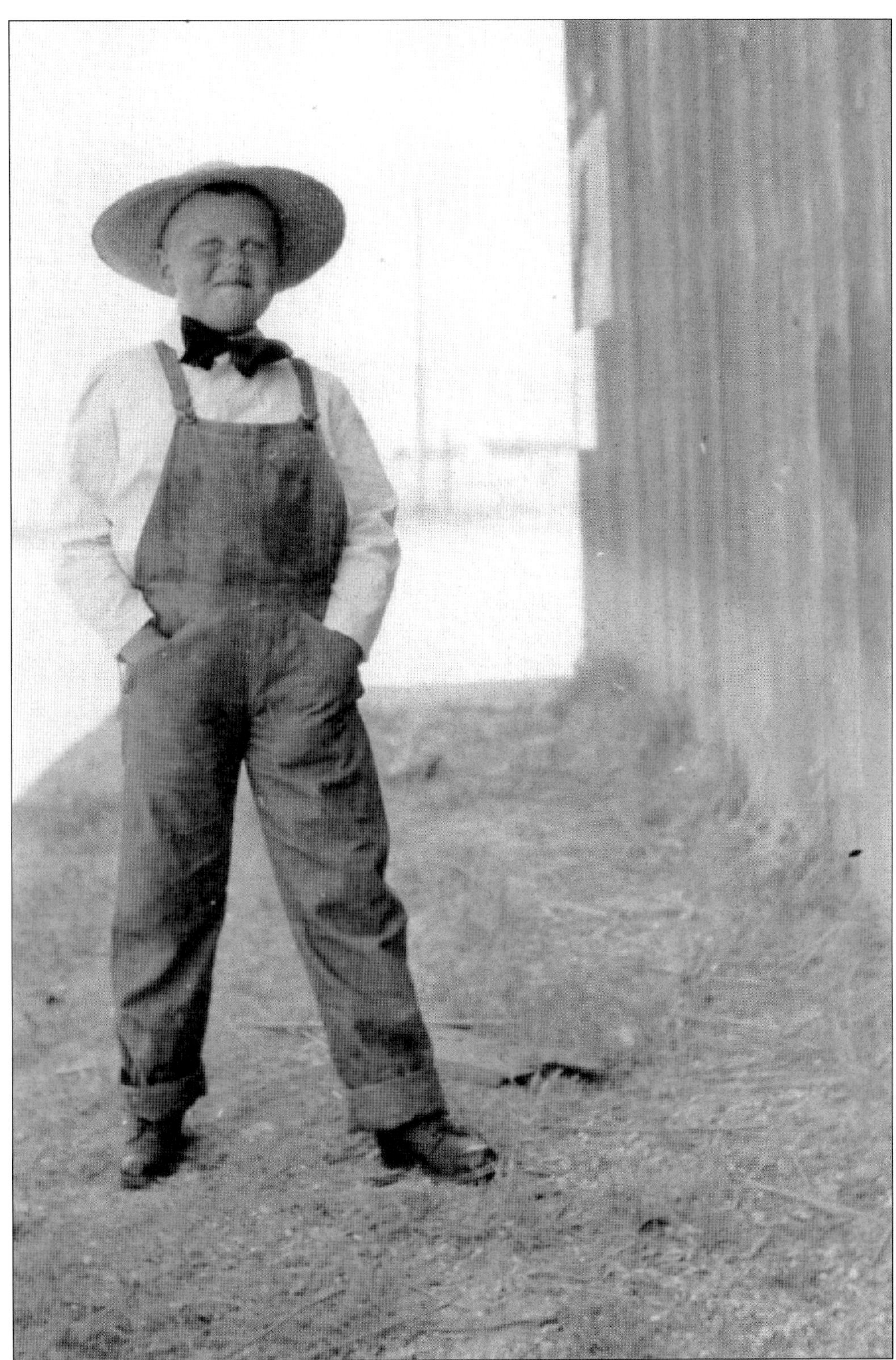

Charles Van Buren Jackson is seen here as a child.

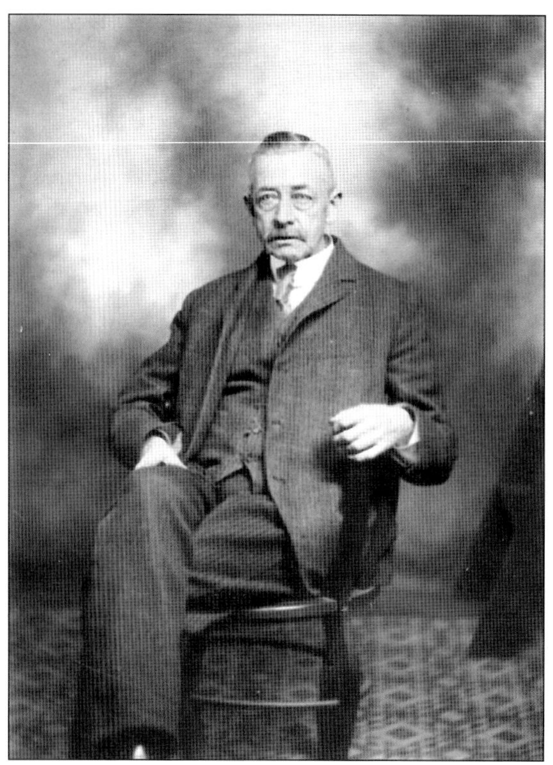

James A. Webster was a member of the Free and Accepted Masons for 50 years and received a gold veteran's button signifying his lengthy membership.

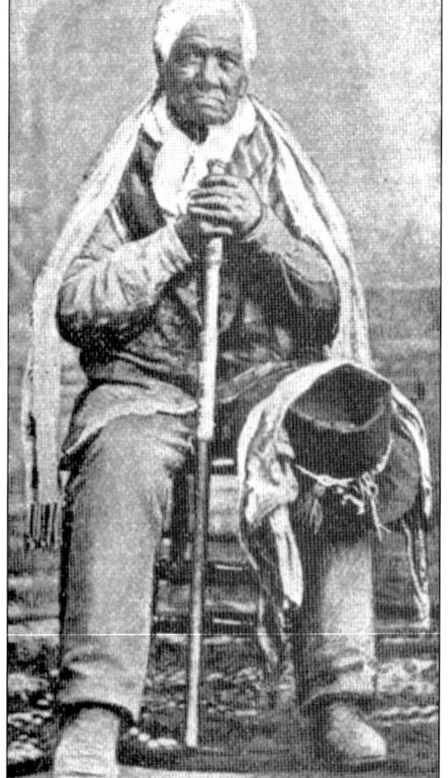

Old Gabriel, a Carmel Mission Indian who is frequently cited as either having lived to the age of 151 or "only" 119 years is pictured on this postcard. He is buried in the cemetery adjacent to Carmel Mission. There are those, however, who question his longevity.

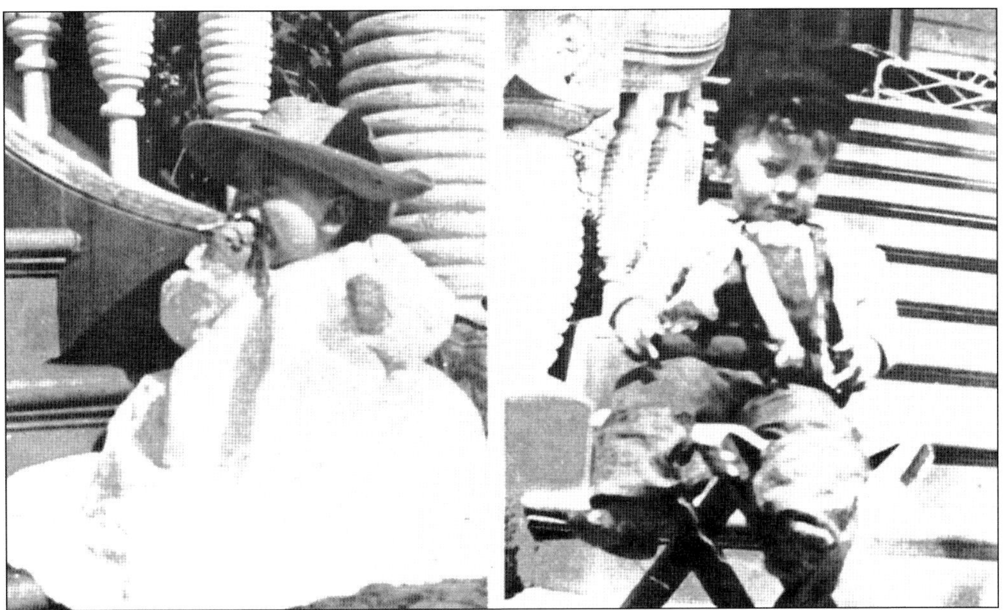

Salinas author John Steinbeck, born February 27, 1902, poses on the steps of his Salinas home at 132 Central Avenue. He won the Nobel Prize for literature in 1962.

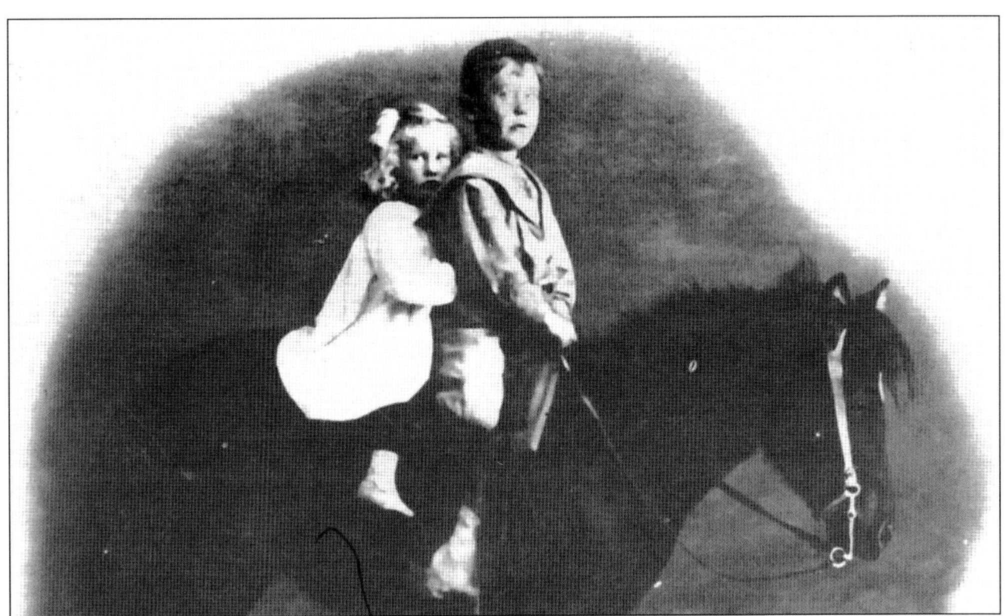

Steinbeck is pictured here with his younger sister Mary. He won a Pulitzer Prize for his 1939 novel *The Grapes of Wrath*. Other famous works of his include *East of Eden*, *Of Mice and Men*, and the travel memoir *Travels with Charlie*.

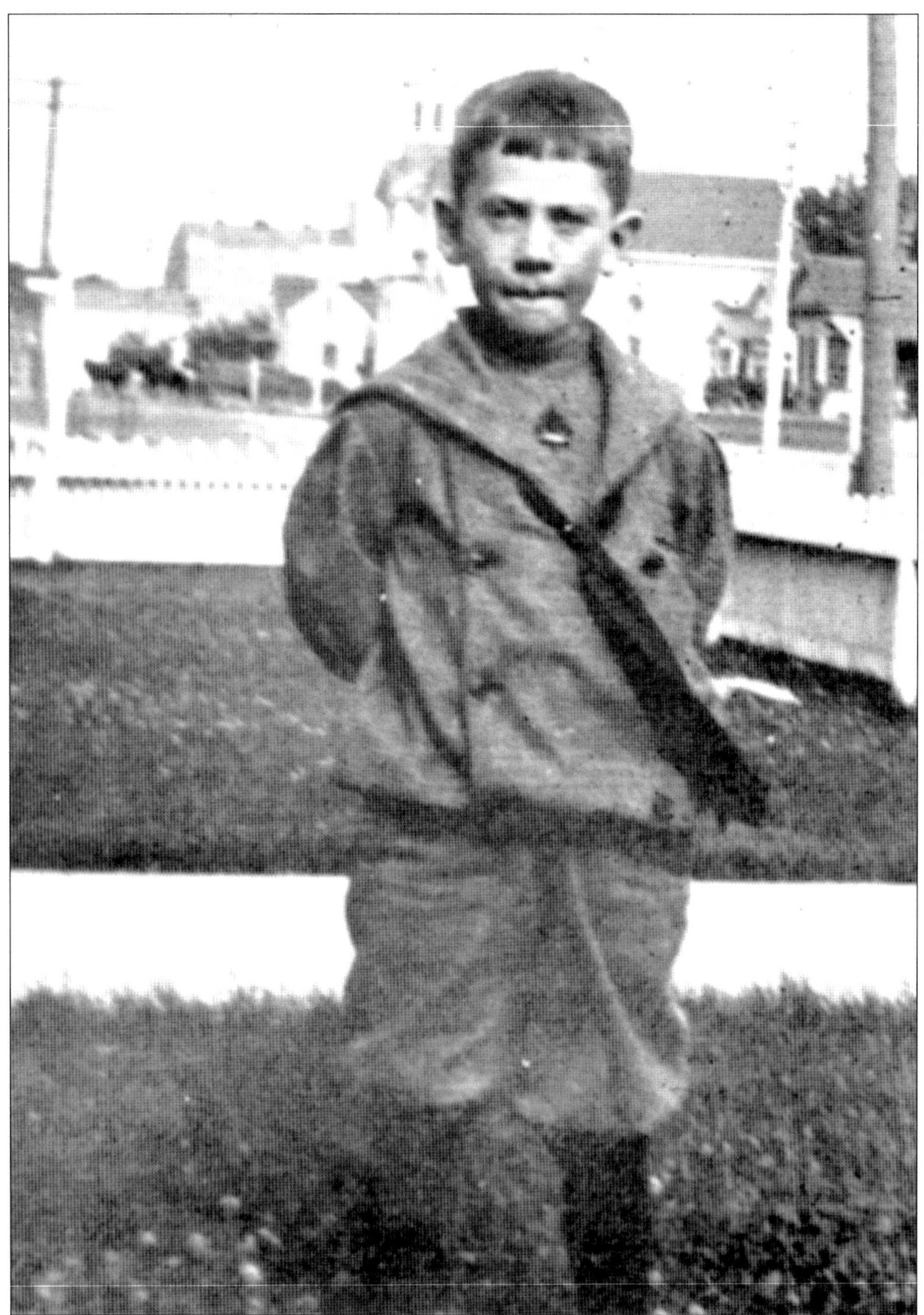

This is another picture of author John Steinbeck. He was a Salinas native, graduating from Salinas High School in 1919. Steinbeck's mother, Olivia Hamilton, had been a schoolteacher, and he spent summers working nearby fields with migrant ranch hands; there is little doubt that both experiences influenced his writing.

Eight

Agriculture and Rural Scenes

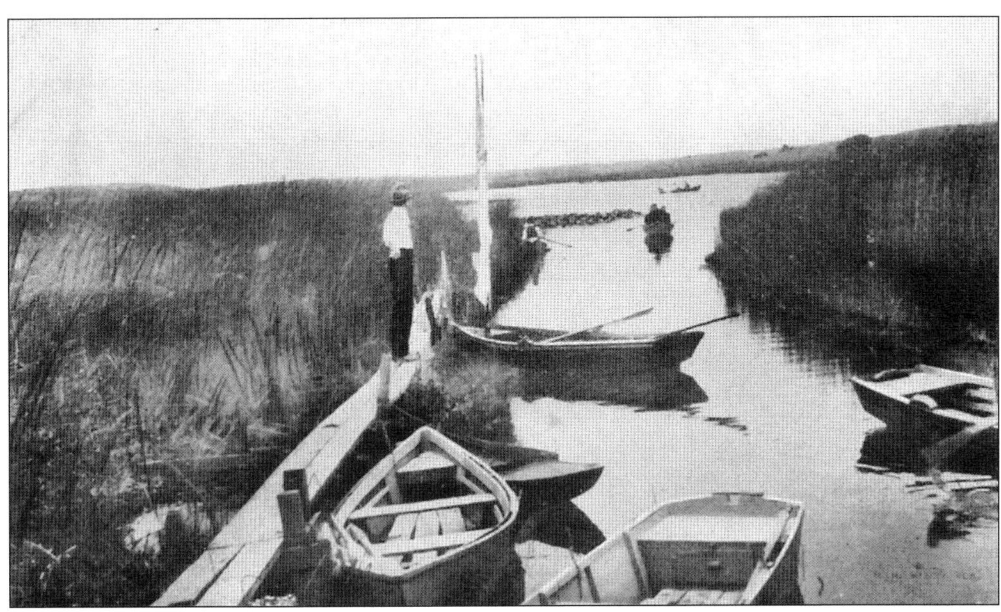

This postcard promotes the Gabilan Gun Club of Salinas and dates to about 1908. The Gabilan Gun Club was one of the best-known duck clubs in Salinas. Its first meeting was held on September 12, 1905, with membership limited to 37. Eventually, the membership was raised to 50 with dues of $2.50 per month. The club leased the Merritt and Espinosa Lakes, and a clubhouse was built on the banks of Lake Merritt. To connect the many lakes, the club members dug canals through the swamp. It was nothing for hunters to get 25 mallards and as many as 20 to 25 different ducks before noon.

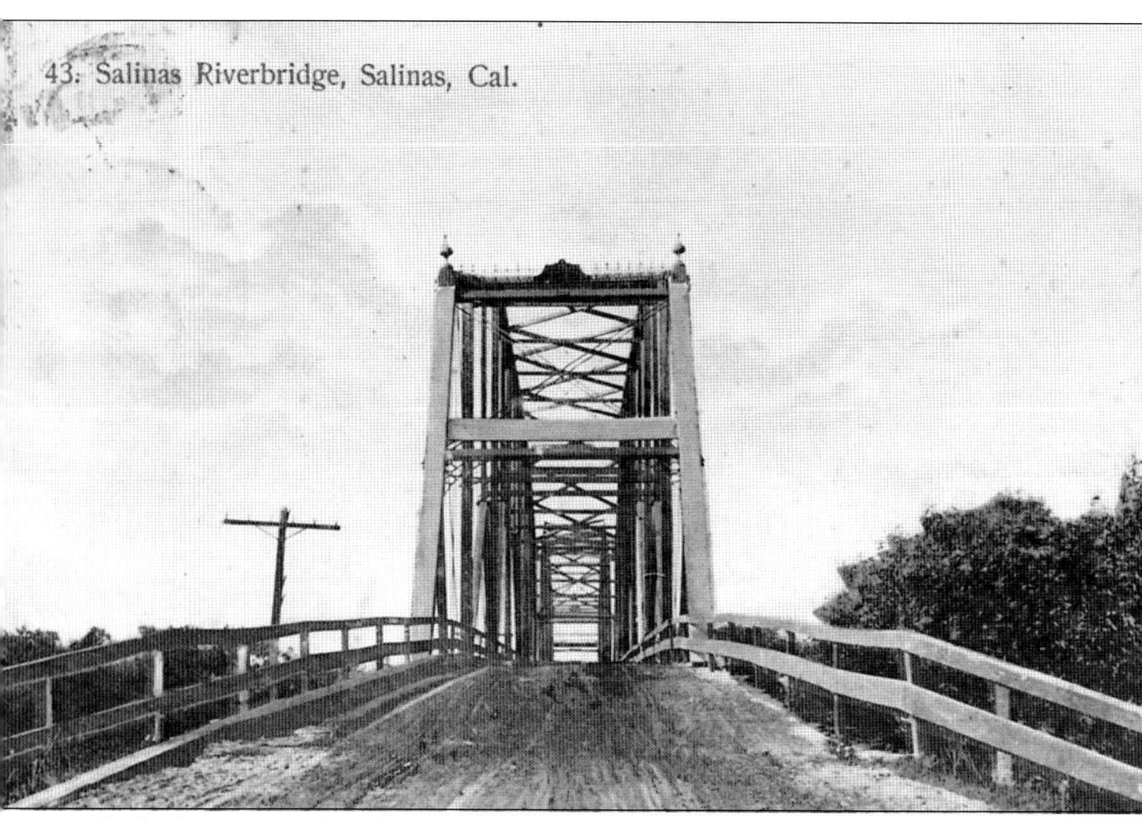

This bridge, spanning the Salinas River in 1909, survived many floods. The Salinas River is one of the largest submerged streams in America; it is also referred to as the "upside-down river," so named by Anne Fisher in her book *The Salinas, Upside-Down River.* Plans for steel bridges across the Salinas River were begun in 1886, and the citizens of Monterey County passed a $150,000 bond to build several in different locations. Hilltown, near Salinas, had a ferry that transported people across the river when it was flowing and was the recipient of $35,000 of the bond. California Bridge Company was contracted and the bridge at Hilltown was completed on February 9, 1889. The ferry, which had served the citizens of Salinas for many years, was retired.

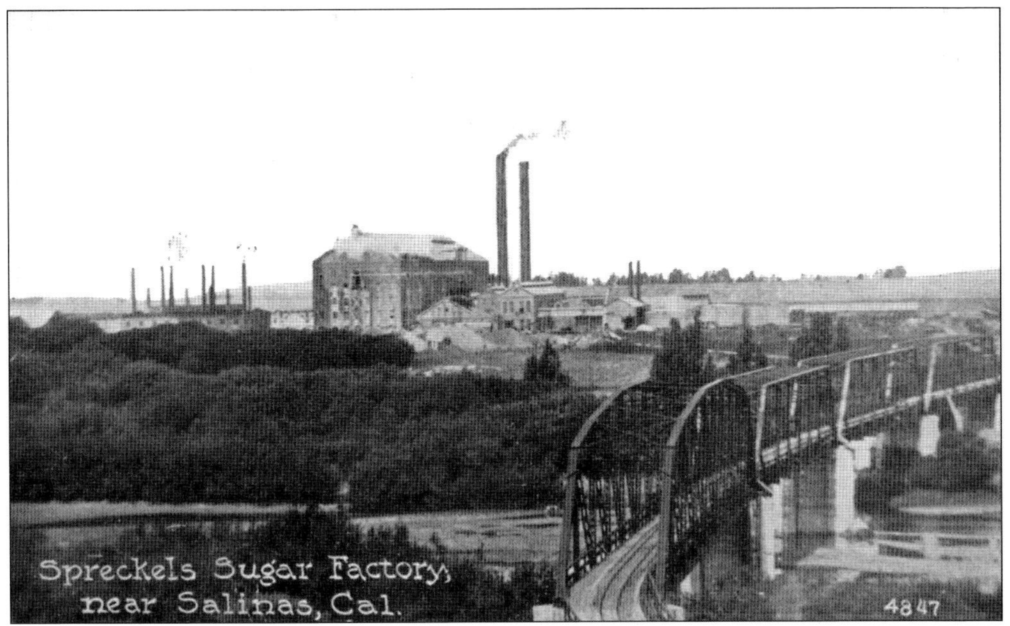

The Spreckels Sugar Factory, located south of Salinas, began operations in 1899. At that time, it was the largest sugar refinery in the world, and Spreckels built his own railroad to move beets and workers to the factory. By 1952, it was able to process 7,000 tons of beets per day. The factory survived the 1906 earthquake but was demolished a few years after the 1989 Loma Prieta quake.

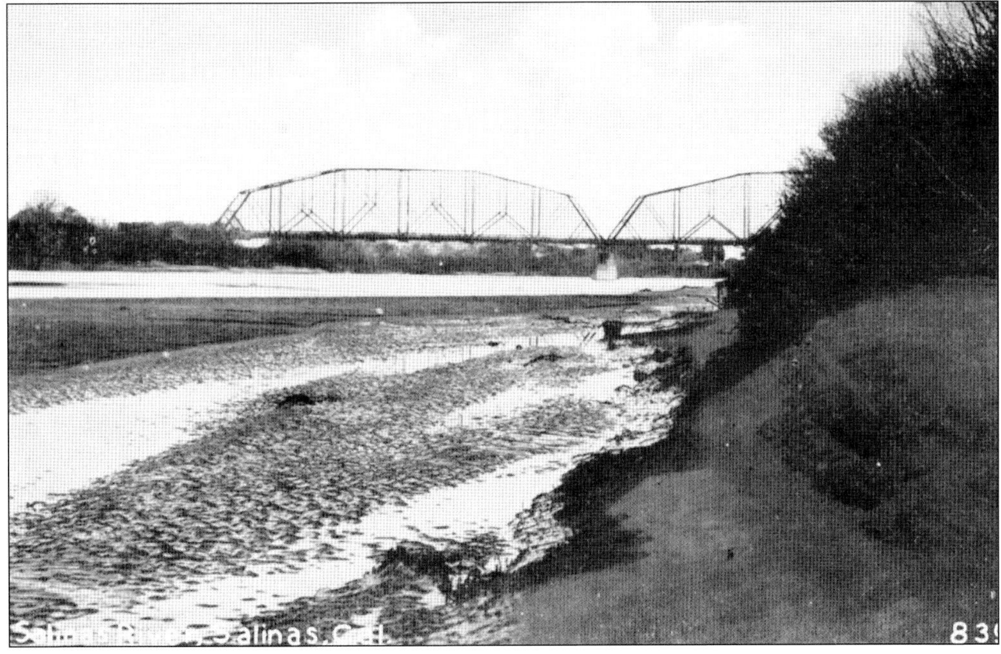

This rare view, dating to approximately 1914, is of the original bridge over the Salinas River on the Buena Vista branch of the railroad. A flood in 1914 destroyed three of the spans, and the west approach to the bridge changed. A new and stronger Salinas River bridge was built to accommodate the heavy train traffic. The railroad had three rails instead of two, allowing the use of both narrow and standard gauge trains on the same rail bed.

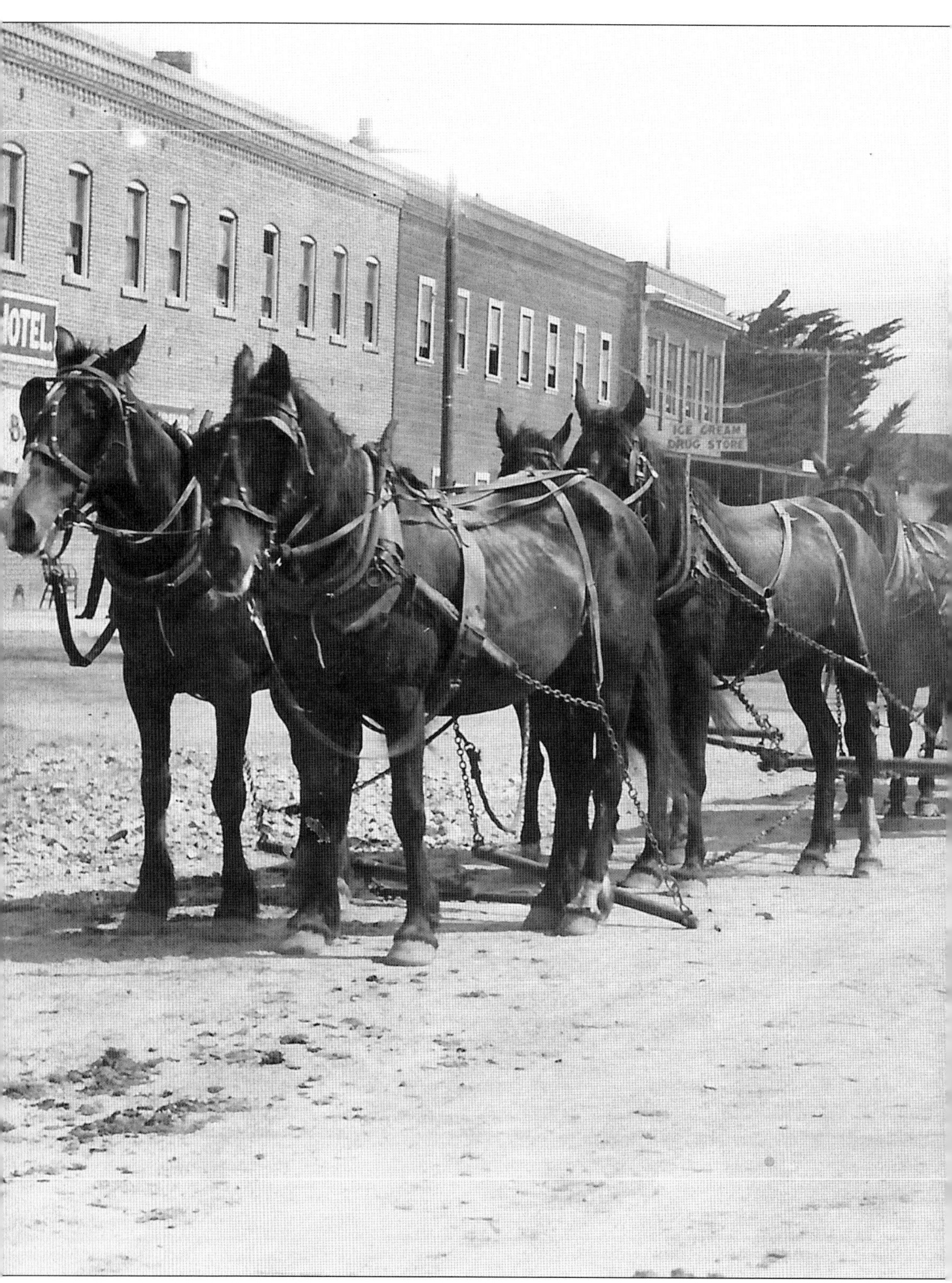

Early agriculture relied on horses and mules for transportation.

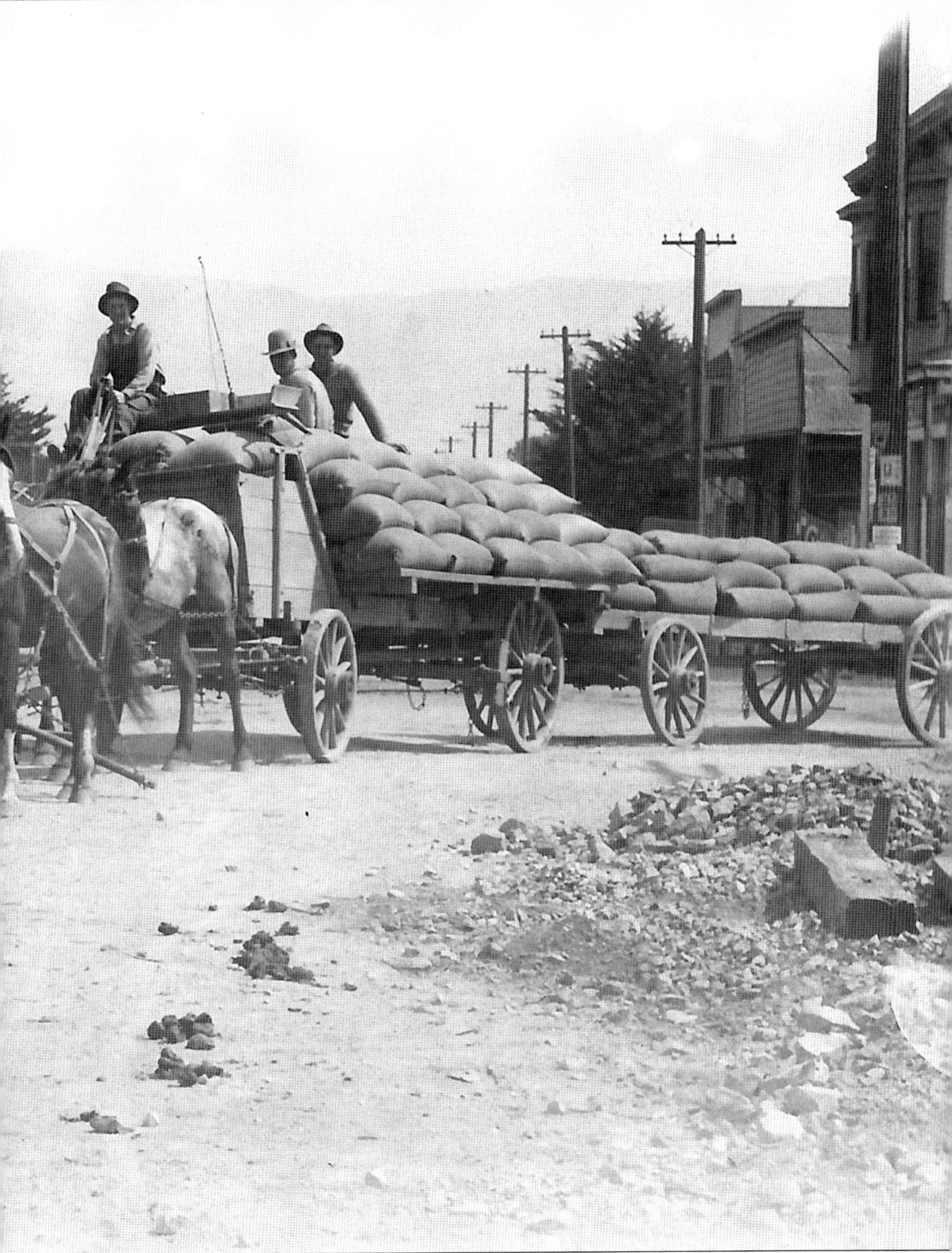

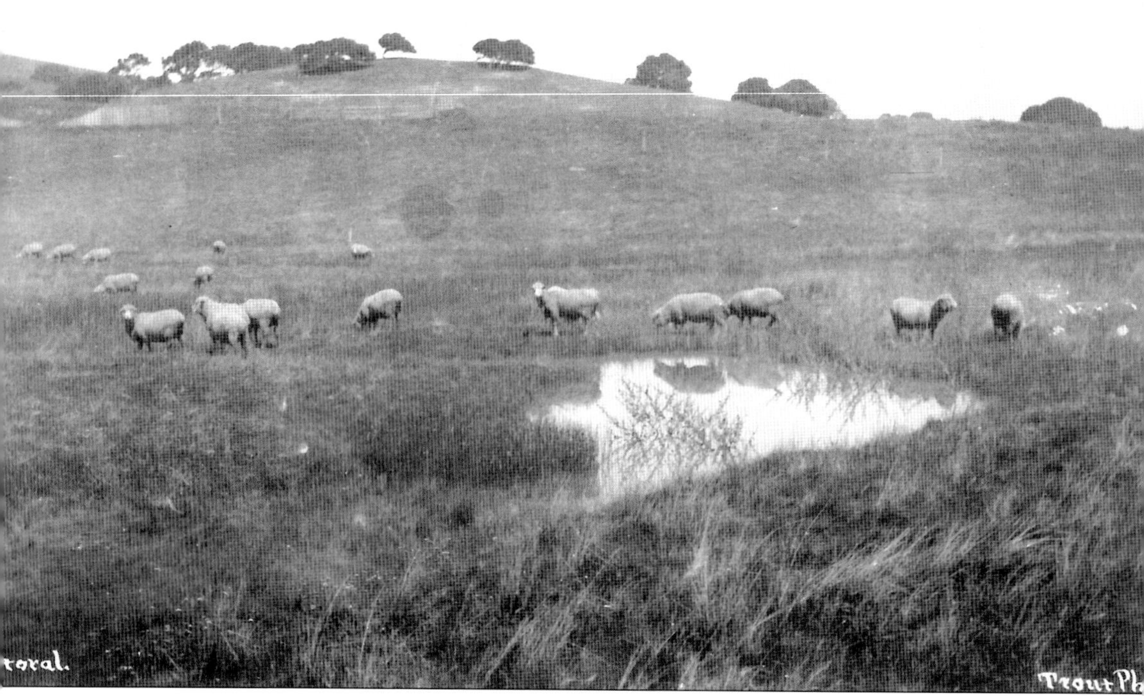

Here is another view of early sheep raising. Sheep raising was a major enterprise in the 1860s when Monterey County contained more sheep than any other county in the United States. Many ranchers hired Basque sheepherders to care for their flock. The sheep were sold for meat, hides, and wool, and were driven to railroads at San Jose, Gilroy, or Soledad. Many of the hides and wool were shipped from Moss Landing to commission merchants in San Francisco.

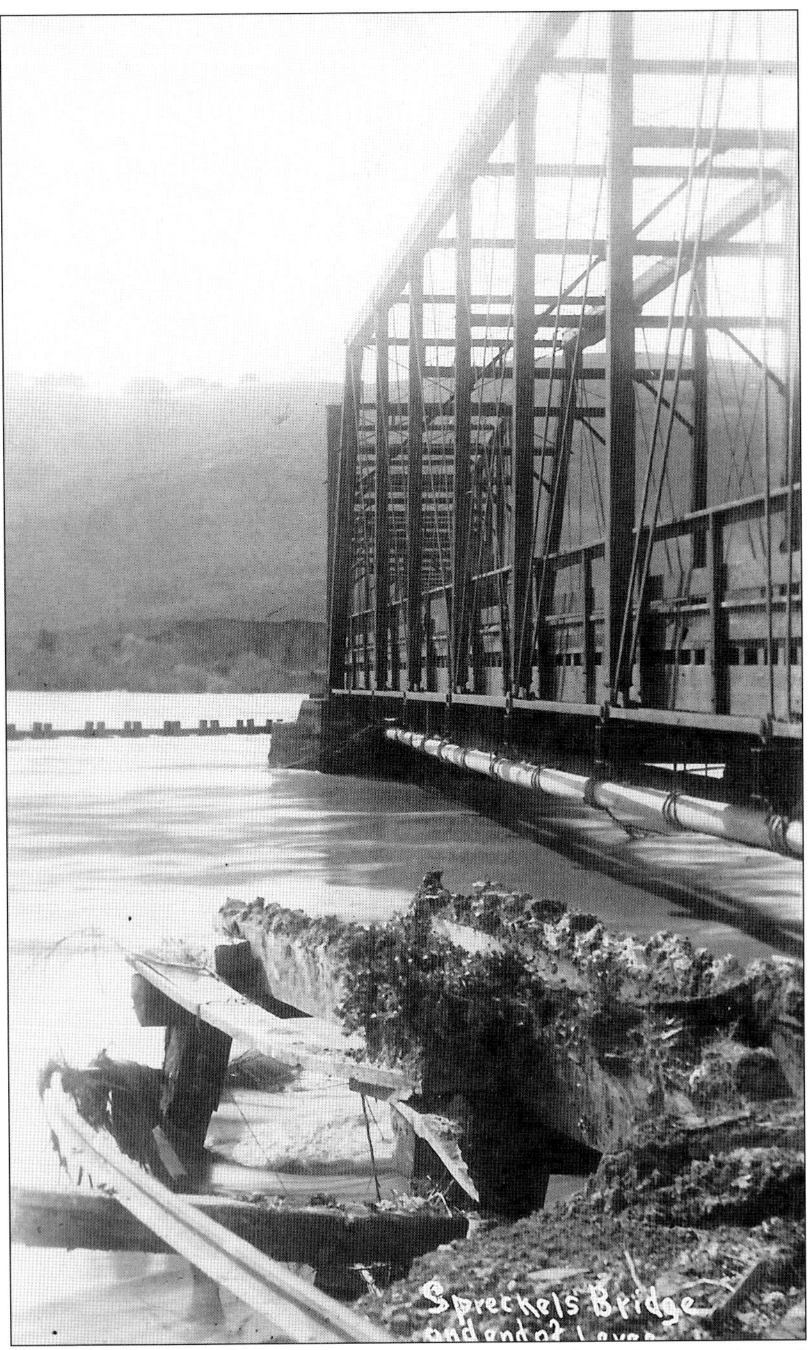

Pictured here is another view of the Spreckels Bridge. Most of the 1890s were focused on Claus Spreckels's proposed construction of a major sugar beet processing plant in or near Salinas. Speculation was high, and despite the national economic recession of 1893, investment and growth were accelerated in Salinas. Spreckels was able to purchase large acreages cheap, and by 1898, enough farmers were willing to change from cereal crops to beets to make Spreckels's promised plant a reality. As early as 1891, a narrow gauge line had been run into Salinas to help supply his Watsonville beet processing operation.

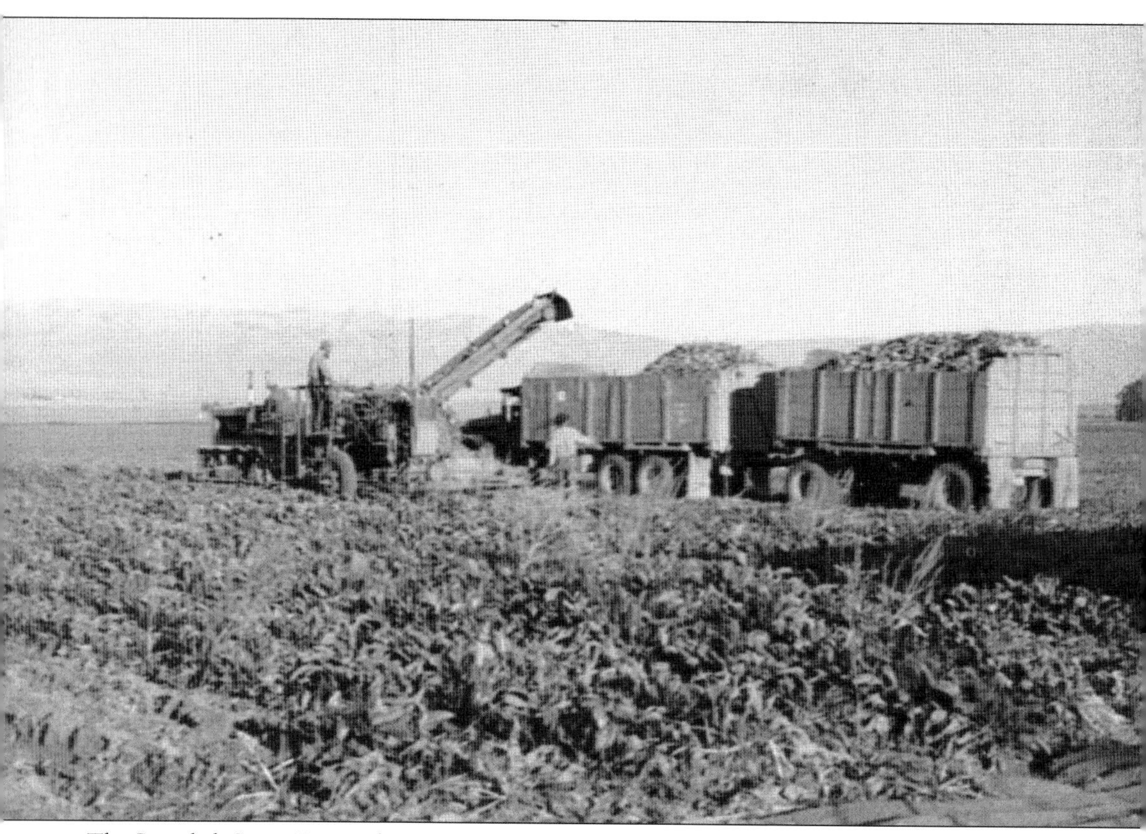

The Spreckels Sugar Factory began operation in 1899 with a capacity to process 3,000 tons of beets per day. That figure gradually rose to 7,000 tons per day. At one time, beets were one of the primary crops of the Salinas area. Interestingly, the irrigation systems that Spreckels developed to water his beet crops made subsequent row crops, for which the Salinas area is most noted, possible.

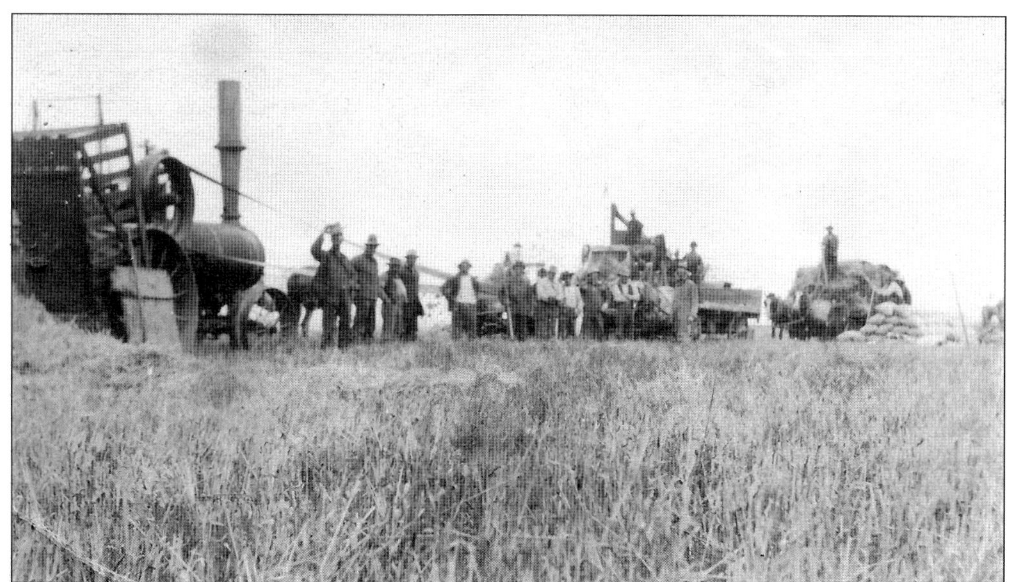

This postcard shows the threshing of grain with an early steam tractor. Note the long belt system running from the tractor to the thresher.

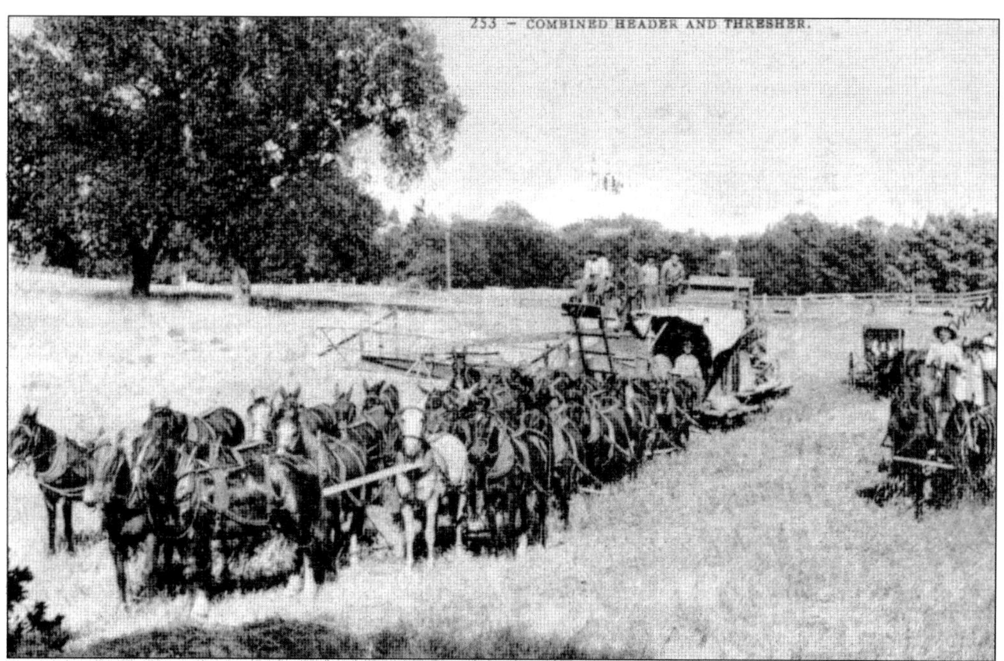

Grains were one of the main crops in the Salinas area prior to the development of irrigation. This postcard shows how intensive the preparations for threshing the grain must have been.

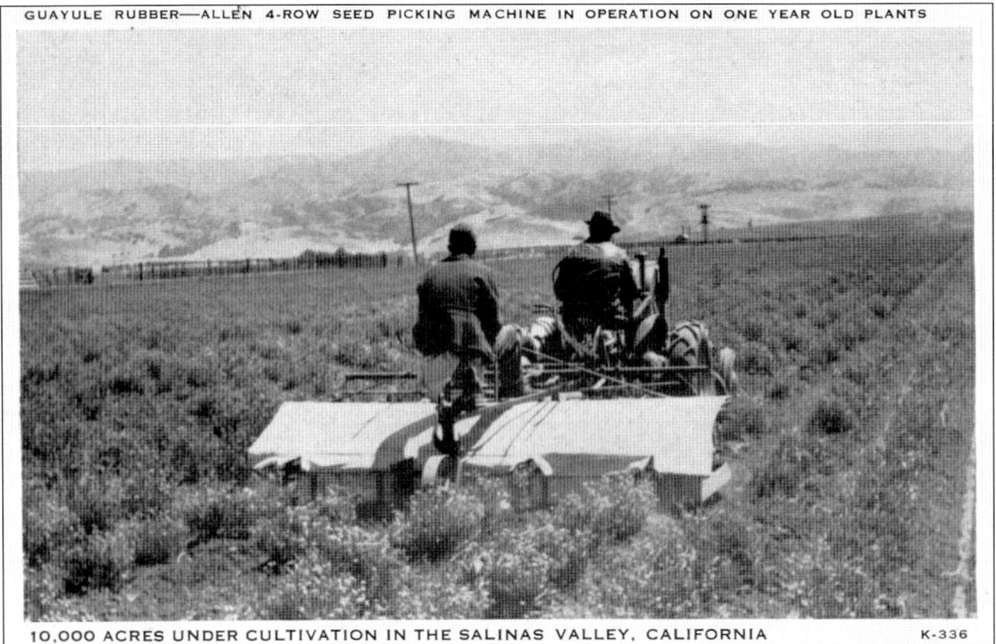

During World War II, with a shortage of rubber, cultivation of guayule was made a top priority. The Emergency Rubber Project set up production sites in three states, and the Salinas area was one of the major producers.

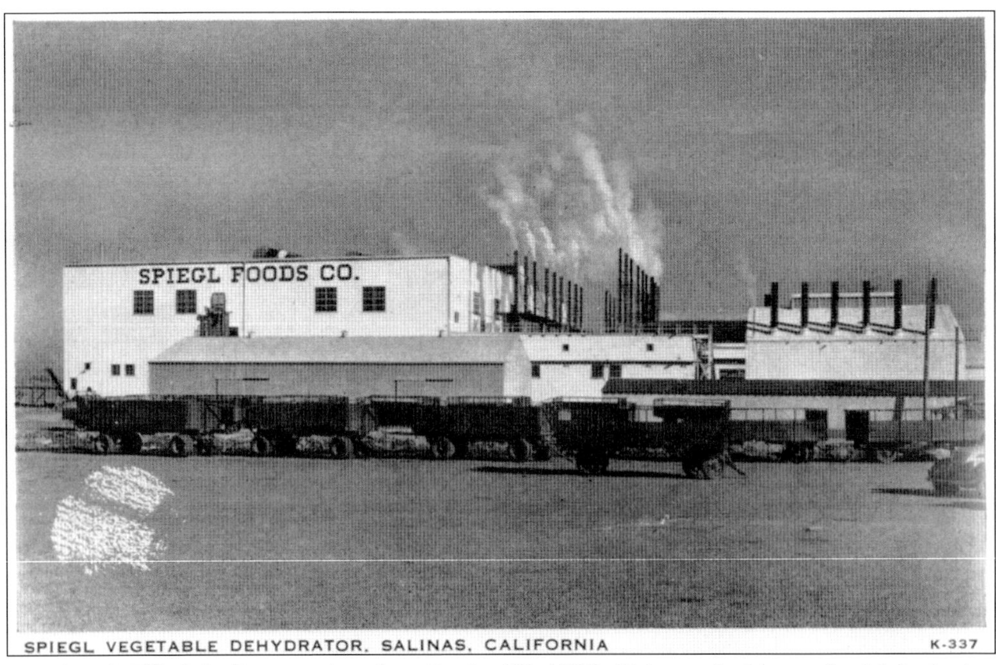

Seen here is Ellis Spiegl's processing plant. During World War II, it was the biggest food dehydrating plant in the world, making it easier to ship food to the troops.

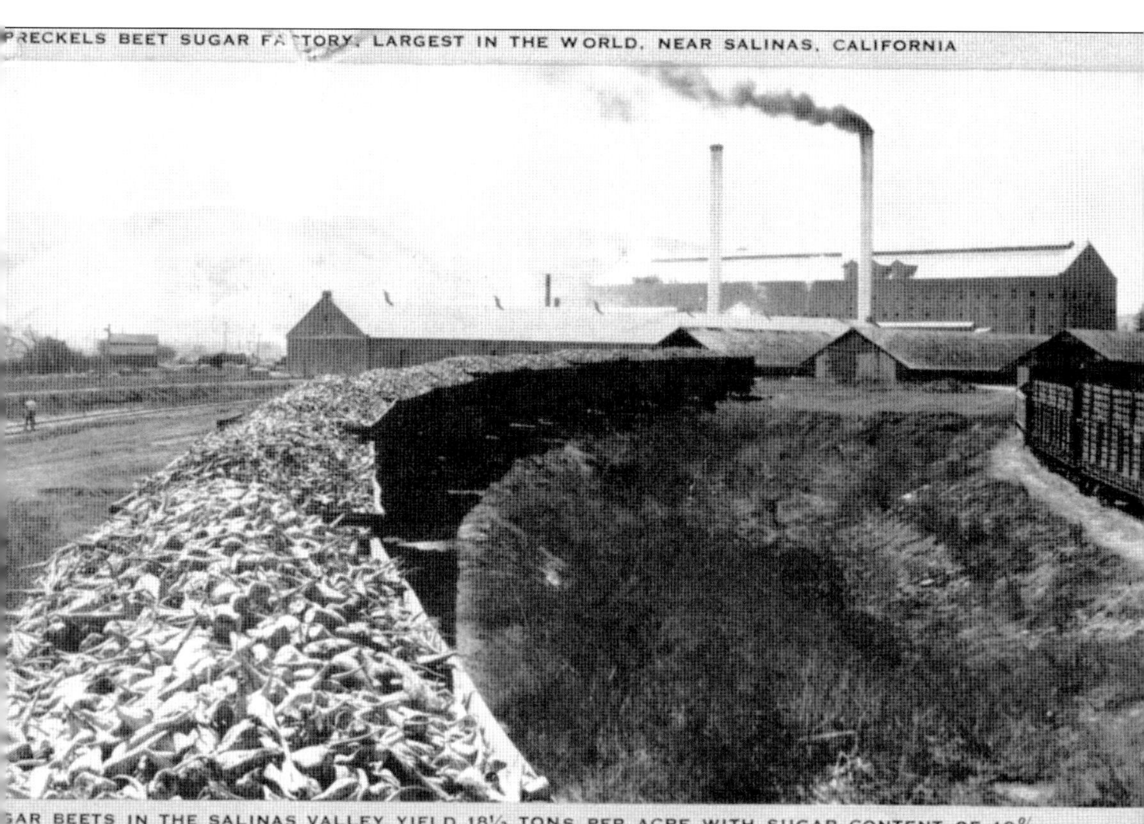

The Spreckels Sugar Factory used thousands of tons of beets per day. In order to move beets to his factory, Spreckels established the Pajaro Valley Consolidated Railroad.

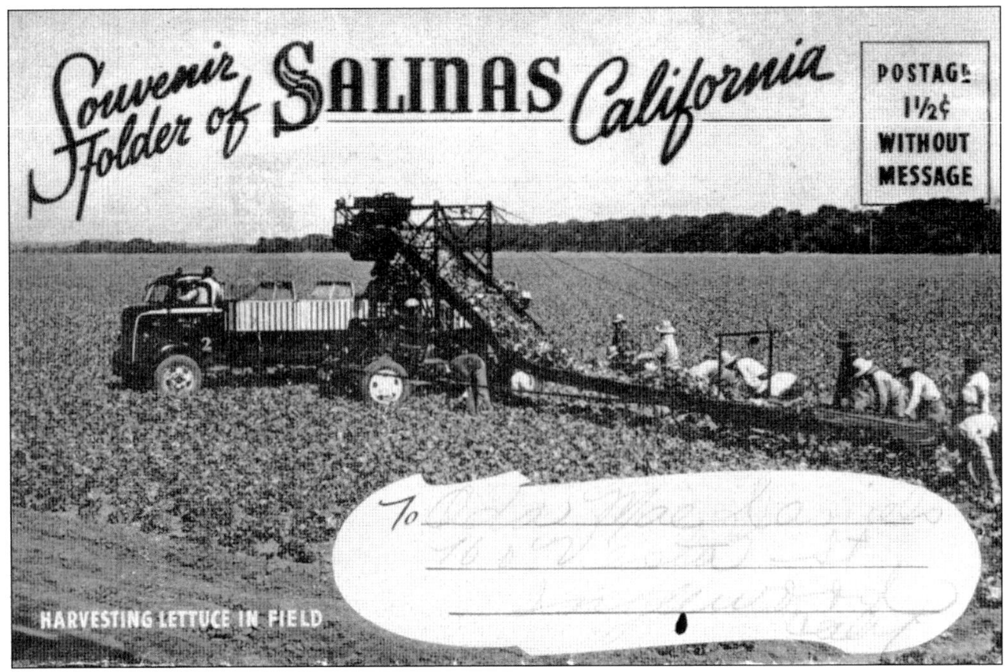

While lettuce was the primary crop in the early years, many other crops are now grown, such as carrots, broccoli, cauliflower, artichokes, and garlic.

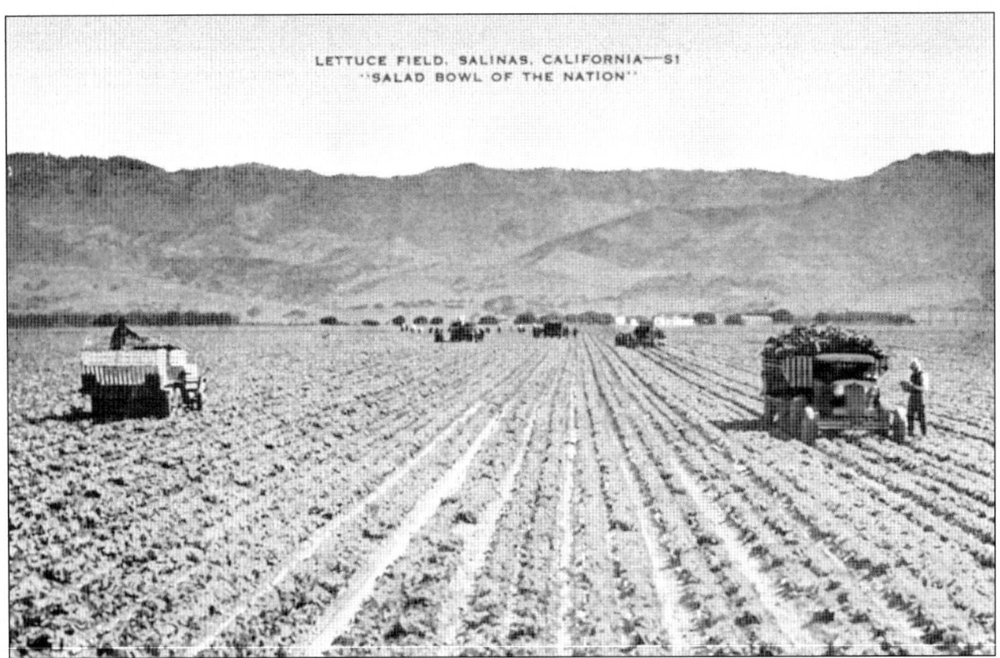

In 1922, approximately 30 acres of lettuce were planted by Kanichiro Takahashi and Kasujiro Maruyama and 5 acres were planted by Ichijuro Kondo. In the years that followed, lettuce became a popular and profitable crop for growers in the valley. By 1930, Salinas had become the "Salad Bowl of the World," a term coined by one of the Cominos brothers, owners of the famous Cominos Hotel.

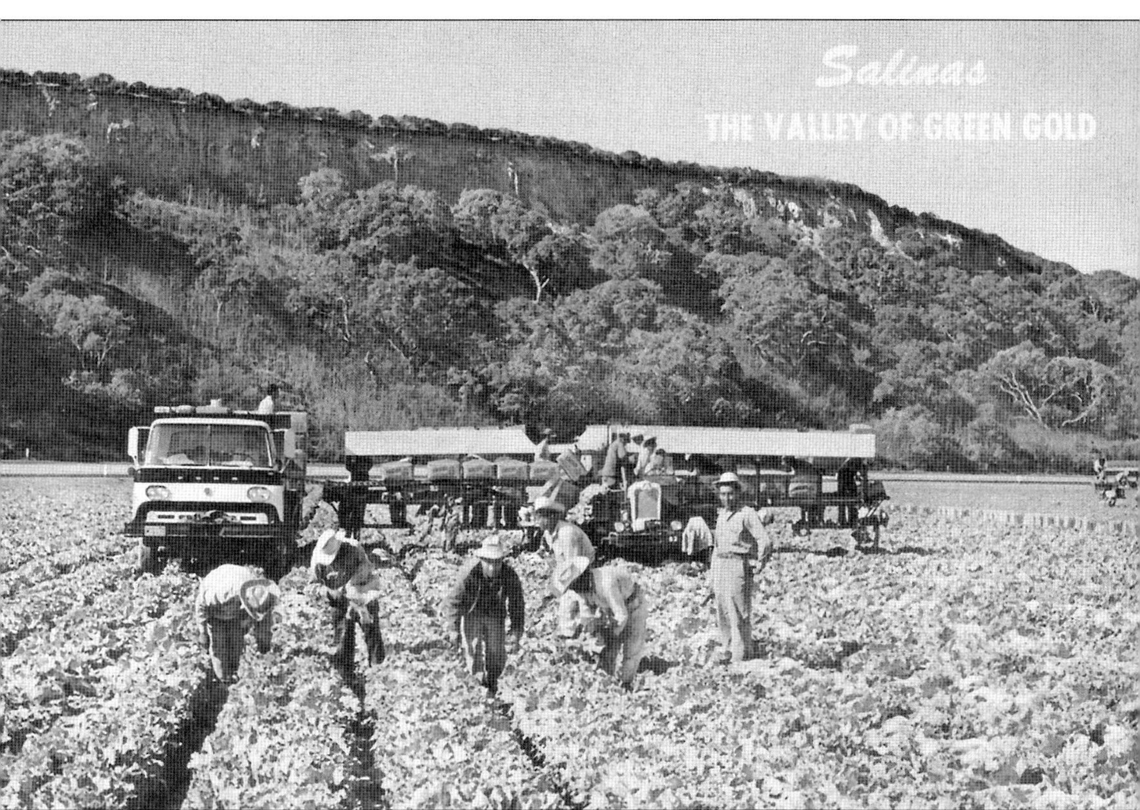

Salinas also earned the title "Valley of Green Gold" when growers were able to ship produce to other states by iced railway cars.

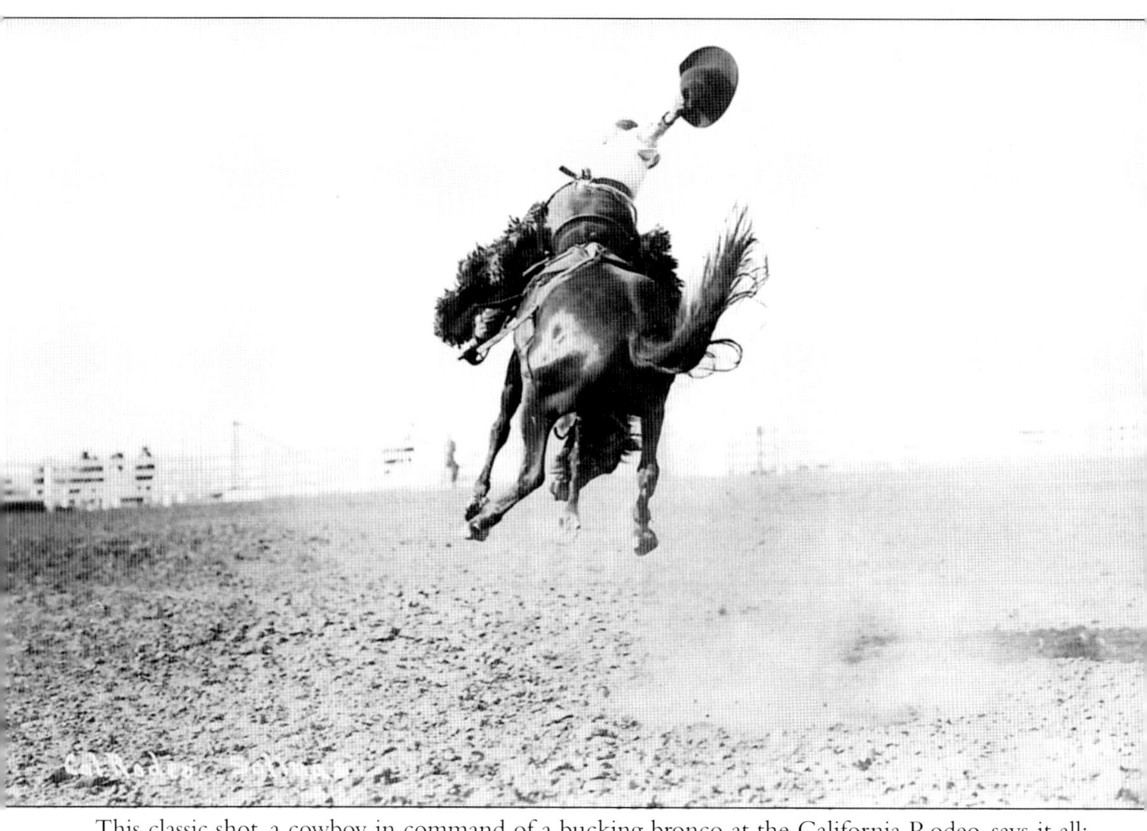

This classic shot, a cowboy in command of a bucking bronco at the California Rodeo, says it all: "the end."

About the Monterey County Historical Society

Founded in 1933, and incorporated in 1955, the Monterey County Historical Society is a nonprofit organization dedicated to the ongoing preservation of our own past. The society is responsible for a massive collection of family, city, and county archival materials. These rare and valuable documents are housed in the society's temperature- and humidity-controlled archival vault. Scholars, authors, students, attorneys, and the public are using these historical documents for research purposes at an ever-increasing rate.

To better serve the public, the society is in the process of building an agricultural museum and research center that will make a significant contribution to the county in the field of education of its youth and outreach to the public. The primary emphasis of this facility will be on the cultures and the people who made this area what it is today.

Proceeds from the sale of this book will help fund the new museum and research center. Visit us online at www.mchsmuseum.com.

Consistent with our mission to preserve history on a local level, this book was printed in South Carolina on American-made paper and manufactured entirely in the United States. Products carrying the accredited Forest Stewardship Council (FSC) label are printed on 100 percent FSC-certified paper.

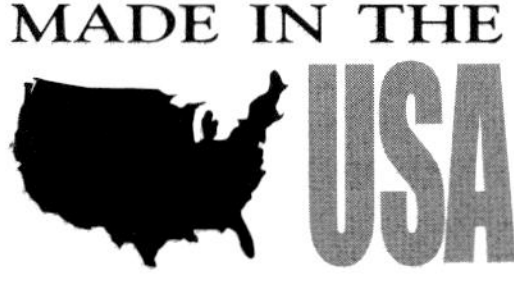